T0367120

African-language Literatures

New Perspectives on IsiZulu Fiction and Popular Black Television Series

African-language Literatures

New Perspectives on IsiZulu Fiction and Popular Black Television Series

Innocentia Jabulisile Mhlambi

WITS UNIVERSITY PRESS

Published in South Africa by:
Wits University Press
1 Jan Smuts Avenue
Johannesburg
2001
www.witspress.co.za

Copyright © Innocentia Jabulisile Mhlambi
First printed in South Africa in 2012

ISBN 978-1-86814-565-2 (Print)
ISBN 978-1-86814-577-5 (Digital)

All rights reserved. No part of this publication may be reproduced, stored in a
retrieval system, or transmitted in any form or by any means, electronic, mechanical,
photocopying, recording or otherwise, without the written permission of the publisher,
except in accordance with the provisions of the Copyright Act, Act 98 of 1978.

Edited by Jennifer Stacey
Cover design by Hothouse South Africa
Book design and layout by Sheaf Publishing
Printed and bound by Creda Communications

Contents

Dedication

To the living memory of my parents,
Emmah Mavis Sis' Sesi
and Ompiyimpi Jeremiah Dhlamini

Acknowledgements

My gratitude goes to my husband, Fanny Benjamin Mhlambi, for his emotional and financial support; a true, loyal and dedicated companion as I wandered about in conferences and lectures to present my ideas to my peers. His support throughout this odyssey is sincerely appreciated. My thanks also go to my sister, Zandile Dhlamini, who played mother to my children, Lwazi, Nolwazi and Lwazisile, as my academic and research engagements constantly deprived them of a mother. Her role playing allowed me all the time and space I needed for writing this study. You, like our mother, documented and continue to archive each and every morsel of my achievement. And to you my children: I have been divinely blessed with the most beautiful and wonderful children any mother can wish for.

For a project of this magnitude, as a researcher, my ways have crisscrossed on numerous levels with a number of fascinating people, scholars, friends and acquaintances, who, when looking back, have been structurally positioned to help me grow intellectually, facilitate my progress and offer words of encouragement and support. The first person, who features largely in mind right now, is my PhD supervisor and mentor, Professor Isabel Hofmeyr. I wish to thank her from the bottom of my heart for her academic guidance, her patience and the opportunities for funding she has directed me to from time to time. Thank you a thousandfold for making time in your extremely busy schedule to read my work as I was transforming it into a book manuscript. Professor Nhlanhla Maake, your cautionary remarks 'balance family life with academic life' and 'children are never the same age again' have constantly reminded me that time spent away from academic pursuits must be diverted to the most important people in life: the family. I assure you, Prof, in my attempts to complete this book, my family has never been neglected. My sincerest gratitude to you, Prof, for the many profitable discussions on African-language politics. It is from these discussions that this study germinated. My thanks also go to Professors Peterson and Ogude for their contributions to my early drafts of this work. Their recommendations helped immensely in the expansion of the scope of this study. Thanks a thousandfold to Bheki Peterson, for being a mentor in my preparing the book manuscript; I profited immensely from the discussions on repositioning earlier drafts. I have also benefitted immensely from the SLLS Seminar Forums. My special gratitude goes to Grace Musila, Carolyn Mckinney and Tom Odhiambo whose contributions to the third chapter helped me in preparing it for publication. Several stellar academics read, with patience, several chapters of this book which have been published in different journals. I am humbled by the attention I received from them. Inge Kosch, Andrew van der Spuy, Sarah Chiumbu, Anette Horn, Michael Chapman and Patrick Lenta, Bheki Peterson, Karin Barber, Mashudu Mashige, Margaret Collins, and Stephanie Kitchen, your intellectual contributions to various chapters in this book are immeasurable. Karin Barber and Stephanie Kitchen's insightful comments on sampled chapters of this book alerted me to other possible extensions of the research focus. I am extremely grateful for this pointer. I also extend my gratitude to Andre Koopman who has been helpful in locating some of the articles that were not readily accessible for they contributed significantly to my intellectual growth. Pumla Gqola, you have been a wonderful friend and have contributed significantly to my intellectual growth. I also wish to thank the Tucker family and Joyce Anderson, a Kumon South Africa specialist, for reading early drafts of my chapters.

To my writing group members Michelle Adler, Kim Wallemach, Libby Meintjes and Judith Inggs: time spent reading, discussing and rewriting some chapters of this book paid off well. The meticulousness with which you went through some chapters is greatly appreciated. And to Leon de Kock I am grateful for your belief in me and the words of encouragement. My sincerest gratitude also goes to Michael Titlestad for your assistance with the administrative expectations of published material. To my research and reading group Liz Gunner, Wendy Willems, Jennifer Musangi, Jendele Hungbo, Maria Suriano and Megan Jones: our fruitful reading exercises and discussions have helped me experiment with the theory advanced in this book to other genres such as Black Opera in South Africa, with special focus on *Princess Magogo kaDinizulu* by Mzilikazi Khumalo and *Winnie* by Mfundi Vundla, Bongani Ndodana-Breen and Warren Wilensky. My gratitude goes as well to my international friends at the Centre for African Studies at Michigan University, Kelly Askew and Naomi André, for the grants and the UMAPS scholarship they procured from the University of Michigan and the Centre for African Studies, so that I could extend my research in the area of black popular culture in South Africa. Finally, my gratitude to Robert Muponde who actually insisted that I consider popular culture and 'new technologies' in South Africa.

My hat goes off to the Wits University Press staff, Julie Miller, Veronica Klipp, Melanie Pequeux and Roshan Cader, who helped with the publishing and marketing side of this book. Special thanks to my editor, Jenny Stacey; the hours you spent many years ago in our English essay writing classes and again in finalising the draft of this book are appreciated.

At various instances I came to a *cul de sac*, especially with the procurement of research materials, and had to depend on support staff to help. My special thanks go to Judy Marshall, a Librarian at Wartenweiller and Margaret Northey and all the staff members at the Cullen Library.

Finally this book would not have seen the light of day if it were not for the generous grants the University offered me. The University Staff Bursary Fund, the Ad Hoc grant, the Carnegie Time-Off grants (2006 and 2010) and the Mellon Grant (2010) helped immensely with the procurement of research materials and for the payment of lecturer replacements, buying me time to further research and to write this book. The University Research Committee of the University of Witwatersrand's publication award (2010), helped immensely with the publishing costs of this book.

Introduction

African-language literatures and popular arts: challenges and new approaches

It is paradoxical that while a systematic study of African popular arts and popular culture has concerned African scholars further afield in Africa for more than three decades, in South Africa such study remains confined to popular arts such as ethno-music, popular music and popular theatre to the total exclusion of indigenous language writing. Numerous descriptive analyses exist that map the contours of South African popular arts and cultural sites, but only a few have paid any attention to both print and broadcast media in indigenous languages as texts that foreground popular imperatives. It seems the African-language literary tradition is confined by approaches derived from earlier paradigms applied in the study of its literatures. These preferred theoretical models (including Structuralism and New Criticism) have consciously precluded certain cultural forms as 'low-brow' and negated their significance as constituting statements of 'proper sensibilities.' Consequently, the African-language literary tradition has a narrow view of what constitutes indigenous literary writing, focusing on formal oral and written literatures and excluding radio drama, emerging popular narratives, theatre, television and film. With waning interest in formally written literatures in indigenous languages and the rise in the quantity and significance of other forms of artistic production, this tradition in South Africa has experienced a paralysis.

A fresh approach to African-language literatures is needed and this is what I hope to introduce in this book.

Works in the African-language literary tradition, with its neatly categorised genres, have been, and still largely continue to be, perceived either as imitations or carbon copies of Western literary models of bourgeois origin or as offshoots of traditional literature. Yet these literatures which have emerged under conditions only remotely similar to those of the Western bourgeoisie and completely different from those which gave birth to traditional literature, shuttled to and fro between the past and the contemporary to articulate certain imperatives. These imperatives, recreated through powerful narratives, poetics and discursive idioms capturing African life experiences, were neither fully traditional nor modern but highlighted the dynamic, multiple, cultural matrix which was forever growing and unfolding into the recesses, crevices, holes, twists and bends of modern life. As Africans flowed with the tide of modernity, responding, interpreting and re-ordering past social orders according to modern demands, other supplementary or complementary forms of expression emerged, responsive to the demands, setbacks, aspirations and outlooks shaped by lived experiences in particular localities. I argue in this book that all artistic expressions of different cultural workers that have emerged through time embody 'authentic proper sensibilities' of Africans in South Africa.

The position I take in this book contrasts with earlier studies in the field both in the view taken of African-language literatures and in the theoretical model applied. The popular arts paradigm I follow allows for critical exploration of a wide spectrum of art products produced by different art workers from different levels of African society. Furthermore, in this approach artistic forms in indigenous writing are not categorised into the oral and the written, rather the focus is on the significance and relevance of repetitions, anecdotes, jokes, allusions, parody, overlaps and the migrations and recycling of textual elements in particular contexts. It is these textual elements that comprise popular discourses and invariably make these texts popular arts. 'Popular arts' is a loose category comprising old and emerging cultural forms that can constitute anything from African traditional discourses to those of the modern African elite. The styles are highly mixed, drawing from local and international influences in their attempt to code and comprehend changing demands in local settings. Contrary to earlier approaches that looked at tradition as in various stages of disintegration and therefore requiring preservation in the face of modernity, the popular arts paradigm privileges a focus which emphasises how this disintegration is re-invoked and continuously re-inscribed by the masses in modern times. This approach is inclusive of all art forms produced since the historical process of contact began. In this book, I draw on elitist cultural products in indigenous languages to demonstrate that the writings of the mission-educated, that set the pattern for later writing, drew heavily on popular culture and this tradition has not changed. This kind of writing, therefore, is firmly located in the popular arts.

There are more commonalities than differences between South African indigenous forms of writing and popular fiction from elsewhere in Africa and in Jamaica. South African indigenous-language writing, together with popular arts from further afield in Africa, is characterised by a specific discourse marked by syncretism, hybridism and creolisation in form and content. Although these concepts have different etymologies involving theology or religion, biology and linguistics respectively, the commonality between them is that they are all marked by a blending of formally discrete traditions or cultures to form new identities. The thematic repertoires of these art forms reflect the life-experiences and consciousness of the masses. These repertoires, focusing on African cultural desires, aspects of religiosity and modernity, and African nationalism, firmly ground these literatures within popular discourses. In addition, plot structures and characterisation strategies are firmly grounded within local realities and are, therefore, familiar. The integrative perspective provided by the popular arts paradigm is a logical solution to constraints imposed by former theoretical models as it allows for a systematic study of a variety of social variables and their interconnectivity with popular art forms. In this book I draw on a variety of contexts: sociological, historical and ideological and bring them to bear on the eclectic mix of tradition and modernity, the local and the international, and the rural and the urban making up the thematic thrust of texts.

Probably a contributory factor to problems posed by conventional theoretical approaches is the wholesale transposition of European cultural perceptions of certain artistic forms as highbrow or lowbrow. These perspectives implied a one to one alignment of the lifestyles and imperatives of the South African black intelligentsia, as cultural brokers, to those found in European societies. However, even a casual glance at the nature of stories churned out by indigenous-language intelligentsia right from the earliest years of this literary form, reveals that their stories were mostly about ordinary people in ordinary local and familiar places, living their ordinary lives. These concerns have shaped the stylistic and thematic repertoire of indigenous-language writing up to this day. Even the forms used by the broadcast media that were to emerge in the mid and later twentieth century based their thematic repertoire on the everyday issues of ordinary people.

During the early years of indigenous-language written literatures, the representation of everyday life allowed the African intelligentsia to express their anguished response to colonial modernity. The narrative genre, which draws simultaneously from traditional and modern discourses to articulate the complexities of modernity and contemporaneity through displays of ordinary lives in ordinary settings, has remained a cornerstone of this literary tradition. As the last century wore on, the African intelligentsia did not remain the only major source of literary output in this tradition as more and more people, drawn from different sections of society, started to reflect, in writing, on what animated their everyday life. So, in this book I have also drawn from post-apartheid authors whose intellectual contexts have not been shaped by the erudite cultures that informed earlier writers in the literary tradition; authors who, by the late twentieth century, had recused themselves from the erudite European high culture. These later authors have been shaped by a variety of contexts and have been exposed to a more complex, eclectic culture which has drawn from the numerous cultures of those races that make up the South African nation.

A fundamental view I express in this book is that the exclusive focus on the assimilated elites' response to colonial and apartheid pressures and constraints denied the parallel existence of the vibrant but less vocal response of the masses whose lives animated most, if not all, of the narratives of the elites. In the context of this writing, lived experiences are drawn upon not as a way of showcasing the plight of the wretched 'others', but as a way of imprinting morals and worldviews, underscored by African middle class sensibilities, which the 'others' have to apply to their life experiences outside the narrative contexts. This will become apparent in the discussion of post-apartheid novels in the first three chapters of this book. Within the contextual framework of the popular arts paradigm, the intense focus on the ordinary reveals explosive energies underpinning and shaping 'micro-worlds' (Jones, 2002: 8), giving a sense of historical reality to lives that were normally ignored or neglected, and provides a number of insights. But more significantly the focus on everyday life shows that 'ordinariness' is neither simple nor banal. The analysis of everyday life makes it possible to uncover the 'microphysics of power', foster awareness of ambiguities and undermine the master narratives of progress, rationality and modernisation (Jones, 2002). The act of drawing from everyday issues by the African-language literary tradition presupposes inclinations that are aligned with popular arts and popular culture thereby highlighting and transcending the foreign constraints that have resulted from theoretical models which have not been informed by local life experiences.

Limits of the field

African-language literatures cover a wide range of black South African literatures in different languages; Khoi and San languages and literatures (which have been precluded and remain excluded in formal studies of African-language literatures), isiZulu, isiXhosa, isiNdebele, SiSwati, Sesotho, Sepedi, Setswana, Xitsonga and Tshivenda. Each of these language categories has its own, but not necessarily distinct, language-bound literary system: a structure which follows the apartheid policy of separate development. The paralysing effect of this arrangement is that African-language literatures remain incapable of realising themselves as, or of achieving a status of, pan-ethnic or national literature. These literatures have been overtaken in this regard by various popular art forms such as music, theatre, film and television which were initially conceptualised within a discourse of control under apartheid but have since outstripped these constricting boundaries to articulate an inclusively popular African culture. Yet, in profound ways, these African-language literatures represent the truest and most uninterrupted forms of black expressive art in South Africa. The processes developed for the production of these literatures from their conceptualisation, writing, the feedback systems authors established and the discourse drawn on are wholly and unabashedly African. This contrasts with the production of theatre, music and television where there is often collaboration between different races, with the problems attendant on that, as well as those caused by the politics of production. In the production of African-language literatures only the publishing sector represents interests outside African cultural interests. However, this sector still remains the major contributor to the low status and negative perceptions suffered by this literary tradition (Evans and Seeber, 2000).

This brief description of the broad spectrum covered by the African-language literatures field indicates that, within the confines of this book, it is impractical for an in-depth analysis of art forms comprising all the different language literatures embraced by this term. Therefore this book will concentrate mainly on isiZulu-language literature and black television dramas as microcosmic reflections of the imperatives encapsulated in the popular discourse of Africans, despite ethnic and linguistic differences. These art forms further provide a fascinating terrain in which extra-textuality, dynamism, multivocality and the interaction of genres operating within particular contexts can be examined.

The isiZulu language as medium of communication between various ethnicities adequately reflects the multi-layered concerns and issues prevailing in the popular imagination compared to other South African indigenous languages. Out of the 50 million legal and illegal citizens comprising the South African population, indigenous South African languages are spoken by almost 77 per cent of the population. The other 23 per cent comprise speakers of English, Afrikaans, a number of minor languages such as modern European, Indian and a host of other foreign African languages that have come to add to the linguistic mix of South Africa's post-apartheid society (Kamwangamalu, 2004). The isiZulu language is spoken by approximately 15 million people in its heartland which is KwaZulu-Natal. It also dominates the linguistic terrain of Africans in the Gauteng province, South Africa's economic hub, and it is spoken fairly widely in other major provinces such as Mpumalanga, the Eastern Cape and in some parts of the Free State, especially in areas bordering Zululand (Pansalb, 2000). As most black South Africans are bilingual or multilingual, isiZulu is one of the languages often spoken by them. The dominance of this language is attributed to a number of social variables that characterised the pre-colonial, colonial and the apartheid periods. The isiZulu language is also part of the Nguni family and therefore has mutual intelligibility with isiXhosa, isiNdebele and SiSwati. Furthermore, intermarriages between differing ethnicities, migrant labour, and the historical displacement of Zulu people through the Mfecane wars in pre-colonial times spread this language variety across a wide terrain. Its varieties, namely Zimbabwean Ndebele and Ngoni, are spoken respectively in Zimbabwe and in some parts of Malawi.

Earlier literary approaches

The study of indigenous language writing, ever since its emergence in the nineteenth century, has been premised on Western bourgeois ideals of what literature is, and particularly on the English literary tradition. During colonial times, when it gradually dawned on missionaries that they should preserve African culture, they, together with anthropologists and philanthropists, collected and edited folklore materials such as songs, poetry, folktales, proverbs and riddles and cultural practices and recorded the history that pertained to each society they worked in. These texts formed the bulk of the first materials collected about African oral literature and the traditional world. The works of Berglund (1889), Callaway (1913) and Bryant (1929) give a glimpse into the nature of the oral world, the world that was to be lamented or lambasted in the writing of the missionary educated Africans. Jabavu (1921), one of the first missionary educated Africans, set the scene for the survey of literature in isiXhosa. His approach gave an overview of what had been accomplished and this became the organising pattern for other surveys conducted for the literatures of different languages. In isiZulu literature, Vilakazi (1945), Scheub (1985), Nyembezi (1961) and Gérard (1971 and 1981) also trace literary production from the earliest publications in 1865 to the point at which they write. These literary surveys are divided into the four subsections of novels, short stories, drama, and poetry. In each subsection a short synopsis of each title and the year of its publication are given. The entries are chronological. Maake (1992) replicated this approach for Sesotho, Serudu (1996) for Sepedi, and Zulu (2000) has provided the most recently updated version for isiZulu literature. The major problem with this form of criticism is that there is not much critical analysis of the texts (Maake, 2000; Kunene, 1989). Also, the survey approach does not look at the different languages' literatures as a collective indigenous discourse but stresses their separateness, playing to the Afrikaner nationalist philosophy of separate development. Another problem is that, although additional background on the titles that were published is also provided, there is a lack of information on the intellectual contexts of the writers and the politics of publishing that influenced a number of the options the writers decided upon.

Valuable critiques of missionary sponsored literature emerge much later in the last century, and collectively give an overall view of both the missionary and apartheid literary production in isiZulu (Swanepoel, 1996). This scholarship provides a critique of the hegemonic worldviews presented in the texts which usually comprised an exploration of a Western lifestyle and an African traditional lifestyle and how the latter would either be imposed upon by, or undermined in favour of, the Western lifestyle. One criticism concerns the lack of any depiction of the socio-political and economic realities of the African population or their inadequate treatment in the texts. Better accounts would have exposed the sources of inequities. Yet another criticism of isiZulu literature involved the question of stylistics; the emulation and the employment of Western literary techniques and conventions which had not been adequately mastered.

The critical materials published during the apartheid period by and large continued the earlier established trend of literary surveys. In addition to the surveys, there emerged a corpus of materials that began interrogating the content of fiction, poetry and drama. Modified structural theories like Russian Formalism and Structuralism coupled with New Criticism, not only became the organising structures for literary criticism but also became the operational mode for creative composition. Numerous African language practitioners and scholars prepared oversimplified, translated versions of these theories for the school market and teacher training colleges or for budding or future writers to use as models.[1] The modified versions of Structuralism and New Criticism eventually became the basic approach to the study of African-language written literatures and have come to form a hegemonic bloc that completely excludes other approaches to indigenous-language fiction. The current syllabus of African-language literatures instruction at schools, training colleges and some universities continues to reflect this trend. No critical analysis[2] of the texts is sought from the students and the authority of the texts is never questioned. The aims and objectives of studying literature do not give students an opportunity to develop a critical approach to texts.

The entrenchment of the Afrikaner Nationalist philosophy in every sphere of life of the South African political economy further complicated the politics of African-language writing (Mpe and Seeber, 2000; Maake, 2000). During the reign of apartheid, there was a sharp increase in the production of African-languages texts and literatures, but the kind of literature that the state-appointed gatekeepers, through the Language Boards and the Department of (Black) Education, prescribed, severely hampered the development of African-language literatures. In the forty-five years of the apartheid regime, the National Party instituted a coercive hegemony that was generally detrimental to the socio-economic and political stability of the country and specifically to African-language literatures. As immediate obstacles, state censorship and self-censorship had resulted in these literatures being concerned with escapism, fantasy and mystic primitivism, noted for its 'safe' historical themes. The writing tended to recapitulate previously explored safe themes: the conflict of cultures, the dramatisation of the move from agrarian societies and cultures into the world of the cities and the attendant overthrow of the system of values and mores that animated the older world. And underlying these themes would be a strong, incessantly didactic, Christian moral outlook. These themes helped create a hegemonic perspective through which writers' representations of Africans lives created and fostered common sense explanations of the disparities and inequities black South Africans experienced in their daily lives. And what perhaps is the most distinctive difference between this literature and that produced during the missionary period, is the marked decline in the quality of stylistics in terms of theme treatment (politics of representation), characterisation, plotting, realism as a mode of narration, focalisations or narrative perspectives, discursive practices and so forth (see also Mtuze, 1994).

At the dawn of the post-apartheid period, African language scholars and critics debated what should be envisioned for written literatures in African languages. Their observations regarding the matter varied greatly. A great proportion still lambasted African-language literatures for their lack of relevance, commitment or realism and their silence about burning political issues. There were also predictions that these literatures would engage with issues that affected all South Africans. Yet strident voices continued to caution against this zealousness, noting that so long as there was no significant change in the obstacles of the past (such as readership, aesthetics and publication processes) change would be difficult to attain. More significantly some critics pointed out that these literatures were still trapped in their old self-definition and that there would not be any significant changes. For this school of thought the literature was largely embroiled in colonial and apartheid mediocrity and had not yet mastered ways in which they could depict the contradictions of post-apartheid South Africa.

Chidi (1989) and Mathonsi (2002) point out that a number of these critics have also been influenced by postcolonial sensibilities. Postcolonial criticism is now an extensive field of scholarship which, in the words of Ashcroft, 'covers all the cultures affected by the imperial process from the moment of colonisation to the present day' (Ashcroft, Griffiths and Tiffin, 1989: 2). The field is now multi-dimensional and covers a variety of topics such as writers in the Diaspora, feminist writing, revisions of the past, the politics of historiography, and aspects of post-colonial crises. However, there have been several criticisms of post-colonial literary theory on the grounds that it is mainly theorised on the basis of Europhone literatures and hence that it overlooks many key features of African-language literatures. Barber (1995b: 3) for example, says

> Post-colonial discourses block a properly historical localized understanding of any scene of colonial and post-independence literary production in Africa. Instead it selects and overemphasizes one sliver of literary and cultural production [...] and this is posed as representative of a whole culture or even a whole global 'colonial experience'.

One feature of African-language literatures that is often misrecognised by post-colonial theorists is their apparently apolitical nature. Given this assessment some critics have dismissed it as socially and politically inconsequential.

All the views discussed above demonstrate the dominant approaches operative in the study of African-language literatures. These approaches have narrow paradigms that cast African-language literature to the margins, parochially sticking to writings by the elite, as self-appointed cultural gatekeepers, to the total exclusion of the varied and often fascinating, emergent, popular forms from a wide cross-section of society.

The popular arts paradigm and generative materialism

In contrast to these stultifying approaches, the popular arts and culture paradigm is seen as useful for a systematic study not only of isiZulu or African-language literatures in general but also for black television drama. This paradigm is interdisciplinary and its intellectual genealogy includes, among others, social history, anthropology, Marxist literary criticism and Birmingham-style cultural studies and literary theory (Haynes, 2000). Significant aspects of this model were developed by Barber in her study of Yoruba travelling theatre which, in composition, drew from a variety of everyday sources. In her work on Yoruba theatrical performances, Barber has formulated a series of analytical approaches that are useful for the study of African-language literatures and television dramas as popular arts (Barber, 2000). Barber's generative materialism, premised on a sociologically inclined approach to the arts, explores the economic, social and cultural levels of text production. Barber has since developed this approach to create a set of literary tools to explain African everyday culture, focusing on the inner pulse, or what she calls the 'meristematic tip', responsible for the continual evolution of African popular culture. Speaking of Yoruba popular theatre, she describes it as a living, contemporary, collectively improvised and continually emergent form (Barber: 7). The observations she makes for Yoruba travelling theatre are also applicable to African-language literatures and black television dramas. Modern African-language literatures likewise evince that internal dynamism that readily predispose them to commentary on topical, contemporary occurrences and happenings, drawing from the lived experiences of ordinary people in familiar localities and using appropriate linguistic resources.

Also significant in Barber's model is her analysis of artistic products that, whilst drawing from popular culture, are able to edify their readers through the demonstration of moral messages flavoured by, and constructed within, local interpretation. The fact that local, cultural producers share the same world as their target audience indicates the close affinity that exists between the producer, the audience and the text. This interrelationship helps produce vibrancy in the production and interpretation of the texts. Thus Barber emphasises that 'in Western Africa, then, people continually produce new forms in order to come to grips with the massive transformation of modernity'(ibid: 5). Although international and transnational media images appeared to be at the forefront of social transformation in the Yoruba context, Barber notes

> that people's overwhelming preoccupation was with social transformations that were perceived as locally rooted and were actually experienced on the ground [...] It was these locally experienced transformations that set the terms in which

images of other lives, other cultures were appropriated – in different ways at different historical moments. And it was these transformations which remained the mesmerizing focus of popular commentary, and which all the new popular genres of the twentieth century – the Yoruba novel, drama, neo-traditional poetry, visual art, popular music – were created to grapple with. In Western Nigeria, as elsewhere in Africa and beyond, it was vernacular genres, representing local experiences that held people's attention (2000: 133).

As I discuss later in the book, this latter aspect of Barber's observation is conspicuous in South African black television series. Similar expressive modalities and extensive overlaps between black television dramas and African-language literatures in this case seem to be rooted in the regeneration and recycling of past themes, plot structures, lessons and styles of characterisation in a manner that Barber's concept of generative materialism demonstrates in her study of Yoruba theatre. She points out that

real experience is narrativized and circulates in the form of anecdotes while existing stories become the templates by which real experience is apprehended […] In this cycle, written texts may participate on the same footing as the anecdotes of experience. Many plays seem to have been an amalgam of hearsay, anecdote, folktale, and written fiction (2000: 9).

In spite of this Barber points out that with Yoruba theatre there is an inherent quest for innovation, exploring the unknown through representations that go beyond the permutation of known elements (ibid: 9). This characteristic of forging forward towards the unknown constitutes the growing point bringing in newness. She points out that 'no rendition of a play or theme is wholly predictable, for though it will recycle much existing material it will also always exceed it in one way or another'(2000: 9–10). These comments are applicable to much of isiZulu literature and black television drama. The revisiting of many themes in television dramas may be seen as recapitulation, but the broadcast media versions, established much later than the print version, always introduce something new that speaks to the topical, the current and the sensational in society.

Barber's approach also considers expressions of 'critical creative metalinguistic consciousness' such as proverbs and epithets. These paralinguistic aspects are at work even in the briefest and most mundane of everyday utterances. Not only are these inherently aesthetic, the consideration of these linguistic features is central, as Barber sees them, not only as the seeds of all the great literary genres but also as their summation. These verbal formulations are mental, archaeological sites that have found ways of being repeatedly cited and of being relevantly applied in contemporary textual productions. These metalinguistic features are encapsulated in a 'discourse of the axiom' as Barber calls it. Barber's (2000: 267) view is that the proverbial sayings in a society constantly act as authoritative, moral codes and can always be used to explain similar situations in different contexts. Messages or themes in African-language written discourses tend to be encoded in 'axiomatic expressions'. These proverbial injunctions constitute generations of folk wisdom from the traditional world, which is shown to be still applicable in modern society.

The repeated stories, observable in different types of media, have been drawn from daily phenomena in order to forge new perspectives on contemporary life styles. Barber points out that

> In the generation of popular Yoruba plays, every moment and every level of production is a site of creative potentiality. Stories are drawn from available repertories but are reshaped; characters are excavated from the repositories of the actors' personal experience, which is always incrementally growing; speech emerges from moment to moment, infused with what is currently in the streets, adapted in the light of the audience's reactions, adjusted to the speech of the other characters in the scene, and fed by the actors' own inspiration as well as the manager's continually updated instructions (2000: 9).

Barber indicates that recapitulations in different periods and their transmutation into popular media like radio and television concretise local experiences. These recapitulations hold lessons steeped in recurrent and other related experiences that have generally been read and interpreted in the same manner. Eventually these assume authority. Barber's premise in the study of Yoruba popular theatre stems from the observation that the stories that were staged mostly dealt with concrete, localised and familiar experiences (ibid: 266). The experiences presented were not only familiar but were also 'real' as the stories were a collective and interactive improvisation by actors who drew extensively from their own reservoir of experience, personality and competence based on hearsay, daily metaphors and proverbial sayings, contemporary events, anecdotes of experience circulating in popular culture, and so forth. Barber's analysis of Yoruba popular culture is useful in explaining the recurrent morality lessons in African-language literatures generally, isiZulu literature specifically and in television dramas.

This way of analysing indigenous expression is supported by Chapman (1996) who points out that an evaluation of South African indigenous literature in terms of realistic criteria is misleading. In a realistic reading the oral 'residue,' which manifests itself in strong storylines, episodic plots, and copious repetitions, might not be recognised. This trend in thinking about indigenous literary expression is not entirely new. As early as the 1960s Ramsaran made a case for 'old mythologies' that propagated themselves anew as signs of the continued growth of a cultural life which, while it evolves, also preserves the vitality of the 'old mythology'. Barber's observations on Yoruba popular plays illustrate this point as does her emphasis on the moral aspects the plays perform as responses to the demands of modernity. When transferred to other contexts, like that of African language generally and literature specifically, these moral aspects contribute to our understanding of the role played by orality in responding to the complexities that resulted from modernity. Furthermore, this insistent recurrence of folkloric material in new textual forms points to both folklore and life experiences as sources for thematic material.

Barber's approach, which focuses on everyday culture through the exploration of textual productions that aim to edify audiences through demonstrations of moral lessons, will be used to explain the recurrence of the old themes in new contexts and the emergence of new themes in both print and broadcast media.

Overview of the book

In this book the texts selected to illustrate the interpenetration between written and oral or popular discourse in post-apartheid written and broadcast narratives are divided into two categories. The first category is comprised of written novels: Radebe's (1998) *Aphelile Agambaqa* (Words have been finished); Buthelezi's (1996) *Impi YaboMdabu Isethunjini* (The War of the Africans is in the intestines); Ngubo's (1996) *Yekanini Ukuzenza* (I have done this to myself); Muthwa's (1996) *Isifungo* (The Vow); and Masondo's (1994) two detective novels, *Ingwe Nengonyama* (The lion and the leopard) and *Ingalo Yomthetho* (The arm of the law). The second category comprises popular television serials: Shabangu and De Kock's *Ifa LakwaMthethwa* (The Inheritance of the Mthethwa Clan), Whener's *Hlala Kwabafileyo* (Remain with the dead), Yazbek's *Gaz' Lam* (My friend/kin) and Mahlatsi's *Yizo Yizo* (This is it).

The first three chapters of the book discuss how proverbs, folktales and naming practices have been redeployed to infuse into the contemporary world aspects of the traditional past. Through such textual analysis, the book demonstrates how older or traditional forms are made contemporary through being applied to the new circumstances. In this way the book shows how apparently stale themes can produce novel readings.

In chapter one the focus is on proverbs. The proverbs in the texts play a central and complex role. In instances where proverbs are used as titles of narratives, or aligned with the leading characters driving the moral of the lesson, the narrative is usually structured in such a way as to refer back to these proverbs at the end. The proverbs encapsulate the known, absolute truth about life experiences which then are re-enacted in the narrative producing similar conclusions. By drawing on Barber's model, we not only understand how the proverb works aesthetically in the text, we also understand it as an implied reading strategy. This strategy provides the reader with instructions on how the axioms in the text should be applied. The intended texts for study in this chapter are Radebe's (1998) *Aphelile Agambaqa* and Buthelezi's (1996) *Impi YaboMdabu Isethunjini*.

In chapter two I focus on those narratives that use folktale motifs as a way of structuring the moral lesson of the story. Ngubo's (1996) *Yekanini Ukuzenza* and Muthwa's (1996) *Isifungo* are representative of a broader class of novels which rely on folktale motifs to construct a didactic outcome. The first novel draws its structural motif from the folktale of the piglet called *Maqinase*, (the self-willed one). In the novel *Yekanini Ukuzenza*, Busisiwe, a self-willed leading female character, is drawn into a life of fast living through crime. The second novel is heavily indebted to the structural motif of the folktale *Mamba KaMaquba* (Mamba son of Maquba). Drawing again on Barber's model, I will analyse these novels to illuminate how such motifs are used to produce a lesson with emphasis on how such texts invite the readers to apply these lessons to the world beyond the book.

Chapter three is concerned with isiZulu narratives which have been influenced by oral forms like praises and naming. According to Masondo (1997) naming has been the most valued practice in the culture of the Zulu people. He points out that there are different reasons why people choose particular names. With regard to names for people, some names are coined even before they are born or when they are born or long after they have been born, in their adulthood. Certain messages are sent by the people who coin the name. Given that praises and naming play such a crucial role in the traditions of the Zulu people, in this book, drawing on Barber's model, I will discuss narratives where the creative use of names and praises in the text reflects not only a stylistic form but a moral lesson which the reader knows to be encapsulated in the meaning of the names. In chapter three I will explore the uses of naming in *Ingwe Nengonyama* (1994) (The Leopard and the Lion) and *Ingalo Yomthetho* (1994) (The arm of the law), which are detective narratives by Masondo.

The last three chapters of the book discuss black television series, in particular the focus is on new themes that emerged in television drama series after 1994. From the early 1990s, the South African Broadcasting Corporation, in their programming, emphasised social engineering policies, such as nation-building and neo-liberalist policies, that were to be aligned with South Africa's new political economy. In the fourth chapter, through a study of two South African drama series, *Ifa LakwaMthethwa* and *Hlala Kwabafileyo*, I will discuss how these African-language television series drew from changing, post-1994 economic policies and popular culture discourses to construct narratives that were 'aspirational' (as defined by Vundla and McCathy, producers of *Generations* and *Gaz' Lam II* (respectively). As part of broader concerns of this chapter I will highlight notions of contemporaneity brought about by the interplay between tradition and modernity, the international world and the local, and the flow of metropolitan meaning through national culture to that of the most remote backwater villages. The change, emphasised by the thematic frontiers of these series, is read against the cultural frames of inheritance conventions which, in both filmic narratives, are signalled by the pivotal use of the genres from oral or popular discourse.

Whereas *Ifa LakwaMthethwa* and *Hlala Kwabafileyo* represent earlier series that signalled the new directions to be taken by the national broadcaster after 1994, the following TV series, *Gaz' Lam* and *Yizo Yizo*, which come much later, after the new dispensation, offer a sober and reflective reality which resonates in intricate ways with the social tone established much earlier by the isiZulu literary tradition. In the next chapters I discuss the intertextual dialogism between the isiZulu literary tradition and these filmic narratives.

These series, as emerging black film in African languages, provide a new site for further exploring and contesting African experiences in post-apartheid contemporary society. In terms of aesthetics, these series illuminate Barber's contentions that there is mutual allusiveness between African artistic products. The porous nature of African artistic products is also visible between these series and isiZulu fiction. The themes treated in these series complement those found in the written literature as well as draw from popular debates in the society. In my discussion I will analyse how older narrative tropes are redeployed to address emergent areas of social concern. I will focus on how the drama series in the post-apartheid context not only offers retrospectively conventional reviews and dispels received meanings, but also how it offers fresh new readings in line with the socio-economic and political realities of the post-apartheid African society.

I conclude this section in chapter six with a comparative analysis of the depiction of crime in *Yizo Yizo* and in one isiZulu novel. Drawing on Altbeker's (2001) ground-breaking research on post-apartheid crime realties and legal consciousness in South Africa, I explore the tensions brought to light in *Yizo Yizo* and *Kuyoqhuma Nhlamvana* (What has been concealed will be revealed) and argue that the parallel existence of the white world, seen as continuous with South Africa's colonial past, and the Black marginalised world, has led to a diminished respect for the law among many Black South Africans. More significantly I will show how *Yizo Yizo*'s perspective on, and treatment of, crime influence this isiZulu novel.

Endnotes

1   See the materials compiled by Ntuli 1983, 1984 and 1985 and Gule 1995 and 1996. The notes that these scholars produced as study guides had simplified explanations of the theoretical model in use during this period. Furthermore, as these scholars are also creative writers, the conceptualisations of their literary works exemplified a symmetrical alignment of theory and the work of art itself, so that there is a one to one reading between the theoretical principle and the different aspects of the work of art. As their works and influence were ubiquitous during this period, budding authors followed these notes religiously when creating their own art.

2   The simplified versions of Structuralism and New Criticism that came to dominate African-language literatures if they have been part of these literary models at all, focused not on critical thinking and objectivity. Instead focus was and still is on measuring rudimentary comprehension skills.

Proverbs in narratives: Seeing the contemporary through archaic gazes in *Aphelile Agambaqa* and *Impi YaboMdabu Isethunjini*

The modern approach to the study of folklore[1] has created a discursive terrain that allows for the reconsideration of the role of folklore material in contemporary society (Thosago, 2004: 13). This approach rejects conventional conceptions of folklore as 'antediluvian', 'backward', 'illiterate' and 'primitive' and instead seeks to regenerate folklore. Thosago's perspective highlights the interrelation between folklore and postmodernity and how technical spaces such as the broadcast media can be exploited for the rejuvenation of folklore, an aspect I explore in the last three chapters of the book. However his views on this matter are not new. Since the inception of isiZulu literature in colonial times, writers have made use of a syncretic admixture of traditional knowledge and Western civilisation when writing about modernity. This has since become a convention of creative writing in isiZulu. Therefore at the conceptual level, re-narrating contemporary experiences entails a need to revisit this ancient tradition, thus creating a hybridised continuity, complex as it might be, between the idyllic, unattainable past and the self-conscious writings that typify post-modern textuality (Obiechina, 1972, 1973; Msimang, 1986).[2]

It is against this background that I discuss proverbs and their re-invocation in two post-apartheid isiZulu novels. The study of proverbs has led to significant advances in our understanding of their nature and their function in discourses of orature, literature, and every day speech acts. The uses of proverbs and other oral genres are various and wide, but their significance lies in their ability to explain language, thought and society (Pridmore, 1991, cited in Zounmenou, 2004). It is not only the thoughts of a society presented through proverbs but also its philosophical views that are reflected and passed down from one generation to the next. In some African societies the use of proverbs in daily conversations is a highly valued verbal experience because it develops the ingenuity seen as linguistic preparation for the performance of lengthy verbal art forms like folk stories or *izibongo* (praises).

Okpewho (1992) discusses the application of proverbs, especially the role of proverbs in everyday conversation and the 'twists' that are discerned in the proverbs used by individuals to 'spice up the talk'. Further scholarly views emphasise their didactic illocutionary function (Monye, 1966; Pelling, 1977; Mokitimi, 1997; Okpewho, 1992). It is the intended didacticism in proverbs that I focus on in this chapter. IsiZulu literature is dominated by didacticism. This didacticism has always been located within a traditional knowledge though accentuated by the advent of Christianity which brought its own moral discourses. The tensions and the conflicts that have existed between these two discourses, tradition and Christianity, with each vying for dominance in literary discourses have characterised isiZulu literature from its inception.

The Christian discourses are not the only prominent force that shaped isiZulu literature. A host of other Western influences shaped its content and form. According to Barber (1999: 20) the use of Western stylistic criteria firstly excluded oral art forms from those texts that are 'constituted to invite comment, analysis and assessment' and secondly, prevented recognition of the fact that these indigenous forms could have formed a basis for an indigenous African aesthetics. When Western literary conventions are applied to isiZulu literature, those oral art forms that have been used in novels, short stories and dramas have been regarded only as 'the author's use of language' rather than as examples of African discursive practices. In such instances the author is praised for including idioms and proverbs in his work and is castigated if their quantity is found to be wanting.[3] According to Barber's model, African discourses are constituted by oral art forms such as folk narratives, legends, riddles, proverbs, axioms and everyday sayings. These oral art forms perpetuate and reaffirm the authority of the traditional world. They are able to improvise, and they are fluid and flexible, which allows them to incorporate new materials and migrate to other genres. In spite of this apparent flexibility and mobility there are certain valuable elements, constituted by unchanging fixed formulations, that make it possible for these art forms to be identified as independent, detached texts. Akinnaso (1985) points out that whenever these forms are performed or uttered, they are experienced as durable formulations that come from outside the current conversation and are thought to transcend conversation or other everyday uses of language. The contribution provided by Barber (1999, 2000) to the study of proverbs, not only as performance texts but also as identifiable discursive practices that underpin African value systems, has never been explored in relation to isiZulu literature. Barber further points out that

> the reification of the utterance in Yorùbá discourses, is signalled by the intense and pervasive presence of quotation […] There is a whole field of texts that are constituted as quotations: rather than being merely uttered, they are cited (1999: 18–19).

Even though Barber's model focuses on the oral art forms of Yorùbá society, the presence of these oral formulations in isiZulu language justifies its application here. The two novels selected for the demonstration of this theory are Buthelezi's (1996) *Impi YaboMdabu Isethunjini* (The war of Africans is in the intestines) and Radebe's (1996) *Aphelile Agambaqa* (Words have been finished).

This chapter investigates the uses of proverbs as an implied reading strategy in isiZulu literature. Proverbs are not only artistic articulations but also critical discourses in which are embedded moral instructions for social cohesion. The close affinities between proverbs as narratives[4] and the plots of *Aphelile Agambaqa* and *Impi YaboMdabu Isethunjini* reveal how the proverbs used as titles, together with others cited throughout the narratives, depend on their linguistic-social authority as pre-existing quotations while they simultaneously comment on, and shape perceptions of, contemporary life. There is 'mutual reflection' at play between the proverbs and the narratives of the novels. What the proverbs encapsulate as the known absolute truth about life experiences is re-enacted in the narrative producing similar conclusions. The narrative is structured in such a way as to refer back to these proverbs at the end of the novels. To bring out the interplay between the proverbs and the plotting strategies of the novels, I explore the proverbs both as titles of the narratives and as propellants of the moral lesson. In discussing the moral I will draw on the many proverbs that have been quoted throughout the novels to highlight issues that impact the central theme of the narratives. These quotations, when detached from the contexts of these narratives, can be used as 'independent utterances' from which various narratives can be derived. However in these texts they have been contextualised as supporting truths that complement or supplement the dominant truth reflected in the titles of the novels.

A summary of *Aphelile Agambaqa*

The narrative opens with the main female character, a single parent, Nomvula, discovering that her son, Sibusiso, has been 'abducted' by his biological father, Makhaya, a journalist on a local newspaper in the Eastern Cape. After Makhaya fails to return the child to Nomvula's Daveyton home late that Friday afternoon, she decides to drive to the Eastern Cape, where Makhaya lives, in order to get the child from its father. She reassures her mother that she will be back on Saturday afternoon. At this moment in her life, Nomvula is involved with Sipho, a lawyer. Over the weekend, talks of her *ilobolo* negotiations are to be conducted. On Monday she is scheduled to leave the country on a business trip.

On arrival in the Eastern Cape she tries to persuade the father to give back the child but she fails, as do her attempts at 'stealing' back the child. Makhaya's reasons for taking the child are, firstly, to get back at Nomvula because she kept him in the dark regarding the pregnancy and, secondly, that he feels he has been denied the chance of exercising his responsibilities as a father for the past seven years. Lastly he has hopes that he can convince Nomvula to marry him since he has learnt that Nomvula is about to be married to another man. On arrival at Makhaya's place Nomvula discovers that he is in a relationship that has problems similar to those in their former relationship which were the basis for her decision not to disclose her pregnancy to him. Tensions between herself and Makhaya's lover arise, but Makhaya's lover cannot openly display her hostilities fearing that such actions and attitudes might cost her this relationship because even though there are problems she is content with the way things are. Thus her support for Nomvula's efforts to get Makhaya to give up the child stems from the realisation that Nomvula's prolonged stay may cause her to lose her patience and eventually expose herself.

Back home in Gauteng province Nomvula's fiancé, Sipho, learns of the reasons leading to her sudden journey to the Eastern Cape. He follows her and on arrival in the area he lays a charge against Makhaya at the police station. By the time he arrives, however, the relationship between Makhaya and Nomvula has developed, and old flames have been rekindled. However, Nomvula has made a promise to Makhaya's lover, and cannot allow herself to be caught up in Makhaya's ways again. Together Nomvula and Makhaya's lover devise a plot for her to get back her child and escape from the province, but it is delayed by Sipho's arrival. Seeing that the presence of Sipho might spoil her plan, Nomvula decides to sneak out unseen and escape with her son. However, things go wrong on the morning of their departure. Sibusiso goes missing and it is up to Makhaya to search for and find the child. By this time Nomvula's family has come to the Eastern Cape because she has stayed away for more days than she had initially planned. They coincidentally meet at the hotel from which Sibusiso has gone missing. When Makhaya eventually returns with Sibusiso, the family is impressed and urges Nomvula to reconsider her decision not to marry him. She is speechless as she allows herself to be prevailed upon by her family to marry Makhaya even though she previously objected to the idea. The narrative ends with the banquet celebrating the re-union and the intended marriage between Nomvula and Makhaya.

A summary of *Impi YaboMdabu Isethunjini*

The narrative opens with Cele, John's uncle, who comes from rural Eshowe, paying an unscheduled visit to John, who lives in Umlazi. John has a good position at work and he keeps to a tight schedule and is thus unable to let his uncle see him until he has made an appointment. An angry Cele eventually secures an appointment but John is not happy to hear what Cele has come to talk to him about. Cele has come to ask John, who we learn is an aspiring petit bourgeois, to take over the guardianship of his sister's children (begotten out of wedlock), since she (the mother of the children) has now married a different man. John refuses to take on this customary responsibility, citing personal and financial reasons. But it emerges later that the real reason is that he is afraid of his wife, Popi, a nagging and domineering wife, who is a matron in one of the local hospitals. It also emerges that John's family life is based on Eurocentric norms and values and therefore the addition of two children to their family budget is out of the question as it would mean he would no longer be able to afford the lifestyle he wants to pursue.

Cele decides to keep the children, Uzithelile and Hlanganisani. They grow up in rural Eshowe, helping him with daily chores and at the same time working as domestics with local white employers. By contrast John's children, Euthanasia and Melody, are juvenile delinquents.

Drastic changes occur with Euthanasia, John's son. After getting into trouble at school, he runs away from home to Eshowe to his grandfather's place where, on arrival, he receives a royal welcome. A goat is slaughtered in his honour and bile is sprinkled over him. He is given a new name, Vikizitha, as the European name did not have much sense or value for the rural people. Eventually he goes back home as a reborn youth who espouses different values to those practiced at his home. Although this places him at loggerheads with his family, particularly with his mother, the family eventually accepts him. He gradually transfers these values to his sister, Melody, who is renamed Vukuzithathe by their rural cousins.

John's lifestyle and marriage disintegrate and because he leads a solitary life in Umlazi he is unable to reconnect with his neighbours who would have given him support. After relocating to La Lucia John abandons his family and leads a hedonistic life of overindulgence in women and alcohol. In his absence his wife manages to get herself educated, acquiring a PhD degree. The children are invited by their rural cousins, who by this time have secured scholarships after matriculating, to come and study in America. The narrative ends with a dejected John eventually coming back home to rural Eshowe where his rural relatives re-unite him with his ailing wife.

Proverbs and axioms as plotting strategies

Msimang (1986) points out that proverbs are witticisms, truisms and maxims that have accrued over generations to explain certain phenomena in the life experiences of a people. They are used not only as artistic utterances but also as instructive sites, which, as pointed out by Mokitimi (1997), relate to knowledge, wisdom, philosophy, ethics and morals. Pelling (1977) observes that through these proverbial expressions certain morals and truths are forcefully extolled. According to Nyembezi, these storehouses of experience tend to influence a society's philosophical outlook and regulate its behaviour:

> As a social unit, the people have certain definite ways of behaviour or conduct, which are expected of the individuals comprising the social unit. Some modes of conduct are embodied in proverbs, which serve the purpose of instructing the younger and ignorant generation, or serve as reminders to the old, who have been remiss in their observance of the rules of conduct expected in the society (1949: 299).

It may appear from this that the use of proverbs can hinder progress and encourage linguistic and social stagnation. But a closer look at various oral forms indicates that they preserve some aspects that are recognisably 'archaic' while processing and incorporating modern items. This is observable in evolving tales, proverbs, praises and witticisms.

Axiomatic expressions, as oral art forms, display similar characteristics. Axioms can be defined as generally accepted propositions or principles sanctioned by experience or universally established principles or laws that are not necessarily the truth. Axioms are patterned formulations which embody moral lessons that the readers work out for themselves after going through a narrative. Examples of axiomatic expressions are 'crime does not pay', 'true love stands the test of time' or 'appearances can be deceptive'. These axioms achieve a state of absoluteness because of repeated retellings of narratives with plot structures that re-affirm their truthfulness. Thus, Cornwall (1996) says, the retelling of narratives inevitably creates an impression that they hold a measure of truthfulness. However, as Barber points out of Yoruba theatre,

> The audience, to get its full measure of edification, could not walk into the hall in the closing moments and 'pick the lesson' from the summary statement made in the final speech or song. They need to see the axiom produced, as the outcome of a chain of events analogous to the events experienced in their own lives (2000: 267).

Barber (1999) explains that the structure of axioms, just like that of proverbs, reveals that they operate on two temporal trajectories: the atemporal past, which always presents the preserved images of the proverbs that give them 'object-like properties' (21); and the fluid or flexible quality that allows the incorporation of newness and freshness. This flexible quality allows the axiom to interact with contemporary realities and projections. Proverbs are structured like axioms because they are old quotations which are able to comment on the evolving trends of contemporary life. The presence of these oral forms in the novels discussed in this chapter points not only to the heightened language used but also to dialogue between the experiences in the novels and other experiences. These experiences are identifiable as 'pre-existing hypotexts.'[5] Hypotexts are secondary texts that embody certain worldviews or orientations that are embedded in a primary text. In these hypotexts, as Mukarovsky (cited in Barber, 1999: 27) asserts, the foreign elements not only retain, 'the aura of otherness' but also give a sense of 'the possibility of reverting or opening out into a different text.' These texts perpetuate and re-affirm the authority of the traditional world and its knowledge. Barber (1999) calls these text(s), 'pre-existent texts', namely, those texts such as proverbs, socio-cultural anecdotes, social or political jokes, witticisms or riddles that are not newly fashioned by the author but which she or he can readily access in linguistic and social repertoires. These pre-existent texts, in the context of this book, are proverbs and other witticisms and observations that are used to propel a traditionalist ideology.

The proverb is a patterned linguistic formulation that has an independent identity outside the text and which can be recognised. The novels under discussion have proverbs as titles. A text, oral in origin has migrated to the written medium. In instances where proverbs are embedded in host texts such as narratives, praises and speech acts, the ideas which are encapsulated in the proverbs are brought to bear on the events in the narratives, songs or praises as these proverbs are viewed as representative of people's life experiences. The titles of the novels, then, are ideas couched in proverbs to explain certain experiences.

Aphelile Agambaqa (they (that is, words) are finished completely) describes the state of being speechless after all attempts at changing realities have been exhausted and the futility of the words has been proven. *Impi YaboMdabu Isethunjini* (The war of the Africans is in the intestine), is an evolving proverb derived from *impi yomndeni isesendeni* (The war of the family is in the testicle). Both operate on the premise that these proverbs are ideas that were formulated centuries ago and have been passed down through generations. In the context of the texts they are accessed to illuminate the actions of the characters that populate and drive the narratives.[6]

Novels that have proverbs as titles have an added advantage because the plotting of the narratives follows already established routes or story lines. Cornwall (cited in Barber, 1999: 26) points out that the experiences embodied in proverbs have been heard before and the axioms deduced from them have been worked out earlier and, therefore, the applications of proverbs and the axioms deduced in new contexts become reaffirmations of already existing perspectives. Thus the proverbs and axioms concretise experiences and reveal an embodied authority in the form of a moral lesson. The narrative experience becomes a template through which moral issues, encapsulated in the proverbs, are accessed.

Proverbs as titles of narratives

The meanings given to the proverbs incorporated in various contexts reflect what social trends are permissible or impermissible in the thought of the time. Nyembezi (1949) maintains that, in instances where the new trends are resisted or completely blocked, that is where social thought is opposed to the emergent trend, and then the interpretation of the proverb would revert to the original. In *Aphelile Agambaqa* the new trends that typify contemporary African society are the diminishing value of traditional families where the father has been the unquestioned head, changing gender roles, diminishing socio-cultural values and problems with cultural relevance. In the context of this narrative, and perhaps generally, these trends which have typified modern African societies since the period of industrialisation, urbanisation and modernisation are disparaged as either causes of, or being instrumental in, the decline of an African cultural ethos. In the narrative the absence of a father figure in the life of Nomvula and again in the first few years of her son, Sibusiso, can be read as a strategy to illuminate problems with dysfunctional families.

The narrative seems to postulate that the absence in Nomvula's life of a father figure, a patriarchal authoritative figure who both acts as guardian of cultural practices and leader of a household, allowed for insidious and deviant behaviour on her part, such as her conception of her child out of wedlock. This observation is made by her sister when she quotes the proverb *'lafa elihle kakhulu … kazi Khabazela uyazi yini lapho ulele khona ukuthi emzini wakho sekukwamachaca impunz' idle mini'*. (Gone are the good old days…I wonder if Khabazela (Nomvula's father) knows wherever he is in the afterlife that his home has been turned into a playground) (Radebe, 1996: 9). These proverbs are used to highlight the decline of values and, in particular, to emphasise the fact that the absence of a father in his family allows his offspring to do as they please. The narrative is concerned with the possibility of this happening to Nomvula's son as well. In an attempt to avoid this occurrence the narrative strategically assigns proverbs to various characters so that all their observations regarding dysfunctional families are underlined by the original proverb or by variants that have a similar meaning to that used as the title. I revisit this notion later in the discussion.

In instances where a proverb's timelessness might encounter limitations because of emergent trends, the linguistic formulation of the proverb is extended, as is the case with *Impi YaboMdabu Isethunjini*. Pfeiffer (cited in Biesele 1993) observed this in Ju/'hoan tales. He asserts that the reiteration of oral tales is an indication that certain values are under pressure. His examples of artistic reiteration examine the idea of egalitarian food sharing and that such reiteration may not reflect abundance but rather the violation of the policy regarding food sharing.

The same could be said in cases of narratives that guard against the violation of social codes. The reiteration of proverbs warns or advises against acceptance of trends that would have a negative impact on the social cohesion established by older generations. Through the use of the extended proverb *Impi yaboMdabu Isethunjini* (the war of the Africans is in the intestines) the author indicates that the applicability of the proverb should go beyond intimate family intrigues, as the original form does not include national and social issues that affect black identity such as class disparities in African society, education, politics, employment and social morality. The tensions that play themselves out in the narrative between the rural and the urban family members are projected as being beyond seemingly trivial family conflicts relating to who is responsible for children begotten out of wedlock in order to touch on socio-economic and political issues affecting Africans in a post-apartheid context. The narrative makes the claim that while change and transformation are essential to progress, certain aspects of this progress are not commensurate with traditional values. Transformational tendencies are therefore carefully sifted through the ordering and structuring of narratives or axioms and their validity evaluated against a pre-existing oral archeology.

Proverbs and gender relations

The narratives are structured so as to refer back to the titles and at the same time explore gender relations through the characters of Popi in *Impi* and that of Nomvula in *Aphelile*. In both instances, Popi's education and Nomvula's business success are positioned as leaving them unfulfilled because these achievements accord them a pseudo-independence that encourages them to 'unrightfully' question their traditional gender roles. Their upward mobility is projected as the cause of gender struggles. Popi's attainment of a Doctor of Philosophy degree and Nomvula's success in the fashion industry are linked to references existing in the society regarding affluent and elite women. In *Aphelile*, where Nomvula cites a proverb or an axiom, her sayings are undercut, first by the irrelevance of her material attainments to the task of raising a child and, second, by the expectations placed by society on a mother within a traditionally conceived family. Her citation of the proverb *'ubucwibi obuhle obuhamba ngabubil'* (it is a beautiful sight to see two birds flying together) is subverted by her refusal to acknowledge the role of Makhaya in her life with Sibusiso as only a life together could attest to the truthfulness of the proverb. The contexts of her citations are ironical and tend to question and cast doubt on her convictions. Her chosen form of motherhood is questioned as shallow and self-centered through such comments as *'umncishe amalungelo okuba ubaba enganeni yakhe'* (you denied him his rights of being a father to his child). Furthermore her depiction hints that she is bordering on insanity in her refusal to accept Makhaya in their lives, especially now that he has shown to be penitent and prepared to marry her (Radebe: 19). Equally, in *Impi*, Popi's observations and proverbial sayings are subverted by the materialistic values she holds.

In these texts such women are held in contempt. They are seen as domineering, controlling, over ambitious, unrestrained and non-conformist. Therefore changes in perspectives, configurations and imperatives within the narratives are curtailed by the geo-archeological boundaries operative in popular culture and traditional knowledge. In both, the narrativisation of gender struggles is processed through the prism of a patriarchal framework which operates through a biased depiction of Nomvula's struggles for survival and Popi's assertion of her independence. Both female characters value their independence and the material benefits of being financially self-sufficient. The conceptualisation of the family in the novel *Aphelile*, is that it has a father-head and a nurturing mother. In the novel *Impi*, the violation of a customary practice, that is, John's refusal to adopt his sister's children because of his wife's fearful disposition and dislike of her sister's children, is the framework within which a range of other themes are raised. I revisit this issue later in this chapter.

In *Aphelile Agambaqa*, the main character, Nomvula, is compelled by the nature of her romantic relationship with Makhaya to raise a child by herself for seven years. Because of his chauvinistic egocentrism, Makhaya becomes an absent father. The romantic relationship he offered to Nomvula removed all commitments and any anticipation of marriage, prompting her to keep the pregnancy a secret and confine herself to single parenthood until he re-appears one day to claim his role as a father and a husband. By the time Makhaya re-appears, Nomvula has established herself as a working mother. The nature of her work, in turn, makes her an absent mother as she has to travel far and wide leaving the care of her son to her sister, Ntombi and her mother, MaMhlongo. This indicates that on her own, without the support of her family, she would have failed in her responsibility of raising her child. The idea of working mothers is challenged, then, particularly if the working mother is a single parent like Nomvula. Makhaya lives with his lover, Thembisile, who is a nursing sister. He has a romantic relationship with her which is similar to the one he had with Nomvula. Thembisile also has a foster child. During her night shifts the foster child is entrusted to the care of relatives until the shift has ended, making her an absent mother.

In both instances children are exposed to bad influences and, to atone, the children are spoiled. Makhaya abducts his son on the day Nomvula has planned to take him out on a spending spree because she will be away from home for a month. Overindulging the child is atonement for affection not given to the child. This is shown in many instances when Nomvula fails to reprimand Sibusiso. In the Eastern Cape, Makhaya, too, is not an innocent party. He atones for the seven-year period he has been absent by indulging the child, winning his trust through material gifts. For Makhaya, the material gifts are used as a vehicle to reconnect with his son and to make him feel the need for a father figure in his life. And it is this need that is exploited by the author to re-unite Makhaya and Nomvula (even though Nomvula initially protests against the idea) and lead them into matrimony, in which Nomvula is expected to fulfil the traditional role of being a housewife because Makhaya will provide for them.

The proverbs that sum up the lesson of ideal parenting are *'ubucwibi obuhle obuhamba ngababili'* (it is a beautiful sight to see two birds flying together) (Radebe: 24) or *'amasongo amahle akhala ngambili'* (this type of bird species normally make similar sounds and they are always together) (Buthelezi,1996: 58). These proverbs are carriers of the central moral in the narratives. In *Impi*, Popi's domineering nature in affairs related to the children is criticised through the proverb *'amasongo akhala emabili'* (Buthelezi: 58). These proverbs lobby for a traditional family. In *Aphelile* the proverb complements the proverb used in the title. In *Impi*, though, the use of the proverb goes beyond surface problems to issues involving the commitment of parents to raising their children and the kinds of values the children receive. For Buthelezi there is a link between social disintegration and the values transferred to children in their families. And together with the axiom deduced from the narratives, that *dual parenting is the best form of parenting,* the proverbs concretise the narrative experience so that Nomvula's attempts at shutting Makhaya out of her life and that of her son are expected to fail. In a similar vein, Popi's domination over her children eventually destroys her family.

Proverbs and traditional practices

Cultural values can also be strategically employed with the intention of directing the reading of the narrative towards the lesson contained in the proverb. In *Aphelile* this cultural value relates to the observance of a customary practice of *inhlawulo* (loosely translated as: paying for the damages), which may be interpreted as a legitimate claim to fatherhood by a father who has children out of wedlock. In the narrative, Makhaya did not show respect to Nomvula's family by observing this practice, not even after learning of his son's existence, therefore, culturally, he does not have a right to the child. With complete disregard for custom (Radebe: 65) he unilaterally decides to reclaim his child, abducting him from school and taking him back with him to Bhizana in the Eastern Cape, with stern directives that if Nomvula wants her child back she must come to the Eastern Cape. His actions are fuelled not only by his knowledge of his son's existence but also by the information he has received regarding Nomvula's impending marriage to another man (Radebe: 59). Makhaya is opposed to another man raising his child (Radebe: 71). Through the abduction of the child from its mother, the narrative directs attention away from this cultural expectation and focuses on the relationship between the parents and the child and on the lovers' estrangement. Makhaya's seven years of estrangement is equated with Nomvula's several hours of estrangement from her son. By shifting locality from Gauteng to Bhizana Radebe symbolically recreates an island without cultural bounds for the estranged lovers to reconfigure their relationship away from the binding traditions represented by families. Radebe attempts to show that the causes of this estrangement are superficial and that it has been unnecessary because underlying the partners' views on why their relationship failed is their undying love for each other which constantly re-surfaces and overwhelms them. Thus their interaction whenever they are alone veers towards rekindling their love. This is captured by a proverb, *'lapho amanzi ake ema khona aphinde eme'* (a pool of water recurs where it once stood), cited by Makhaya's lover in desperation at seeing the natural attraction between Nomvula and Makhaya (Radebe: 50).

This focus on the relationships emphasises Makhaya's biological right to the child as opposed to a social or cultural right that could have been occasioned by his observance of *inhlawulo* (Radebe: 65). This reading is deduced from his retort, '*Anginamsebenzi nomthetho [...] Ungowami, uyindodana nendlalifa yami ngokwemvelo. Akukho mthetho ongangiphuca ilungelo lami lemvelo*' (I do not care about the law [...] He is mine and naturally he is the one to take on my inheritance. There is no law that can deny me my natural right) (Radebe: 65). Although the cultural observance of *inhlawulo* is key in such cases as the narrative intimates, there is a reading that suggests that Radebe emphasises the biological claim above customary laws. Makhaya's views regarding which claim is weightier reveal the underlying ambiguity of the narrative, where patriarchal views are allowed to be selectively applied and observed by the male members of the society. Makhaya, who espouses the patriarchal values of the author, is given greater scope in his interpretation of the social or cultural values that strengthen his case as he attempts to reclaim his son. The fact that *inhlawulo*, which is a necessary cultural bridge between parties and families, is downplayed is indicative of the room given to patriarchal members of the society.

The centrality of the patriarchal head in Radebe's conception of a family unit goes against emerging truths concerning the success of single mothers. Radebe seems to imply that Nomvula's pregnancy and the untraditional manner in which it has been handled occurs as a result of the absence of the father figure who would have ensured that proper traditional practices were followed. For Radebe the presence of the father would have been instrumental in extracting *inhlawulo* (payment for the damages) from the man who impregnated Nomvula. Her mother has not questioned Nomvula's pregnancy because, it seems, she understands and knows about the probability of success in single parenting. However, single parenting as a contemporary reality in many African societies is not fully explored in the narrative because the depiction of this reality would have questioned all the proverbs on display that allude to the fact that it takes two parents to raise a child. The narrative underplays the fact that material acquisitions are equally important in raising children and instead focuses on questioning the character and intelligence, particularly of Nomvula, in her determination to be a single mother.

Proverbs and the boundaries of the family

The narrative's exploration of the nature of relationships reveals the author's preferred reading of the traditional knowledge around the family. By exploiting ideas about what constitutes an ideal family, Radebe has not only reconciled Nomvula and Makhaya but has also been able to discount contemporary views that families can be constituted by adults who are not the biological parents of children. This is illustrated through the impending marriage between Nomvula and Sipho. Their relationship is subjected to a series of tests through which it emerges that Sipho has always despised Nomvula's son. Consequently Nomvula is left with no option but to terminate her engagement. The proverbs used to describe Sipho's actions and personality illuminate his position as an intruder into Makhaya's family unit and, significantly, show how unnatural his role as a father will be. Sipho is said to have '*bhodlela emswaneni*' (a belated grumbling) (Radebe: 22) when hearing about the abduction and how Nomvula has gone after Makhaya to beg for the return of her child. However, even though he grumbled he saw in Makhaya's act a solution for getting rid of Nomvula's child. He had intended to send Sibusiso to a distant boarding school after the wedding but Makhaya's actions create an opportunity and prompt him to negotiate for the child to be handed to his father through a legal process. Sipho's actions point to the axiom that a man cannot raise another man's child, a concern that led Makhaya to abduct his son from Nomvula.

Nomvula's entrapment between Sipho, who she has realised harbours a deep-seated hatred for her child, and Makhaya's chauvinistic demands, makes her desire to escape. When the three of them are supposed to discuss the status of the child she disappears and the proverb '*usele nesisila sehobe*' (he was left behind holding a feather of a wild dove) (Radebe: 79, 82) is cited. This saying predicts that Sipho will be jilted in favour of the biological father of the child. This proverb also describes Sipho's destitution after he has been deserted by the woman he loves; he feels as though Nomvula has dumped him like '*inyongo yenyathi*' (the gall bladder of a deer). Thus axioms deduced from these proverbs foreground Sipho's deceptiveness, warn against raising another man's child while that father remains alive and emphasise the sanctity of the family. Makhaya's re-appearance in Nomvuyo's life helps her to see Sipho for who he really is. Sipho is found to be morally repulsive as she is drawn back to Makhaya. The union between herself and Makhaya occurs despite Nomvula's earlier protestations of '*lingawa licoshwe zinkukhu*' (it [the sun] will fall and be eaten by the chickens) (Radebe: 28) meaning she will never be involved with Makhaya again. However, this union has been predicted through numerous proverbs strategically located in the narrative.

In the application of the above proverb as associated with Nomvula, there is an implied understanding that the father acted within his rights to take the child because Nomvula's family had warned her that getting the child back might not be as easy as she thinks, saying '*uyodela uMakhasana[7] oyozibona zingqubuzana*' (It is well with Makhasana who will see them fight) (Radebe: 19). The truth of the proverb works in tandem with the pressure that her family exerts on her that questions her decisions about single parenting. These decisions are made to appear thoughtless and egocentric. This causes her to lose confidence in her convictions and to see the need for dual parenting (Radebe: 10, 53). Equally, the events of the narrative are structured in such a way that all her attempts to get her child back fail and the proverb '*ufe olwembiza*' (breaking up to little pieces like a clay pot) (Radebe: 80) describes her state of 'speechlessness' after all her attempts have failed.

Regarding Thembisile's involvement with Makhaya, there is a proverb in the text that indicates that Makhaya will be compelled to choose between Thembisile and Nomvula. When the narrator says, '*akukho zinkunzi zimbili zakhonya sibayeni sinye*' (two bulls will never stay in the same kraal) (Radebe: 96) this introduces the author's perspective on the sanctity of family. Even though the proverb creates suspense, it is anticipated that Makhaya will opt for Nomvula since it has been prefigured in the use of the proverb '*ubucwibi obuhle ngobuhamba ngabubili'* as discussed earlier on.

A number of other structural devices have been employed by the author to channel the interpretation of the narrative. These are the dream artifice, ancestral intervention and nature as reflected in the ecosystem. The dream artifice has been structured in such a way that in all three instances Nomvula is saved by Makhaya (Radebe: 36, 64), prefiguring their reunion at the end of the narrative. In the second technique, the author has drawn on the traditional belief system, in which the ancestors are supposed to intervene in human destinies (Radebe: 52). The last strategy makes use of natural phenomena. For example, the author dramatises the capture of a frog by a snake (Radebe: 92). This occurs in a scene where Nomvula has failed for the third time to take her son back from Makhaya. Conveniently, it occurs at Makhaya's place in the Eastern Cape, where the belief in *inkwankwa* (a snake believed to be representative of the ancestors) takes precedence in matters relating to the ancestral acknowledgement of children. Both on the literal and symbolic levels, the natural relationship between the prey and the predator is unavoidable. Thus there is a reading of the narrative in which the matrimonial bond between Nomvula and Makhaya is an inevitable occurrence in which Nomvula's individuality will be swallowed by the greater demands of social expectations.

Proverbs and the moral lessons of post-apartheid society

Buthelezi's application of the proverb as a title in *Impi,* and its extension to encompass social development issues, race relations, gender relations, class politics and rural and urban dialectics allows him to comment on evolving trends within the life experiences of contemporary South Africans, while attributing the tensions and conflicts characteristic of these life experiences to the inequality and social injustices that prevent access to basic human needs. There is a sense that Africans in South Africa are simultaneously engulfed by the traps of modern life and reeling from colonial and apartheid legacies. By considering post-apartheid as the third epoch (colonialism and apartheid being the first and second) Buthelezi is able to suggest the direction in which Africa should develop. Buthelezi seems to suggest that true development would stem from past values.[8]

The first example that demonstrates Buthelezi's manipulation of the plot relates to the customary practice of adopting nephews and nieces begotten out of wedlock which has been a valued practice in African society. It is viewed as a familial responsibility underpinned by the philosophy of *ubuntu* (African humanism). Through this philosophy Buthelezi has been able to satirise and critique modern lifestyles that have denuded urbanised, elitist Africans of their sense of nationhood. The juxtapositioning of rural and urban dialectics seems to suggest that vestiges of *ubuntu* can still be found in the rural areas.

The traditional world not only controlled the sexuality of youths through the system of *amaqhikiza* (regimentation of girls) and *ukubuthwa kwezinsizwa* (regimentation of young men), but the problem of children begotten out of wedlock was normally solved by assigning a widower to the 'fallen' girl. A classic example of this practice in Zulu history is the marrying off of Nandi, Shaka's mother, to Gendeyana. With the imposition of colonialism and industrialisation, the age-old practice gradually changed to be replaced by the adoption of these children by their uncles. It is believed that in modern times it is *ubuntu* not to burden a new husband with the children of another man. There seems to be an underlying understanding that uncles assume responsibility for the girl's failure to control her sexual desires (Buthelezi: 25). That failure should be contained within the family and thus male members of the family are assigned to raise these children and of course they rely on the material benefits accrued by the family. Also implied in this custom is that the wives of these patriarchs, as they are foreigners in the home themselves, are not consulted on matters related to the adoption of the children and are expected to raise these children as their own (Buthelezi: 22–23). They are called *umalumekazi*[9] (female gendered uncle).

The wives become the extension of their husbands in all motherly duties. They have married into the family knowing that it is '*ubuntu nobuzwe bethu*' (African humanism and nationality) that the uncle '*uyozibutha zonke izingane zikadadewenu. Uyozibutha noma zingaba yishumi noma amashumi amathathu'* (will collect and raise all the children of his sisters. He will collect and raise them all even if they are ten or thirty) (Buthelezi: 65) because it is their right to be raised under their uncle's law (Buthelezi: 26). Cele, the character representative of the traditional position in *Impi*, fails to understand John's refusal to add these children to his family. What comes into sharp focus is the Eurocentric and the Afrocentric conceptions of what constitutes a family, and how these conceptions affect an urbanised, educated African financially. In this text the clash of cultures, which was dominant in the writings of the first generation of isiZulu writers, is propelled beyond pitting Western and African values against each other, in the course of which the superiority of the Western values is emphasised. In this novel traditional African notions that kept the society intact are revisited and used to question accepted and normalised Western notions.

Buthelezi retrieves and re-concretises African values by activating numerous proverbs which are strategically distributed throughout the narrative. The proverbs work in tandem with axioms derived as moral lessons in the narrative. For example, the narrative's conflict is based on the violation of a fast declining social code, the adoption of children out of wedlock, which is captured in the quotation *'kwakuyothenga ilala'* (it is dead). However, the subsequent structuring of the events indicates that throwing away good social practices is tantamount to throwing away one's identity and humanity and this act only contributes to the state of poverty and underdevelopment witnessed in the country. The axiom that captures the loss of identity and nationhood becomes the basis for the exploration of the general state of affairs within the African nation.

That Buthelezi's narrative depicts the multi-layered intricacies besetting urban African lifestyles is captured in the proverb, *'insumansumane imali yamakhanda'*[10] (an anomaly, the head tax issue) (Buthelezi: 3, 6). This proverb not only captures a sense of loss but emphasises the absurdity of urban lifestyles. Cele, who was once a migrant, is not averse to change but his fundamental criticism of urban life stems from his realisation of the lack of foresight, from urbanising and modernising Africans, regarding the nature of this change and the indifference with which valued customs are treated in the urban areas.

The fact that in the cities life is different and people lead their lives differently to those in the rural areas is captured in '*seligaya ngomunye umhlathi*' (it chews on another side) (Buthelezi: 7). This proverb sets the tone of the narrative, establishing the moral depravity, materialism, hedonism and decadence of city life which illustrate the change from traditional life to an urban Westernised and elitist lifestyle. This proverb channels the reading to a conclusion, '*lafa elihle kakhulu*' (the beautiful (land) is dead) (Buthelezi: 14), which is a lament for the good past that will never be retrieved.

By comparing the lifestyles of blood relatives in the rural and the urban areas, Buthelezi is able to direct readers to a conclusion regarding the causes of the evils that beset African urban dwellers and their lifestyles. Life in the urban centres is at all times bound by monetary considerations. As a result, city dwellers are seen to have sold their humanity because they are now known as people '*abangabekelwa nja*' (those for whom one does not keep a dog) and their homes have turned into '*kukwanja yotha umlilo*' (it is the house of a dog sitting near the hearth). This implies that they are stingy and inhospitable, the treatment received by Cele when he paid an unscheduled visit to John, his nephew.

Given this cluster of proverbs it is expected that John will not accede to Cele's request to adopt Uzithelile and Hlanganisani. John gives different reasons for declining this request, one of which is the very old adage, '*intandane enhle ngumakhothwa ngunina*' (the beautiful orphan is the one licked by its mother), implying that the children will be well raised if their mother takes care of them. Because he violates the custom by discriminating among his own children, for his sister's children are his own, Cele points out that John's mother '*akazalanga ubole amathumbu*' (she did not bear offspring, but her intestines were rotten). The proverb and particularly the emphasis on the metaphor connoted by the words *ithumbu* (singular) and *amathumbu* (plural) operate in the same way as in the proverb '*impi yomndeni isesendeni*' because both allude to the feuds in the family. In the narrative John is the metaphoric rotten and selfish offspring of the Ngubane family. John's Eurocentric conception of a family is interrogated and shown to be based solely on selfishness without compassion. This materialistic selfishness makes him reject his own children. John's parents died when he and his sister were very young and his uncle, Cele, because of the customary duties expected of him, raised them (John and his sister) as his own children (Buthelezi: 26). When he adopted John and Lenolo, Cele's material position bordered on poverty whilst John's current affluent status puts him in a position where he can afford anything.

The second example through which Buthelezi directs the plot to preferred readings involves class politics and how the peasant and working class is predestined to observe culture while the values harboured by the educated are a barrier to cultural observances. Some of these values relate to the position of women in educated families from which they abuse the powers accorded to them by their educated husbands, as is the case with Popi, John's wife. Popi's role in this family is depicted as having a negative impact because she neglects the African values that should be inculcated in their children.

Changing gender roles that are based on Western formulations shift power bases and adversely affect the family structure in urbanised, educated families. The choices and decisions made regarding traditional culture are based on material acquisition. Popi's values are those that look up to European mores at the expense of African ones, creating 'umlungumnyama' (a black white man) out of her children. The location of these children in a black urban township worsens matters because they become islands. Their cultural disconnection is witnessed in the white friends they have, their use of English as a first language, the white schools they attend, the white manners they display and their consciousness about status. This explains Cele's retort, 'izingane zikaBafana ngeke zilibone eliwinayo, uyongibuza ungiphale ulimi' (Bafana (John) children will not be able to see the winning one, you will ask and scrub my tongue) (Buthelezi: 48). Buthelezi's picture of class distinctions in urban areas establishes Cele's class as 'izinqe zoluntu' (the bottom of humanity) but as far wealthier in human values than educated people, 'izingengelezi zezimpandla' (the bald heads) because their financial success and education 'igugule ubuntu basala bezingebhezi, benqunu' (has eroded their humanism and left them bald and nude) (Buthelezi: 10).

Equally disparaged is the kind of education provided by the white schools which black learners attend. For Buthelezi, these schools are far from being multiracial. They remain white, in spite of their multiracial composition. Buthelezi is of the opinion that true education is only offered in the rural areas where it is related to their material conditions. Evidence is provided by Uzithelile and Hlanganisani's performances in class and in sports and their subsequent success in Ongoye and American universities. The tendency of black parents to enrol their children in white schools and universities only heightens their deculturation and the crises in their identity as has been the case with Melody (Buthelezi: 223, 224, 228). Euthanasia eventually defies his mother and goes on to study at Ongoye, like his rural cousins, where he is successful in his studies. According to Buthelezi, studying in what were known as 'bush universities' seemingly prepares one sufficiently to be able to cope with any educational situation. Thus Euthenasia is also successful in American universities. The kind of veiled racism operative in white schools and universities limits the freedom of black children and hence their excellence is always restricted to sporting activities (Buthelezi: 137) However, American institutions still hold a glimmer of hope for such children as seen in the achievements of Euthenasia and his cousins.

Buthelezi's concept of education is that it is based on life-long learning during the course of which individuals take an active role in pursuing programmes for social development. He conveys this by juxtaposing John and Popi's social involvement after completing their studies and John's nephews' involvement in agricultural, economic and social politics. John's education only procures him a certificate. He studies for the first degree that enables him to get a good job and spends the rest of his life siphoning material benefits for himself and his immediate family. His kind of education creates class divisions between the educated and the uneducated and contributes to structural underdevelopment and intellectual poverty (Buthelezi: 140). John fails to use his education to find solutions to problems besetting the society. The elite class, those of John's calibre, are intellectually emaciated and given to escapism as a way of dealing with the anguish faced by their society. They drink heavily, live in perpetual lethargy, indulge in hedonistic lifestyles, listen to ghetto music and seek affection and fulfilment in sexual overdrive, diluting values and contributing to the general depravity, decadence and social entropy that typify urban lifestyles (Buthelezi: 140).

Popi's education is equally castigated. She engages in life-long learning of the wrong kind since her learning only increases the number of degrees she obtains. Her education fails to broaden her mind and she cannot translate it into tangible aspects that can contribute to social development or, at least, identity-definition. Her learning contributes to her financial viability and status that she uses for career advancement in her insatiable desire for top positions at the hospital, but it also causes the disintegration of her marriage (Buthelezi: 65, 187–189, 191). For Buthelezi, Popi's education does not lead to development because, despite her appointments to high positions, she does not have the skill and knowledge that can lead to true social development when correctly applied.

Uzithelile and Hlanganisani's life-long learning, by contrast, contributes to social development. Their return from America is marked by their involvement in social politics that seeks to effect change through agriculture and education. This change is not only for rural women in the informal trading structures (Buthelezi: 231, 236), but also in politics where women participate in political structures that seek to uproot all causes of poverty and underdevelopment in African societies (Buthelezi: 153–158). Through these siblings Buthelezi demonstrates the kind of educated people that Africa needs for true development in all spheres of modern living.

The dramatisation of racial politics and interracial relations in the narrative also reflects the infighting that is characteristic of family life. The politics of race is reflected in educational, religious, political and economic matters which are all causes of interracial tensions and racial exclusions that lead to underdevelopment and poverty in the country. Buthelezi postulates three categories of white people to assess their contribution to the state of black people in the country. The first category comprises dubious, colonial Christians (Buthelezi: 226) and their role in causing social strife, particularly the clash of civilisations that is characteristic of modern African life and the accompanying poverty and psychological violence to which African societies have been subjected.

Affluent liberal capitalists constitute the second category represented by John's employer. These capitalists contribute to the state of apathy witnessed among black South Africans. People in this category are characterised by self-deluding tendencies based on fallacious outlooks. In their eyes offering poverty-inducing wages to the majority of Africans, and extraordinary salaries to a few blacks, brings about social development. However, as far as Buthelezi is concerned, this outlook is based on *'ubugovu bedlazana'* (aggrandisement of the few) (Buthelezi: 258, 259) which is poverty-causing. For Buthelezi, this category of white people denudes the majority of their sense of self and pride as seen in the character of Velemseni, renamed Williamson for the convenience of his white employers. But this category of whites also creates a class of affluent Africans who are delusional about their identities and human value as evinced by the character of John.

The third category, represented by Martin, consists of good white people who are true Christians, and who are socially conscious and have a sense of duty towards the underprivileged sectors of the community. They are characterised by respect for other cultures. Their involvement with the disadvantaged in the society does not stem from the desire to benefit but the desire to advance humanity in general (Buthelezi: 74, 78, 81, 84).

Both in *Aphelile Agambaqa* and *Impi YaboMdabu Isethunjini* the application of the proverbs as title of the narrative presupposes that the narrative will be read in such a way that its truth is demonstrated. At times, however, evolving trends in contemporary life produce a certain flexibility in the linguistic formulation of the proverb that manages to capture and interpret these from the traditional perspective. Moving from the family infighting produced by the violation of a cultural code as captured in the proverb *'impi yomndeni isesendeni'* (the war of the family is in the testicle) to *'impi yaboMdabu isethunjini'* (the war of Africans is in the intestines), allows Buthelezi to transcend the original application and interpretation of the proverb bringing into the narrative issues that never would have been captured by the old adage in its original meaning. He has thus been able to raise socio-political and economic issues as reflected in the cultural interaction of different racial groups in South Africa.

Conclusion

Proverbs are independent texts which can be incorporated into a variety of genres. As embedded texts their illocutionary role cannot be underestimated. Whole narratives can be formulated to reflect the truth they espouse. The two novels discussed in this chapter apply a similar underlying proverb used in the title differently.

In *Aphelile* it is applied to gender politics, to warn against working mothers because they are no longer able to perform the traditional role of raising children. There is a nostalgic lament for the past roles of women in society because their strict adherence to the roles they performed ensured that the social order was not disrupted. In *Impi*, the proverb is applied in a different situation and a general outrage against city life is registered (Buthelezi: 14). The significance of both applications lies in their lamentation for the transient nature of time that forever pushes the societies into the intricacies of modern life. Those proverbs quoted in the texts embed moral imperatives, and the axioms derived from their application reinforce the absoluteness of accepted norms and values. As Barber (1999: 36) points out 'anything that is constituted as quotable can be recruited for new purposes, expanded or inflected in new ways, attached to new textual forms'.

Endnotes

1   I have used folklore in accordance with Okpewho's (see Introduction, 1992) definition to mean oral literature and indigenous literature.

2   African folklorists since the middle of the 1980s have moved beyond the conventional folklore study that focused more on the cultural contexts for its rendition or performance. They now study the relationship between orality and literacy. Their views are succinctly captured by Emanuel Obiechina (1972 and 1973). The *Southern African Journal for Folklore Studies*, 2003, 13(1) devoted the whole journal to a treatise on the presence of

oral forms in literary genres. In relation to the isiZulu literary tradition, C. T. Msimang (1986) advanced a theory of the oral influence on the early Zulu narratives. However, his treatise creates an impression that it is only earlier narratives that manifest oral influence. However, this book establishes that there is unbroken continuity with current narratives.

3   Russian Formalism and Structuralism played a significant role in shaping isiZulu literary criticism. The tendency to collapse certain concerns of these two approaches as they relate to the artfulness of the poetic language or the literariness of the poetic diction or that of the language of literature created a perception that the oral art forms which are inherently artful were used in a similar way to the poetic language in European literary traditions.

4   Proverbs in oral lore have been derived from lengthy narratives of observed phenomena. The repeated re-narrations of these proverbs over time in different contexts have resulted in them being shortened expressions which in turn stood for whole narratives.

5   Robert Stam, 2005 has used the terms to refer to film adaptations but has drawn from Bakhtin and Kristeva's concepts of intertextuality and hybrid construction of the artistic forms. These theories hold that the artistic utterance is always a mingling of one's own word with the other's word. One's word/literary form becomes a hypertext spun from pre-existing hypotexts which have been transformed by operations of selection, amplification, concretisation and actualisation.

6   In the period under study, there are other narratives that have taken their titles from proverbs. These are Wanda's *Izibiba Ziyeqana* (some medicines are stronger than others, 1997), Vilakazi's *Aphume Nobovu* (they came out with the pus, 1998), Msimang's *Igula Lendlebe Aligcwali* (the gourd of the ear never fills up, 1995) and *Walivuma Icala* (s/he pleads guilty to a charge, 1996), which is also a derivative from *icala ngumphikwa* (a charge is denied). There is also another category of texts whose titles have been articulated through idiomatic sayings (*izisho*). These are not necessarily proverbs but are axioms, truisms and maxims that command the same kind of absolute authority that is characteristic of the proverb, and that are used to highlight the actions and realities of the characters. Examples are Gininda's *Ukukhanya Kokusa* (The dawn of the morning, 1997), Masondo's *Ingalo Yomthetho* (The arm of the law, 1994) and *Ngaze Ngazenza* (I myself am to blame, 1994), Mbhele's *Izivunguvungu Zempilo* (The whirlwinds of

life, 1995), Shabangu's *Kade Sasibona* (We are sages, 1997), Mngadi's *Umbele Wobubele* (The udder of kindness, 1995), Bhengu's *Seziyosengwa Inkehli* (They will be milked by a spinster, 1998), Cele's *Ngiyokhohlwa Ngifile* (I will forget when I am dead, 1996), and Mbatha's *Amanoni Empilo* (The fats of life, 1996).

7   Makhasana was a war commander-in-Chief in pre-colonial KwaZulu. It was custom that the King/Chief remained behind when his regiments went to war, except during the reign of Shaka who usually led his armies. Makhasana as an army commander would come back from these wars and re-narrate to the King/Chief and other council members who remained behind all that transpired in the actual battle. Giving minute details regarding how the regiments were sectioned (*ukuphakwa kwempi*), how they advanced and attacked and who stood out as fearsome brave warriors deserving of branding and how the enemy was defeated. This re-narration replayed the storytelling sessions with all the paraphernalia that went into them and thus was an occasion that was looked forward to by the whole Kingdom/Chiefdom.

8   This view certainly concurs with those of leading African developmental scholars like Azikiwe (1969), Davis (1962), Davidson, (1964) and others.

9   The morphology of the word is: Malume (uncle) + kazi (suffix denoting a female gender).

10   The head tax promulgation in 1906 and the poor translation of the concept Poll Tax as *Intela Yamakhanda* in isiZulu elicited responses from the peasants that alluded to the fact that it was an anomaly to pay for one's head. Subsequently all ideas that did not make sense in the isiZulu language and culture were said to be *insumansumane imali yamakhanda*. The basic definition of *insumansumane* though, relates to a folktale that has mythical origins which is called *insumo*.

2

Nested narratives: 'Some are seated well [...] while others are not seated at all'

The last chapter illuminated the function of proverbs as discursive practices underpinning the African value system, and how they perpetuate and reaffirm the authority of the traditional world. In this chapter, I discuss two post-apartheid novels that have used folktale motifs to provide structural and aesthetic patterns for these modern isiZulu novels. The use of folk narrative motifs has always been a marked feature in novels in the isiZulu literary tradition. These folktale motifs signal themselves as 'nested' narratives where aspects or whole narrative motifs are embedded in new contemporary constructions. Certain allusions or intertextual references draw the readers' attention to known folk narratives structured in similar ways to the novels. Ngubo's (1996) *Yekanini Ukuzenza* (I am to blame) and Muthwa's (1996) *Isifungo* (The Vow) are representative of a broader class of novels which rely on folktale motifs to construct a didactic outcome. The first novel draws its structural motif from the folktale of the piglet called *Maqinase* (the self-willed one). The second novel is heavily indebted to the structural motif of the folktale *Mamba KaMaquba* (Mamba son of Maquba). Barber's (1987, 2000) popular arts and culture model makes clear how these embedded narratives initiate a dialogue with the newly constructed narratives and how novels that have drawn on folktale motifs produce lessons that favour traditional conservatism.

The emphasis will be on how these texts are constructions of popular discourse.

The impact of traditional oral expressions on modern literature is a phenomenon that has shaped modern African-language literatures and, as Lindfors (1973) points out, has contributed to the creation and exploitation of new aesthetic opportunities. Most isiZulu novels, from the early stages of literary development, have shown a tendency to absorb as much as possible of the narrative devices of folk stories. These devices can be detected in the plotting strategies, archetypal characters, thematic considerations, or the use of predetermined motifs like that of the journey, or binary oppositions especially between good and evil and how good always prevails over evil. According to Schmidt:

> Even though the content of the fiction may bear little resemblance to that of oral tradition … the primary narrative nature of the fiction can be traced to [it] as can be the use of proverbial references and praise names for description and the use of proverbs and tales for providing commentary on the actions of the characters (cited in Lindfors, 1973: 11).

Further stylistic devises derived from folklore, as pointed out by Chiwome, include:

> The formulaic beginning of the story, regular repetition of information to maintain coherence in an oral tale, use of traditional poetic discourse side by side with prosaic narrative, use of make-believe, references to love and adventure, prevalence of overstatement as well as use of significant names (cited in Thosago, 2004: 14).

Different writers have accessed these oral aesthetics to engage with a variety of issues. Of writers who draw from these indigenous sources of inspiration, two very significant aspects about their applications are emphasised: the first is that everything will depend on how the material is used, that is, how well it is integrated into the authors' writing, and second, folklore, like any other ingredient, must not be used to effect authenticity but must have an important role to have any significant value (Lindfors, 1973: 3, 32). There are novels in the isiZulu literary tradition that represent this class of writing. For example, Dube (1929) in *Insila kaShaka* (The body servant of Shaka) has drawn on the folktale tradition. Dube's emphasis is on the journey motif through which he illuminates Jeqe's psychological development as he overcomes adversities on both the physical and the metaphysical level. Bhengu's (1965) *UNyambose noZinitha* (Nyambose and Zinitha), which bears striking similarities to Dube's novel, has also drawn on the folktale tradition. Here the emphasis is on the picaresque hero. In the novel the hero's bravery is celebrated in the tradition of the Zulu warrior of the past. The first drama in isiZulu literature, *UGubudele Namazimuzimu* (Gubudele and the Cannibals, 1941), by Ndebele is also drawn from a folktale. In this drama Gubudele, just like Phoshozwayo in the folktale, single-handedly annihilates the cannibals for eating his father. Although *UGubudele Namazimuzimu* dramatises a simple plot, scholars like Zondi (2001),[1] have drawn our attention to its political significance as it is regarded as a commentary on the colonial question.

The novels discussed in this chapter can be seen as creolising, supplementary narratives that comment on the contemporary by recasting the past with the aim of demystifying emerging phenomena. This is achieved through implanting an authoritative, traditional interpretation of the emerging phenomenon, not only to direct the evolution of the emerging practice, but also to make the point that the emerging behaviour strikes chords with past occurrences and, as such, tradition has been able to 'deal with it'. In developing this line of thought, as well as drawing on the allegorical potential of these folk narrative motifs, I discuss how Ngubo's *Yekanini Ukuzenza* and Muthwa's *Isifungo*, engage with contemporary lifestyles, whereby aspects of modern lifestyle are challenged through introversion. (Introversion is an active process in the popular imagination of selecting African and western values which at times might be contradictory to the African value system.) However, in the narratives under discussion, although this process is apparent, the themes are structured to illuminate didactic outcomes that privilege traditionally prescribed values.

Chiji (1998) makes a significant observation regarding the interconnections between oral literature and written forms.

He observes that the tendency to privilege the written form has, to a large degree, contributed to considering oral aesthetics as functioning only to embellish or add colour to the written narrative. This tendency overlooks the fact that oral resources can be the basis and the pivot on which the meaning of the narrative rotates. As we shall see in the novels *Yekanini Ukuzenza* and *Isifungo,* lessons embedded in the oral imagination of the traditional knowledge system form the basis of the texts. In both novels the representation of gender sensibilities is drawn from the archetypal representation of women in isiZulu folktales. This representation is brought to bear on the reality of present day African society in the face of the onslaught on traditional cultural values. The revisiting of the past through these archetypal representations is a means through which writers attempt to halt what they obviously regard as an onslaught on past sensibilities. And, most importantly, it is an attempt to recreate and reinvent cultural practices that have been known to be capable of holding the society together. The spirit of these novels is captured in Biesele's observation that:

> Stories can be understood as effective, ongoing mechanisms both for educating the young and for sharing information and creating consensus about attitudes which continue to be important throughout adult life in an oral culture (1993: 60).

The reconfigurations of traditions that govern gender sensibilities in isiZulu literature are authoritative and absolute. Groenewald (2001), in *Traditions and reconstruction: the culture play in Zulu,* traces the early stages of isiZulu drama to the late 1990s and focuses on the centrality of the topic of love and marriage which brings aspects of gender relations into thematic focus. In most of these narratives, the events that lead to marriage revolve around 'courting, acquiring a husband and the choice of a husband.' These cultural values are expressed from a generalised perspective in which general rules apply. As Biesele points out, the multiplicity of these stories is important since 'not only one story is told but many and the truth of what they say is believed to be somewhere in the dialogue of them all' (1993: 54). Her comments reveal that there exists a web of cross references that attests to the truthfulness of the depiction of gender issues in these texts.

Barber (2000) also points out that the interaction of oral forms and written texts produces an abundance of repeated narratives. These webs of stories are disseminated via the broadcast media and through their repetition listeners or readers are drawn to the life-like realities of the narratives so that they see in them 'real' experiences. However, in isiZulu literature these gendered perspectives are normally conveyed from a patriarchal point of view. These literary materials form a web of mutual references that direct readers to predetermined interpretations of the narratives. The discussion in this chapter focuses on gender as a site for understanding the interaction of folktale and written forms in isiZulu novels.

A summary of *Yekanini Ukuzenza*

The novel's introductory scene depicts MaMsomi, Busisiwe's mother, having just alighted from a taxi. She has been to town where she witnessed a heinous crime committed by Busisiwe's boyfriend, Sipho. She talks to her daughter about this and also mentions other devilish crimes committed by the boyfriend against people in their neighbourhood. Some of the people that have fallen victim are family members. MaMsomi is worried about her family's image if the relationship between Busisiwe and Sipho continues. Busisiwe is head over heels in love with Sipho and she tends to be on the defensive whenever her mother cautions her about her relationship with Sipho. Even though Busisiwe seems to be a well brought up child she is too materialistic to care about the repercussions of her involvement with Sipho. When Sipho proposes to her that they elope she does not hesitate. Sipho has killed the leader of another gang on the previous night hence his sudden desire to leave his hometown, Harding. He deceives Busisiwe into thinking that his affluent uncle in Richmond is about to die and has called on him to help in his businesses.

Sipho's true nature is revealed to Busisiwe when they arrive in Richmond. They are financially stranded because the little money that Sipho has is gambled away. It is in this state that they meet iNswephe, a seasoned criminal. All three devise a scheme through which they extort large sums of money from local businessmen. However, Sipho and iNswephe are eventually killed in an accident with a fuel tanker and Busisiwe is arrested and sentenced to 15 years in prison for her complicity in the crimes committed by the two men.

A summary of *Isifungo*

Gcinekile is a young nurse at Scottburg Hospital. Her relationship with her boyfriend, Thami, is strained because Thami has been unemployed for several years. He seems uninterested in doing something about his life and seems content with the occasional part-time jobs that he gets from time to time and with his poetry writing. The relationship is under pressure and eventually both decide to call it off. This is a painful process, particularly to Thami, who still remembers their promise not to part before death. He even attempts suicide but his friend, Sibusiso, comes to his rescue. Eventually Gcinekile marries a local tycoon, Pita, but because she married him for money, she is unhappy and constantly lonely in her marriage as her husband is forever on business trips. Eventually she reconnects with one of her previous suitors, Frisco, a car hijacker. Her husband eventually finds out about her infidelity and when they are celebrating their second anniversary he exposes her to her family and friends.

Thami wins a prize in a poetry competition. He establishes a small business and eventually sets up a taxi business too. He falls in love with Zime, who later turns out to be Gcinekile's stepsister. At their wedding the police attempt to arrest Frisco. During the scuffle Gcinekile is paralysed by a stray bullet when Frisco shoots at the police and misses. Her parents are too old to care properly for her. Zime and Thami decide to take her in as their responsibility.

Adaptation, hegemony and folktales

Biesele conducted research into the verbal art forms of the Ju/'hoansi community. Her observations and conclusions have far reaching consequences for the study of other African communities. In her study of the verbal art forms of the Ju/'hoan Biesele outlined the role that these stories play in cognition and communication. While the community she studied is very different from contemporary Zulu society, some of the approaches she outlines can be usefully applied to isiZulu folktales.

One of the concepts Biesele uses is that of adaptation. Adaptation refers to the cognitive ability to 'recreate situations to convey what has been found to be of interest and of value and for which it is worthy to adapt' (1993: 42). In Zulu society, this idea of adaptation can be explored in relation to the idea of the family, a recurring trope through which themes of social change and urbanisation have often been explored. The focus is generally on the urban family since the rural family is thought of as being suitably 'traditional'. The family becomes a favoured novelistic site for exploring and re-exploring a range of ideas regarding tradition and modernity.

A second notion outlined by Biesele is that of 'sense and consensus making'. Sense or common sense formation entails a positive representation of all aspects of the social activities that are perceived to be vital for the continued balance and sustenance of the community. She concludes that:

> Sense must be made, for human beings, of biological and social life, and consensus based on the sense must be reached concerning the rules by which social activity will gain its end, the perpetuation of the society. What is more, social agreement or consensus must be reached not once and forever but repeatedly in the lives of each group and generation in order for the human life as such to continue. This is true whether the intervening time has been characterised by great change or has been relatively changeless. The process of incorporating new meaning into understanding is fundamentally the same as the process of reiterating old meaning: both are recreations, performances of already accepted and newly accepted imaginative realities which bear a relationship felt to be vital to the concrete realities of living. (1993: 47)

There is obviously a close relationship between consensus making and tradition. In consensus making certain features of social life are selected and constantly re-iterated and hence attain a hegemonic status. In the view of many writers there are certain vital traditions that are needed for the continuous survival of the Zulu community. In isiZulu novels the hearth of this vitality is the family. The family is a centralised and highly valued institution in Zulu culture. It serves as a site for the instruction of the young members of the community in the ways of the people. Not only is cultural consciousness actively instilled in the family unit but also certain prejudices and stereotypical views regarding people and their environment are internalised.

The social context into which *Yekanini* and *Isifungo,* as post-apartheid texts, insert themselves and to which they respond is fed by several social variables and intellectual currents. Perhaps the underlying discourse comprises the paradoxes of modernity on the one hand and the post-1994 call of the African Renaissance on the other. In African popular imagination in South Africa, the call of the African Renaissance was interpreted as an antidote to the cultural domination of Western modernity. In different public spheres and in the media, the call of the African Renaissance was responded to through various public displays and pledges to tradition. In the African-language literary tradition, this social discourse found a favourable site replete with ideological armour against Westernisation that had all along been perceived to be responsible for the endemic social disintegration in African communities. Therefore popular discourses such as those critical of colonial reconfigurations of gender relations articulated an intricately ambiguous back-to-roots campaign. In print and broadcast media, visuals and sound images reflected this ideological stance. Yet, at the same time, foreign images that fed into the hedonistic culture of glamour and affluence and that were vigorously circulated by the popular media elicited excited responses from the majority of people. These images were integrated into the cultural production of the community, in Appiah's (1991) sense. Both *Yekanini* and *Isifungo* participate in the cultural production of the people because they have been able to express issues and concerns as the particular discourses of the majority of people. These novels, while incorporating emerging viewpoints are, at the same time, attempting to establish routes that will take their communities back to their African roots. Furthermore, in a true Bakhtinian (1981) sense, these texts are a polyglot or heteroglot, as their discourses are an admixture of knowledge systems that blur constantly.

Gender identities and folktale patterns in *Isifungo*

In isiZulu literature rules about gender relations and the socially gendered differences that justify inequalities between women and men in the family and society are among those issues that are most often depicted in a biased manner. IsiZulu literature has conventionalised these notions. Indeed, only a handful of narratives question the apparent inequities between women and men. The most noticeable writer in this regard is Buthelezi, an expatriate and a new comer on the isiZulu literary scene. In the vast majority of these novels there is a sense of a tradition being played out, of women being assigned their traditional positions despite the fact that times have changed. In instances where feminist discourses are part of the thematic treatment in the narratives, these are trivialised and postulated as the libertine views of Western thinking. A growing feminist consciousness in African societies seems to have ruffled the dominance of the patriarchal setup, and, to a large extent, disrupted the presumed harmony that characterised gender relations in African societies.[2] Currently, in the cities, the relationship between the genders is very complex. The strain between the genders seems to be a sore point which African-language fiction writers use to explore fissures in feminist discourses, an ideology that has not found sufficient acceptance in the African popular imagination.[3] In narratives these complexities are usually played out in generational conflicts which also tend to run across gender lines between fathers and daughters and between females and males who are in a love relationship. In considering the studies conducted so far regarding the position of women as both storytellers and as characters, one is struck by the way these stories marginalise women and insist on their inferiority and subservience. However, Biesele's findings reveal a difference in the nature of stories narrated by males and females in the Ju/'hoansi community. Those narrated by males reveal chauvinistic male-centred interpretations of reality whereas those narrated by their female counterparts not only celebrate their femininity but the

heroines' roles most often undermine male power so that there is a
constant equilibrium in the visions of reality between men and women.

Novels seem to have adopted one tradition from isiZulu folk
narratives which is that isiZulu folktales rarely deal with gender
reversals even in stories narrated by women.[4] In the folktale about the
Mother-in-law and the sour milk (*Umkhwekazi namasi*), for example, the
mother-in-law is punished by her son-in-law for putting on his loin
skin cloth and for eating with his utensils. This is viewed as her way
of reversing gender roles and the position of mothers-in-law within
the household (Canonici, 1993). Consequently this deed is met with
a harsh punishment. This folktale indicates the rigidity of culturally
constructed gender roles in Zulu tradition. There are many other
folktales that explore hierarchical relations with regard to gender in
which the lesson conveyed warns against tampering with established
norms and instils a deep observance of societal injunctions to mainly
female members of the society. Linked to the rigid gender relations
within the family are those associated with the institution of marriage.
The matrimonial bonds presented in both oral folk narratives and
novels reveal a philosophical element in the Zulu conception of life.
Matrimony and the matrimonial preparation of young members of the
community, particularly female members, make up a big proportion of
all cultural values. All other cultural observances revolve around this
fundamental aspect of Zulu culture and tradition.[5] The two folktales
which are the basis for our reading of the narratives have structural
similarities to the novels in terms of this preoccupation as well as in
plot structure, characterisation and the symbols and metaphors used.

What emerge from an examination of *Mamba kaMaquba* and
Isifungo are numerous symmetrical structures as well as social practices
which are core cultural codes. Zulu social organisation commences
with the home and the relationship that exists between members of
the family unit. This is the form of organisation in the folktale. In the
novel, *Isifungo*, and the folktale *uMamba kaMaquba*, the family base is
only implied because there is a presumption that the girls have had a
proper upbringing and therefore are at the stage where they can make
independent decisions. *Mamba kaMaquba* is a tale about two sisters
who set out to find a husband. The older one had been socialised

successfully and was respectful of elders and other people she came across. The younger one was bad tempered and disrespectful to everyone she met: she was not properly socialised into her role of being a woman. Along the way they met an old woman whose eyes oozed so profusely that she could not see properly. The old woman asked the girls to lick her eyes. The older sister licked the mucus until the old woman could see but the young one ridiculed the old woman. The old woman showered blessings on the older sister and the sisters continued with their journey. They met many other people who asked to be helped in various ways and the older sister helped all of them while the younger ridiculed and mocked them. They eventually arrived at their destination and the husband-to-be turned out to be a black Mamba, a snake. The older girl submitted to the snake but the younger one screamed and ran away. The snake, *Mamba kaMaquba,* was so furious that he gave chase. As the younger sister was approaching her home, her family, on seeing that a snake was chasing her, came to her rescue. They killed it and burned it. The older sister cried on seeing her new husband being killed. Out of grief she collected the ashes, returned with them to *Mamba kaMaquba*'s home and buried them in his hut. After some months a young handsome man arose out of the ashes and the older sister was overjoyed because he was to be her real husband. In the novel, Gcinekile and Zime are already young government employees. Gcinekile is a nursing sister and Zime is a schoolteacher. Both girls are also at the stage of searching for a husband. In both texts the message is that girls should be properly brought up so that they will be eligible for marriage and be good wives. Properly brought up girls are those who conform to social expectations regarding womanhood. Ill-reared girls do not conform to social expectations as noted in the depiction of Gcinekile in the novel and the younger sister in the folktale.

There are numerous cultural differences in the discursive distance between this folktale and its rendition in novel form post-1994, yet in striking ways hallmarks of the earlier form also dot the latter. In terms of Barber's (2000) generative materialism, what could possibly spark a re-narration of this story in African popular discourse? As mentioned earlier, anti-Western views, African Renaissance discourse, the growing assertiveness of a feminist consciousness all necessitated this revision.

These ideas appear in the narrative sheathed in the discourse of a 'dysfunctional modern family' where gender and generational relations no longer follow traditional organisation. Muthwa seems to suggest that in dysfunctional families such as the one depicted, the continuity of traditional values is subject to strain. Muthwa's exploration of the dysfunctional modern family, however, is revealed through a traditional family where both parents are present but where confusion around the roles that they should play in the family leads to a collapse in the values instilled in the younger members of the family. Zondi, Gcinekile's father, instead of reproaching her regarding the manner in which she handles her courtship with Thami, complains to his wife, MaNtuli, who is very defensive of Gcinekile's actions (Muthwa: 6). In his failure to get MaNtuli to admit knowledge of Gcinekile's wayward activities he says, *'Ngizithulele-ke mina wako-Zondi. Funa kuthiwe ngikhuluma kakhulu njengomsakazo'* (I, of the Zondi clan will keep quiet. Otherwise it will be said I speak continually like the radio (Muthwa: 6). In families such as Gcinekile's, even when certain cultural practices are observed, these are misunderstood and the distortions resulting from these malpractices can be catastrophic as observed towards the close of the novel.

The powerlessness of the patriarch in Gcinekile's home is depicted as one of the bases of dysfunction in contemporary families. On the other hand, the education women receive which inevitably positions them beyond traditional and patriarchal control, is criticised:

> *Uthi kuseyikho ukufundiswa lokhu okwenziwa amadodakazi enu?*
> *Kuseyikho ukuthi ngoba nakhu eyizifundiswa ezinkulu sekumele*
> *ahamba ema isidana nabafana phambi komphakathi?* (Muthwa: 6–7).

Is it still education, the things that your daughters are doing? Is it because they are highly educated and therefore they can stroll about parading with boys in full view of the public?

Gcinekile is representative of such women and is thus depicted as wayward and this is symbolised by her many love affairs and her ambiguous aspirations to respectable womanhood crystallised in marriage. Gcinekile's views of marriage reflect contemporary values where material comforts are sound ingredients for a happy marriage. But in the narrative her views are infantilised and her mental state is shown to have been compromised by the Western trappings she uses to define her identity:

> *usibona kahle isimo somnotho ukuthi sitsheke kanjani. Ngakho-ke uma ukumgcina kwami uThami kuzongenza ngiphile impilo enswemphu, neNkosi isiyongithethelela* (Muthwa: 25).

> do you realise how bad the economic state of affairs is. Therefore if my keeping Thami means that I lead a difficult life, God will forgive me.

There is double objectification at play in her assessment of her identity: in the one she is depicted as enjoying all the male attention and in the other she engages only with herself (Muthwa: 33). The latter self-objectification plays itself out in her narcissism which operates between the private sphere of self-reflection and the public sphere that reflects its image of an individual's identity. The fear of being consumed and having her identity swallowed by the public image is what drives her to redefine her private image to attempt to override and transcend the public one. One such attempt at redefinition is through her status because with a different status she will stand out from her peers and colleagues at work. Gcinekile's self-love and concern with status make her give up the only person who has true regard for her,

> *UThami ngiyamthanda. Akukhona ukuthi ngimthanda ngenhliziyo yami yonke, kodwa ungukuphela kwento eyigugu esengake ngaba nayo empilweni* (Muthwa: 25).

> I love Thami very much. And I not only love him with all my heart, but he is the only and most valuable thing that I ever had in my life.

However, because she is materialistic and sees people as possessions, she says '*into eyigugu iyagcinwa, nami bekuyisifiso sami ukuthi uThami ngimgcine njengegugu laphakade*' (priceless possessions are kept, it was also my wish that I keep Thami as my most valuable possession for

ever) (Muthwa: 25). She terminates her relationship with Thami and
marries a local tycoon.

Her search for a husband seems to be doomed from the moment
she jilts Thami. Thami, as in the folktale's snake metaphor, embodies
another identity more positive than the emasculated one he showed
while they were together. The snake metaphor in the folktale not only
conjures up phallic interpretations but also points to deeper religious
meanings. In most Nguni societies the snake symbolises the presence
of the ancestors. Xhosa people show respect for *inkwankwa* (python),
respectfully called *uMajola*. Zulu people revere *iNyandezulu*, a non-
venomous green snake normally found at *emsamo* (the back of the
Zulu hut), a sacred ancestral place in the hut. The significance of the
snake metaphor is that it directly points to ancestral approbation and
the sanctioning of certain modes of behaviour amongst the women
in the society. In the case of *uMamba kaMaquba* there is an implication
that women who have been properly socialised benefit from ancestral
intervention in their choice of husbands. The implication this
philosophy has for the older sister and for Gcinekile's actions in *Isifungo*
cannot be overemphasised. Gcinekile's materialism and narcissism and
her constant belittling of people, especially of Thami, her boyfriend,
are indications that her interpersonal relations are flawed and therefore
cast doubt on her success in married life since sound interpersonal
interaction, characterised by love, loyalty and compassion are essential
in marriage.

Thami's transformation is similar to that of *Mamba KaMaquba*
in the folktale. Thami's thwarted suicidal attempt after being jilted
by Gcinekile results in his metamorphosis which not only includes
changed perspectives on life but also a changed identity. He adopts
a new name, Thulasizwe Phungaza, starts up a small business and
pursues the affections of Zime, a Christian girl who turns out be
Gcinekile's half-sister (Muthwa: 47–68). The inclusion of Zime,
Gcinekile's opposite, is an extrapolation of the contrasting female
images conventionalised in the isiZulu literary tradition and also has
the effect of leading readers to those socially desired interpretations
that affirm social codes. The oppositional relation between Zime
and Gcinekile revolves not only around their personalities but also

their professions. IsiZulu literature has tended to stereotype certain professions: nurses, hospital sisters and matrons are disparaged for their libertine behaviour and questionable morality in contrast with those in the teaching profession whose virtues are exalted. The depiction of these two sisters operates in this manner. Zime is virtuous whilst Gcinekile is a villain. Commenting on how certain genres pre-empt the reading and impose desired interpretations, Zounmenou notes that oral genres reflect 'the conception of life of the community who produced it' (2004: 128). The behaviour of the female characters in these narratives reflects desired constructions of female identities. Furthermore, in view of the fact that they are stories constructed under the auspices of a patriarchal set-up, their ideological implications for social control cannot escape notice.

Linked to this is the emergence of Christian discourses in *Isifungo* which illustrates Biesele's principle of adaptation. The interaction of Zulu tradition and Christianity is well documented. The merits and demerits of this interaction as they are interpreted in isiZulu literature depend on the stance taken by different authors. An overwhelming majority of writers, beginning with Vilakazi (1934) in *Noma Nini* (Whenever), have assumed a stance that supports the acceptance of Christian ways as logical alternatives to the traditional way of life. In the last century Christian discourses in isiZulu literature underpinned the hegemonic framework operative in African-language literatures. But its recurrence in post-apartheid literary production points to a broader realisation regarding the centrality of Christianity in the life experiences of Africans. Christianity has become a necessary adaptation strategy, not only for religious purposes, but also for the continuous survival of certain cultural values. Its association with selected traditional values, especially those regulating social relations, has made its inclusion within the traditional cultural value system almost natural. In *Isifungo*, the education of women is not questionable when it is aligned with Christianity. Zime's teaching profession finds acceptance because she involves herself both in the school environment and the church (a site of Christian education and modernity) where she actively manages the church choir (Muthwa: 60, 62), but education is found to be problematic in other professions. It is apparent that

Muthwa's ideological purposes are informed by the material and cultural conditions that govern the social construction of women.

Some discourses 'are seated well' [...] they are traditional authority!

In *Isifungo* the patriarchal construction of male identities is beyond reproach. There is a reading that projects the view that the failures of males should be sympathetically understood. This observation holds when considering Thami's portrayal. His inability to secure employment or further his education is not fully explored or linked to other social realities known to exist in the South African context. Instead Gcinekile is blamed for raising these concerns. As a result she is trivialised and infantilised throughout the narrative as though she is indecisive and incapable of knowing what is of worth to her (Muthwa: 5, 24, 25, 42, 71). This notion is symbolised in her paralysis which connotes a permanently infantile state.

Equally Zondi's irresponsibility, both in neglecting Zime, a child born out of wedlock, and in failing to intervene meaningfully in Gcinekile's life, is not questioned. Instead his infidelity and adultery is said to be *'ukubhokelwa ubusoka esenomuzi'* (womanising spree when married) (Muthwa: 86), which is not portrayed as necessarily morally questionable. In traditional society a young man who keeps numerous girlfriends at one time has been affectionately called *'isoka'* (a ladies man) a term that bestows respect and high esteem. The writer's indecision regarding Zondi's misconduct stems from past matrimonial practices that privileged men by allowing polygamous marriages. This view is further supported by the ambiguity with which the author closes the narrative. Gcinekile, in a vegetative state, is cared for by Zime and Thami. It emerges that Thami has feelings of love for Gcinekile, and he still wishes to keep their vow to be together in both good and bad times. Her ill health provides him with the opportunity to fulfil that vow. He asks Zime's permission to do this.[6] He says,

> ... *ukuthi ngangenze isifungo noGcinekile sokuthi ngiyomthanda kuze kube sekugcineni. Ebuhleni nasebubini. Ngeshwa-ke leso sifungo sengisenze nawe. Ngingazi-ke nami kuwena. Ngokwami*

*bengibona lisekhona ithuba lokuthi ngigcine isifungo sami ngokuthi
ngimnakekele nami uGcinekile kuze kube sekugcineni. Singazi-ke
phela ngoba nesikhwele sibuzwa kinina* (Muthwa: 96).

… it is just that I made a vow to Gcinekile that I will love her
until the end of time, in bad and good moments. Unfortunately
I have now made that vow with you. As far as I am concerned
the opportunity still remains for me to fulfil that vow, to care
for her until the end. But I would not know because I know
women can be jealous.

Acting contrary to her Christian upbringing, Zime agrees to Thami's
proposal,

*kuhle ngoba nangu ubaba ukhona. Kuzomele umnike ilobolo lakhe
kusashisa nje. Angazi noma umfundisi uyosamukela yini isithembu
sakho* (Muthwa: 96).

it is good because here is father, he is still alive. You had better
pay him his *ilobolo* immediately. However I would not know if
the reverend will accept your polygamous marriage.

This utterance illustrates that Christian doctrines are viewed not as
an end in themselves but as values that can be harnessed and infused
with traditional mores so as to favour a traditional value system. The
eclecticism of both traditional culture and Christian doctrine points not
to the negation of either, but to the tendency to selectively engage in
habits and practices that are necessary for the survival and continuation
of core social codes, in this case, codes privileging patriarchy.

Muthwa's silence is not confined to Zondi's conduct: there is an
implied understanding and tacit acceptance of male misconduct that
is pervasive throughout the text. It is not only Zondi's adulterous
past that remains unquestioned. Thami's role in breaking Gcinekile's
virginity (Muthwa: 40–41) and the fact that he eventually marries her
younger stepsister also remain unquestioned (Muthwa: 93–94). Instead
Gcinekile is made to feel guilty for her complicity in the act. While
Thami is repentant for his actions, his self-justification absolves him of
any wrongdoing so that the guilty party remains Gcinekile alone:

Ngifisa ukuxolisa kakhulu ngobuntombi bakho. Empeleni ngangingaboni iphutha uma ngibuqeda ngoba ngase ngenelisiwe ukuthi sesiyofa silahlane nawe. Kubuhlungu-ke nokho ngoba ngisho ungaze ushade nenkinyankinya yesikhumukane, kawusenaso isipho esiligugu oyosiphathela umyeni wakho.Kawusenakumbonga ngalutho kukho konke ayobe ekwenzele khona, kwazise nokuthi ubuntombi bomuntu yibona obuyisisekelo somshado onenjabulo (Muthwa: 40–41).*

I apologise profusely about your virginity. Actually I did not see any problem consuming it because I was sure that only death would tear us asunder. It is a shame though that even if you could be married to a tycoon, you no longer have a priceless possession that will be a proper gift for your husband. You will never be able to thank him enough for everything that he will do for you. It is known that the virginity of a maiden is the foundation of a happy married life.

The one-sidedness of Muthwa's belief leaves unexplored aspects of male sexuality and virginity; Thami is equally a fallen man. This belief operates on the social level where it has become natural to conclude that it is women who fall and, as a 'weaker sex', they bear the brunt of the blame.

In isiZulu literature, disrespect for the law has frequently been paired with failed romantic relationships. Biesele's principle of sense and consensus making provides a way of understanding these literary situations. One reading of such literary situations is that self-willed uncontrollable female characters invite the attentions of anti-social outcasts such as criminals. This representation has been a steady theme from as early as Dhlomo's *Indlela Yababi* (1935) (The way of the wicked). Delsie, the protagonist in this narrative, and the prototype for this form of characterisation, attracts a corrupt and abusive police officer. The end of the narrative is marked by her returning to the rural area dejected and rejected by the world. Numerous publications spanning the period from the 1930s to the present day revisit the theme, instilling an acceptance of traditional ideology. The law plays a crucial role in reinforcing the repercussions of disobedience and disrespect for social codes which are integral to society. Gcinekile's relationship with Frisco is a doomed one; she is paralysed because of his involvement in organised crime (Muthwa: 94).

Straight out of traditionalism: *Yekanini Ukuzenza's* didacticism

The overt didacticism in *Yekanini Ukuzenza* is an example of one of the most central and recurrent features in African popular arts and culture. The simplicity with which this didacticism is structured in the novel resonates with that normally found in folktales, particularly, in this case, the folktale *UMaqinase*. *UMaqinase* is a story about a little pig called *Maqinase* (The self-willed one), one of a litter of ten. Her mother was very strict and kept a tight watch over her litter. She forbade them from going outside their enclosure because she feared for their safety. However *Maqinase* was pig-headed, and would not listen. She made a habit of sneaking outside their enclosure on hot days when she knew that her mother and the rest of the litter were fast asleep. One day she sneaked out as usual, intending to go to a farm where she had once noted an abundance of delicacies. She had the high gait characteristic of pig-headed pigs. On her way she met a donkey who greeted her enthusiastically, but *Maqinase* dismissed the donkey, saying it should mind its long, ugly ears instead of being a nuisance to her. She did the same with the toad, citing its ugly, protruding eyes. Many other animals that she met along her way were subjected to her scathing ridicule and they were all disappointed in her. By the time she approached the fence that demarcated the farm, *Maqinase* was furious with everyone she had come across because they just could not let her be. That is probably why she did not notice the greyhound rapidly approaching her. The dog pounced on her just as she jumped over the fence. She screamed, scuttling through a small hole that she spotted in her state of fright. The fence tore her skin and the dog bit her behind. She raced back home, encountering all the animals she had belittled on her way and asking them to help her. All of them told her they were minding their own business. She got home covered in bruises and her mother was so furious on learning that she had been outside their enclosure that she punished her all over again.

Yekanini Ukuzenza's didactic discourse is structured around the dislocation of African society in an Americanised, fast-paced, criminal infested, post-apartheid, city existence, where African youth, against all social injunctions, create a parallel existence away from parents and social prescriptions. Busisiwe, Maqinase's equivalent, is warned against her involvement with Sipho, a local gangster (Ngubo: 9–11), but she ignores the warning and the rest of the narrative documents the consequences: her elopement, criminal life in Richmond and imprisonment. The city lifestyle this novel depicts has traces of the television and filmic vocabularies of the American gangster genre on the one hand and post-apartheid socio-economic realities on the other. However, the novel is quick to set up the boundaries to the interpretations of these Americanised images and how they affect the local context. It achieves this feat through foregrounding local conditions which reduce the glamour and prestige normally attached to these images.

Busisiwe's search for independence and the hedonistic lifestyle is shown against the local realities of poverty, deprivation, social abnormality, lack of education, a crime culture and many other endemic social ills that have the ability to overwhelm young people like her. Foreign, popular images of independent, model-like, affluent and ruthless *bella mafia* (mafia women) are vigorously circulated in the media and have created in the popular imagination impressions of truly liberated women capable of doing anything that their masculine counterparts can do. These are drawn upon to emphasise the extent to which Busisiwe's psychological outlook is misguided. Through Busisiwe's adversities in her pursuit of this version of the good life, Ngubo is able to weaken its hold on local youth particularly on female youth. It is young females who, because they yearn for a life outside the confines of their realities, are attracted to social miscreants whom they believe will take care of them. Furthermore, these celebrated images are shown to be directly opposed to the reality of South Africa's women's lives as Busisiwe is dependant for everything on her male counterparts with whom she is involved in the scam. More significantly, the fact that she takes all the blame for the gang's activities, since the other two members are killed by the police, underpins this observation.

In African communities women bear the brunt and burden of the actions of their male counterparts and in the narrative this is illustrated by the heavy sentence she receives which she will serve alone.

The construction of gender identities and roles across generations in this novel leads to a reading that asserts that contemporary African social reality is flawed, as it is susceptible to a variety of influences that compromise traditional Zulu customs and values. This reading is established as early as the opening sections of the novel which employ a folktale technique, a state of lack or disequilibrium to represent instability. In *Yekanini Ukuzenza* the lack of equilibrium foregrounds the loss of parental power experienced in contemporary African societies. Parent-offspring relations in Zulu culture altered with cultural changes and were also susceptible to foreign influences. The adoption of foreign, cultural practices which could not be integrated into traditional practices, made these relationships complex. Traditionally, issues affecting parent-child relations could be mediated by strong institutions such as the regimentation of male youths and the *qhikiza* (Girl Guide) systems that governed socially acceptable behaviour for young people. The absence of these institutions in contemporary settings meant that parents directly involved themselves with issues affecting young people, including issues relating to romantic relationships. There is general agreement that contemporary parents have always been unsure of the extent to which they can be involved in the love affairs of their children.

Their involvement, at times, is characterised by two extremes: being too relenting or too stern. Furthermore, underlying these contrasting states is a sense of apology, as if the precautions they offer to their young are interfering with their children's right to freedom. This can be noted in MaMsomi's remonstrance:

> *Ukuthi mntanami angazi ukuthi ngizokubonisa ngithini. Yebo, khona kakufanele ngigamanxe kangako ezindabeni zakho. Ngihlala ngikutshela njalo ukuthi kangisho ukuthi ngiqonde ukukukhethela. Kodwa mntanami ngakutshela ukuthi mina njengomzali wakho, kungumsebenzi wami ukuthi ngikubambe ngengalo ngikuhlenge uma ngikubona uyokhalakathela eweni* (Ngubo: 9).

It is just that, my child, I no longer know how to get through to you. Of course I am not supposed to interfere extensively in your affairs. And I have always told you that I do not intend to choose a suitor for you. However, as I have once said to you, my child, as a parent, it is my duty to guide and protect you.

MaMsomi's apologetic, emotional outpouring reveals not only her helplessness in her failure to influence her daughter regarding her choice of suitor, but also her uncertainty regarding the role she should play at this stage of her daughter's stormy adolescence. The depiction of MaMsomi points to a bigger reality: the receding influence of parents over their offspring.

The other way in which the didactic discourse of *Yekanini Ukuzenza* is structured is around family and social values. With regard to family norms, issues such as respect for parents, single versus dual parenting, whereby the father figure is the enforcer of values, and the hierarchy of members within the family unit are shown to be extremely significant. In Busisiwe's case, she lacks all of these basic values. In her home the absence of the father figure throws all basic social values into disarray. This disorder is reflected in the choices she makes and in the broader society where her social relations are improper. The latter example is brought into the narrative through a description similar to that in the folktale *Maqinase*:

> *Indlela ashesha ngayo uBusisiwe eqonde kubo! Impela nethwasa lishesha kangaka nje, hhiya! Lalingadlela ogageni. Wayekhabuzela. Nempangela kuthiwa iyashesha nje, impela sengathi yayingeke ilibone elidlalayo ngalolo suku. Wayeshwabuzela. Wadlula ngakwaMdlalose indodakazi yakhona endala usisi Ntombi eme egcekeni. Wathi uyambingelela, wavele waphakamisa isandla uBusisiwe wachitheka eyosithela ekhoneni. Ikhehla lakwaJali elalizimele egcekeni kwalo, lathi lingambona eza ngalo mfutho, lasondela ngasesangweni. Lelula umqala lafifiyela, kwathi lapho edlula ngakulona, wezwa likhuluma lodwa lithi: "Kazi kuthiwa yini-ke igama lalo mdlalo osufikile. Impela izingane zethu! Sengathi lukhulu esisazolu ..." Akabange esezwa ukuthi laqhubeka lathini, ngoba wayengenaso isikhathi sokulalela lezo zinto* (Ngubo: 24–25).

The way Busisiwe sped towards her home! Even a trainee diviner, known for his/her speed, would not catch up with her. She was walking like a mad person. Even the guinea fowl would not catch up with her that day. She was shuffling so quickly. She passed by Mdlalose's home, their older daughter, Ntombi was standing in the yard. She greeted her, but Busisiwe simply answered by raising her hand and disappeared from sight. The old man from Jali's home was also standing in the yard, when seeing Busisiwe in such haste, he approached the gate. He stretched his neck blinking, and when Busisiwe passed by the old man, she heard him saying to himself: 'I wonder what the name of this new game is. Really our children! There is still more to be ...' Busisiwe could not hear the rest of the utterance, because she had no time to listen to such things.

As in the folktale, her lack of respect contributes to her fate at Richmond. Busisiwe's indifference to the neighbours, on the level of social codes, is similar to Maqinase's mockery of the other animals. The narrator implies she should have made some time to greet and speak to the people she met. Culturally one does not only inquire after the other's health during greeting sessions, but a variety of issues come up such as one's intended actions or journeys. The individualistic lifestyle that is a norm in contemporary society has prevented Busisiwe from respecting perennial customs such as greeting elders who could have been instrumental in protecting her from the catastrophic consequences she experienced in Richmond. This mirrors the way in which Maqinase could have been warned that her intended stroll held danger in the form of a dog.

Conclusion

Folk narratives are reservoirs of references to a shared worldview. They also provide metaphors, symbols and images that, when recreated in another form, provide varied and complex stories that affirm the values and beliefs of that worldview. Canonici points out that *insomi* (folktale) images reflect a need for an ideal, ordered society and the themes emphasise that adherence to custom is the most effective means of ensuring the continued equilibrium of the human community.

Some of Canonici's (1993) observations relate to Biesele's principles. These principles refer to selected unchanging and flexible worldviews that have to be repeatedly communicated to the younger generation in order to reach consensus. In spite of the colonial and Christian assault on the Zulu tradition there still remain certain immutable codes. Writers hope that these literary recreations will eliminate anti-social behaviour and also promote the moral order and ethical values that have always defined social organisation.

Endnotes

1   Personal interview, 2001.

2   The convention of isiZulu literature regarding gender issues fails to acknowledge that the female sense of independence is not just a recent occurrence but can be traced back to the establishment of the earliest urban centers in Kimberly or Barberton. Furthermore the literary tradition fails to recognise that prostitution and general lawlessness amongst urbanised women not only reflects their loss of grip on female sexuality but also their strong will for adaptation and survival in harsh environments.

3   There are texts which, whilst attempting to foreground a feminist consciousness, are trapped in a contradictory consciousness because the patriarchal sensibilities associated with female characters in the texts outweigh the feminist discourses.

4   For a discussion of isiNdebele storytellers, see Isabel Hofmeyr (1993).

5   This notion is derived after observing the extent of the cultural forms like rituals, verbal expressions, and observances associated with the institution of marriage.

6   According to Zulu custom the man discusses with the first wife his intention of taking up a second wife. He can only take up the second wife if the first one approves.

3

Acts of naming: The detective plot in Masondo's fiction

Masondo is amongst the few isiZulu writers who have written detective stories. He produced six detective novels and one anthology of crime fiction short stories within a period of four years, from 1990 to 1994.[1] Although he eventually wrote outside the detective plot, he is particularly celebrated for his detective stories.[2] His first trilogy,[3] *Isigcawu Senkantolo* (A scene at the court), *Iphisi Nezinyoka* (The hunter and snakes) and *Ingwe Nengonyama* (The leopard and the lion) set him up as amongst the first to introduce novel ways of dealing with contemporary reality in the literature of isiZulu, especially in the face of the crime crisis and waning confidence in the South African law enforcement agencies.[4] But perhaps even more intriguing are the naming practices in his detective stories. Masondo's act of naming in these narratives is peculiar and might be regarded as fortuitous. In this chapter I demonstrate that far from being fortuitous these naming practices can be seen as extraordinary strategies for disrupting expectations.

An overview of Masondo's acts of naming in his fiction

There is an established tradition in the use of names in isiZulu novels which is a practice copied from centuries of orality and of literary writings in dominant languages. As Ragussis (1984: 4) claims, the novel 'emerged as a genre by organizing its plots around acts of naming'. Masondo's naming techniques, particularly in his detective novels, take on an unconventional, non-standard but refreshingly unique approach. While his naming of personages in the detective narratives serves to highlight their personalities, capture their mannerisms, and centralise their roles, his application of similar names in his other narratives explores entirely different psychologies. In other words, the name he assigns to a character in a particular text, exploiting his or her physical attributes, temperament and psychological or emotional state, could denote a completely different personage when the same name is used in a different text. This means that whilst he exploits archetypes with the roles the personages represent in the narratives, he disrupts and defamiliarises their conventional meanings in the Formalist and Structuralist sense.[5] This simultaneous stereotyping and de-stereotyping is seen in the prevalence of the same names across his detective narratives. These names are consistently drawn from different personalities across the social fabric. In spite of this unusual naming practice, the common names and migratory patterns and the intertextuality of issues and concerns not only contribute to the framework of the narratives but these names ironically also create continuity and familiarity, and predetermine the interpretation of the narratives.

The major paradox introduced by Masondo's acts of naming is the realisation that, whilst names act as a central locus of meaning in the narratives, the way he exploits them as pointers, indicators or shadows makes clear they can never be representative of the whole, they can only be units of a whole. In Masondo's novels different facets of the characters' personalities are glimpsed, not by relegating their meanings to received archetypal notions, but by recreating personalities within particular contexts in contemporary urban or rural spaces. By not following established trends, Masondo unravels unexplored terrain in relation to characterisation and representation that grants him the liberty to explore the contradictions, the bizarre and the absurd, the intrigues and the complexities that typify modern African societies from an angle beyond constraint or convention.

IsiZulu literature has long since established a convention regarding the manner in which personalities representative of localities (rural vs. urban) can be read. This conventional reading takes into account social variables such as class and economic status, racial politics, historical politics, education and elitism, the politics around literacy, gender and notions of masculinity, urban and rural and traditional folklore, youth and the generation gap. However, Masondo's naming practice introduces novel ways in which contemporary African societies can be looked at. He toys with the established foundations and questions some of the assumed principles of characterisation. In this manner he introduces alternatives that not only demonstrate the pitfalls of straight-jacketing representations or character portrayals, but that also open up other possibilities of representing and reading characters through the names assigned to them. The disruption at the heart of his naming practices across his detective narratives does not reflect a lament over past morality or a Christian re-proselysation. Rather, it is reflective of a contemporaneity where new values and lifestyles, (a consequence of the cultural mix of many nationalities), have shaped modern values in South Africa. And it reflects how these values are continually evolving and, therefore, requiring continuous re-inscription. His idea of the identity of a modern, black South African is not confined to traditional perceptions. It is in this way that Masondo defies the norm. The spread of similar names in his detective stories does not result from a lack of ingenuity on his part but attests to his realisation of the complexities of human psychologies in contemporary African societies.

Literary Onomastics: Analysis of character through names

According to Alvarez-Altman literary onomastics

> is a more specialized literary criticism in which scholars are concerned with the levels of significance of names in drama, poetry, fiction and folklore. These include names of places, characters, cosmic symbols, etc. as they relate to theme, structure and other literary considerations (cited in Neethling, 1985: 88).

However, literary onomastics does not necessarily explore cultural aspects beyond the literary texts and so, in this analysis, literary onomastics will be supplemented with the ethnography of isiZulu naming practices. This latter approach can point to the derivation of names, the philosophical relationship between individuals and their names or to customary practices such as different forms of address as well as changes in society. All of these Masondo exploits to depict different personalities across the social fabric. Koopman (1990 & 1992) provides a detailed account of the changing nature of the use of names within isiZulu cultural life. He points out that

> [...] other linguistic processes such as adoption of words from outside the language, neologisms, coinages, and compounds of various linguistic sorts [...] are part of the linguistic strategy which Zulu uses to adapt to modern times (1992: 99).

Nicolaisen (cited in Neethling, 1985: 88) argues that literary names and naming admit three significant levels of meaning. The first is the lexical level which examines the meaning of names in a manner equivalent to dictionary entries. The second is the associative level which looks into reasons why particular words are used in the naming process. The third is the onomastic level which looks into the denotative meaning of a name in terms of its origin (see discussion below). Stewart (1986), Pyles (1986) and Fairclough (1986) have devised various onomastic schemes for an in-depth analysis of names associated with these levels. However, the most rewarding is Alvarez-Altman's (1981) classification scheme. She identified twelve classes of literary names and all of them in some way relate to these three levels of meaning. The first class comprises the anonymical family of literary names. According to Alvarez-Altman, these names do not give a sense of individuality or personality but rather suggest anonymity like an idea that has no exact term to express it. Neethling (1985: 88) gives examples of these types of names drawn from the isiXhosa repertoire, for example, *uBani* (who), *uSobani* (the father of whom), *uNozibani* (the mother of whom) and *uMasibani* (the wife of whom). In Masondo's novels these names refer to individuals whose names are relatively insignificant for the narrator.

The second class consists of proper names. They function on the denotative level as labels referring to individuals. Many of these words are lexically meaningless. Alvarez-Altman (1981: 223) refers to them as 'purely invented fantastic names', names like *Taga* and *Kabasa*. These have no meaning but are nevertheless names used to refer to certain individuals. However, there are meaningful names that could appear as contextually meaningless. They function on the onomastic level. Their application is both on the denotative and associative level. Names like *Themba* (hope), *S'fiso* (yearning), *Popi* (doll), and *Thandi* (loved one) are well established and their usage in both *Ingalo Yomthetho* and *Ingwe Nengonyama* does not contribute to thematic development but merely brings variety to the characters populating the text.

Some names in this class indicate personality traits that have bearing on the meaning of the theme. Makgamatha (1992) explains that in such characterisation, the roles of the characters are encapsulated in the names. This contributes to the moral and social polarities revealed in the formal patterns of the text and advances the aims of the narrative. Names like *Magwegwe* (crooked legs), *Vika* (take cover), *Bhadi* (ill-luck) and *Mamba* (a poisonous snake) have particular significance in the texts because through them the narrator underpins certain thematic issues. Their names are semantic axes because they exert influence on events.

The category of personal names also includes names whose characters are presented symbolically and through whom certain epistemological and cosmological aspects of the African community are revealed. In *Ingwe Nengonyama* names like *Makhosonke* and *Makhosazana* invoke ancestral beliefs that represent a way of life and the hierarchical positioning of the name bearers within isiZulu society. Their significance in the text points to certain aspects of ancestral belief and social organisation considered very significant in African society as will be shown later.

Ethnographic study of names

Harder (1986) and Neethling (1994) mention that names are rooted in culture and are fixed in connotation and are used as a form of control in society. This is true of African society, where naming takes on a very particular cultural significance. In certain African societies an individual goes through three important naming stages at different stages of his or her life. According to Thipa (1984) the individual is named as a newborn child. During and after initiation she or he assumes a new name that points to the stage attained and in married life yet another name is given to him or her.

Herbert (1995) delineates some of the key issues with which the ethnographic study of names is concerned. These relate to the name bestowed at birth, public or private coinage of names, stages of life and name usage and alternation in forms of address, for example the use of kinship terms. The name given at the birth of a child can be influenced by significant happenings which occurred during the time of birth. Names like *Majalimani* (the Germans) or *Mangisi* (Englishman) or *Mpiyimpi* (war) refer to particular situations or moments in history. Names may allude to the status of the family during the time the child is born like *Nomcebo* (wealth) or *Mhlupheki* (suffering) or *Nokufa* (mother of death). Another influential factor at the time of the child's birth is the status of the name giver and how the name giver has gone about the process of selecting the name. In this regard Neethling (1985: 88) points to an underlying motive for the naming of children in African society, namely that 'it is common practice for parents to embody in a name the expectations they might have for that child in the future'.

When names are coined it is necessary to look at whether the coinage has been done privately or publicly. This is important for our discussion, because in isiZulu culture both circumstances prevail in naming. An individual is given a name privately when she or he is born, but as she or he goes through the significant stages of life she or he creates his or her own new names or other people bestow new names on her or him. Canonici (1993) states that an individual obtains these names through his or her actions and involvement in the society. These become a string of names revolving around certain events, utterances or actions and are called *izibongo* (traditional praises). Canonici defines *izibongo* as:

> praise poems in honour of individuals. Any person may have
> 'praises'; in fact one may even compose one's own praises.

> Izibongo are developed from initial 'praise names', that an individual is given or gives himself, which briefly describe or epitomize an event or action in his life, his achievements or failures, or a peculiar physical characteristic. A praise name may soon become a 'praise phrase' or a 'praise sentence': this may constitute the nucleus of a praise poem, which will then grow with episodic and occasional additions as demanded by events (1993: 9).

Gwala and Gunner (1991) point out that the word 'praises' is misleading because *izibongo* is primarily concerned with naming, identifying and therefore giving substance to the named person or object. As Turner points out, these *izibongo* are praises that extol

> the virtues of manly prowess, of courage and fighting skills, of exceptional hunting ability, of brave leadership and outstanding physical and behavioural presence (1999: 196).

Gunner comments that *izibongo* are

> manifestations of cultural power broking, where the values the poetry espouses, validate the righteousness of war and conquest, of heroic struggle and of courage through physical action and endurance (1995: 196).

The last issue relates to the alternation in the form of address, for example addressing an individual with his *isithakazelo* (singular)/ *izithakazelo* (plural) (clan praises). Canonici (1993: 17–18) defines *izithakazelo* as clan names for 'adulation' or a 'flattering phrase' or a 'tribal salutation' or a 'term of polite or friendly address peculiar to each clan'. *Izithakazelo* are ancestral names that have been assumed by the whole clan as names identifying them. They can extend to several praise phrases and they reveal a myriad of interconnections in relations. In the past these were recited in full and in that way the interrelationships between clans were revealed and intermarriages were avoided.

However, today these phrase names are no longer recited in full. Only the initial *isithakazelo* is recited. Herbert (1995) looks at the impact on naming practices of the many changes in the social organisation and the culture of everyday life. This may include the modification of naming practices, because of Christianity or modernity, or the general decrease in the art of naming which has led people to draw names from the stock of available names. Neethling (2000: 208) observes that 'personal names reflect the sociology and psychology of the era in which they are or were used.'

Disrupting and de-stereotyping archetypal representations

Following classical detective narrative structures, Masondo's act of naming is structured around fixed categories of characters that propel the narratives.[6] In his detective novels, and one collection of short detective stories, the framework around which characters are structured are: the owner of the private investigation company, the detective, the prime suspect and the criminal(s), who all fall into the category of major characters, as well as a motley cast of minor characters, and the general populace, constituted by faceless and nameless characters. Equally, the developments of the plots in all the stories follow classical formations where clues, digressions and omissions are designed to bring about suspense and twists.

I use the two tables below to highlight some of the points made about Masondo's naming technique and to demonstrate the structural framework for the characters' roles. The tables summarise Masondo's naming technique across all the detective novels in his first and second trilogy.

The similarities of the names of the law enforcers, *Themba Zondo* and the company holders, *S'fiso Ngubane*, in the first trilogy and the resurfacing of the name *Themba Zondo* in *Ngaze Ngazenza*, of the second trilogy, does not necessarily mean that the names denote the same personage with the same personality. Actually, across the four texts both these characters are constituted differently in terms of their physical makeup, psychological outlook and mannerisms. Furthermore, there is no continuity or progression from the first character so named to the one found in subsequent texts. To illustrate further, take the name of *Taga Nxumalo*, in the text *Iphisi Nezinyoka*. This character is considered

Table 1: Naming of character roles

First trilogy		
Isigcawu Senkantolo (1990)	*Iphisi Nezinyoka* (1991)	*Ingwe Nengonyama* (1994a)
Detective *Themba Zondo*	Detective *Themba Zondo*	Detective *Themba Zondo*
Owner of PI Co. *S'fiso Ngubane*	Owner of PI Co. *S'fiso Ngubane*	Owner of PI Co. *S'fiso Ngubane*
Prime suspect *Mrs. Kubheka*	Prime suspect *Taga Nxumalo*	Prime suspect *Magwegwe Buthelezi*
Corpse *Mr. Zikode*	Corpse *Bheki Hlophe*	Corpse(s) *Mrs. Kubheka, Taga, Nxumalo, Themba's family and fiancée*
Second trilogy		
Kanti Nawe (1994b)	*Ngaze Ngazenza* (1994c)	*Ingalo Yomthetho* (1994d)
Detective *Zimisele Wela*	Detective *Qodlwana Mthethwa, Themba Zondo*	Detective *Makhosonke, Ndima, Popi Hadebe*
Owner of PI Co. *Bongane Simelane*	Owner of PI Co. *Qodlwana Mthethwa*	Owner of PI Co. *Moyeni Hadebe & Makhosonke Ndima*
Prime suspect *Makhanda Zuma, Mbamba Mlaba, Mamba Luthuli*	Prime suspect *Thoko Ntsibande, Mginsa Nxumalo*	Prime suspect *Dr Bhadi Shongwe*
Corpse(s) *Zodwa Sihlahla, Jabulane Mthiyane, unnamed characters*	Corpse *Bhekani Ndlovu*	Corpse *Mamba Nxumalo*

a prime suspect. However, in a different text, *Ingwe Nengonyama*, his structural role is that of a corpse whose murder should be investigated. The name acts on a primary level signifying 'nothing but the ideas that are in the Mind of the Speaker' at the time (Locke cited in Ragussis, 1986: 4).

The same can be said about the prevalence of certain surnames across the narratives. These surnames do not refer to any relation between the personages or refer to the clan so named, they are just surnames. In all texts where frequently used surnames like *Nxumalo* occur, these refer to entirely different individuals. One interpretation of this is that Masondo recycled names and surnames from a bank of common names without any particular ideological imperatives in mind simply because he was eager to narrate a situation that warranted investigation. The emphasis for him seems to be on how the investigation is carried out more than on the shadows of meaning carried by the names.

The same observations can be made for Masondo's naming of major characters and minor characters whose structural positioning propels the plot. The similar names assigned to certain characters do not necessarily allude to a 'type' but represent a wide variety of the psychologies and emotional states of contemporary black South Africa, as demonstrated in Table 2 below.

Table 2: Naming of major characters

First trilogy		
Isigcawu Senkantolo (1990)	*Iphisi Nezinyoka* (1991)	*Ingwe Nengonyama* (1994a)
Major criminals	Major criminals	Major criminals
Magwegwe Buthelezi, Mhlobo Mvubu, Vika Kubheka	*Magwegwe Buthelezi, Mhlobo Mvubu, Vika Kubheka*	*Vika Kubheka, Duduzile Kubheka, Bheki Nxumalo*
Second trilogy		
Kanti Nawe (1994b)	*Ngaze Ngazenza* (1994c)	*Ingalo Yomthetho* (1994d)
Major criminals	Major criminals	Major criminals
Khende Sibisi, Popi Xaba, Magwababa Shange	*Mrs Kubheka, Mpondlela Xaba*	*Makhosazana Xaba, Jona*

An intriguing name is that of *Magwegwe Buthelezi*. The name *Magwegwe Buthelezi* in the first trilogy operates in a similar fashion to the names in the first table. In *Isigcawu Senkantolo* and *Iphisi Nezinyoka*, this name is assigned to criminals but in *Ingwe Nengonyama* it is assigned to a prime suspect who is later absolved and acquitted of any wrongdoing. The interest is not so much in the first name but in the surname *Buthelezi*. The recurrence of this surname in the two texts of the first trilogy could have suggested typification[7] and signalled a comparative reference to the name of *Buthelezi* because at the time these texts were written this surname had political connotations. But the role given to the character bearing this name in *Ingwe Nengonyama* does not support such connotations.[8] However, the ambiguity implied in this name in the narratives makes for a fascinating reading of the dark, political intrigues associated with the political figure bearing the name of *Buthelezi*. This would have been especially relevant in the early 1990s when the ravages of *Inkatha Yesizwe*, a quasi-cultural/political group he led, were felt in the eastern townships of Gauteng. In the three texts the characters bearing this name are also implicated in double worlds, the underworld and the mainstream, with intrigues, secrets, murders and double dealings trailing behind them. In this way the inclusion of the surname operates like names do in allegories. According to Fletcher (1964), Honing (1959) and Whitman (1987), allegorical writings say one thing and mean another. Fletcher (1964: 7) mentions that allegory does not need to be interpreted because it makes sense on the literal level without an interpretation. But the literal surface suggests a peculiar doubleness of intention that invites an underlying reading. And this gives the narrative a richer and more interesting interpretation. Key to the use of Buthelezi's name is the invitation to its possible allegorical implications, however fleeting or peripheral. Finnegan (1970) and Turner (2001) also raise an important observation regarding such names. Both agree that names in African society are not only used for surface meaning but may also serve as a

> way of 'working out tension', or for social function in 'minimizing friction' or even more importantly […] as a useful form 'for providing a means of indirect comment when a direct one is not feasible' (Finnegan 1970: 470).

It is not only *Magwegwe Buthelezi* that is repeatedly used, there are also *Vika Kubheka* and *Mhlobo Mvubu* whose personalities are different in each text. A similar table of minor characters in all six narratives can be drawn up and it will show the same migratory patterns of names from different structural roles. Throughout both trilogies these names are drawn from different social backgrounds and made to characterise and depict different aspects of contemporary black society. The similarity of names and their migration seems to suggest that Masondo has drawn from a stock of common names reflecting personality traits across the social strata. Only at a structural level does Masondo's naming technique operate as captured in Sucksmith's (1970: 250) observation of Dickens's art of narrative,

> the psychology and social realism of Dickens's characters, their evolution from originals, their relationship to the structure of the novels in which they appear […] may not be related to the structure; it is itself structure and may be related to effect and vision.

In order to understand how Masondo's names function aesthetically, we need to follow what Culleton (1994: 4) says of Joyce's naming process,

> studying names in Joyce we not only find largely untapped resources that extend our study of genealogy, history, sociology, folklore, literature, philosophy and other disciplines outside of linguistics, but we enhance our ultimate understanding of the writer with whatever information we can harness about the processes [he] went through when he selected names for his characters.

The study of Masondo's names can also be enhanced, not by looking for archetypal representations in his act of naming, but by looking at these names broadly as given names drawn from a bank of popular names in contemporary society names that, while loaded with meaning and showing clear genealogical or typological information, resist straight-jacketing at all levels of meaning. Although there is a strong temptation to explore Masondo's naming technique in all his detective novels because of the prevalence of his cross-referencing of certain names, I will only look at two narratives, *Ingwe Nengonyama* and *Ingalo Yomthetho*, which are part of the first and second of Masondo's trilogies respectively.

The paradox at the heart of Masondo's acts of naming and characterisation

The use of anonymical names in both *Ingalo Yomthetho* and *Ingwe Nengonyama* does not hold any significance because in most instances when Masondo refers to anonymous characters in the text, he uses the terms indicating their employment. These characters do not have any significant role except to function as auxiliaries. For instance, in *Ingalo Yomthetho*, when *Makhosonke* checks in at the hotel in *Maseru*, we hear of the luggage assistants and hotel receptionists whom he questions regarding the people he is investigating. Their presence adds flair and variety to the characters populating the texts and enhances the credibility of the scene and setting. In most instances mention is made of them only once and then they fade out of the plot.

Perhaps the most interesting class of names is that of 'purely invented fantastic names'. Whilst they mostly do not hold any imaginative value, they are meaningful and some of the characters represented by these names are central to the plot and reflect the migratory pattern mentioned earlier. The name *Taga* is one such example. Similarly, names like *Bhoyi* and *Sambo* in *Ingwe Nengonyama*, appear in more than one text. *Lasi, Skero* and *Mamba* in *Ingalo Yomthetho* are also invented personal names which according to Ngonyani (2001), the writer purposefully invented and used because they are meaningful and contribute in different ways to the narrative. They are descriptive of qualities or the trade of the characters. For example, the names *Lasi* and *Skero* do not exist in isiZulu. They are street names or nicknames that locate the characters in a non-conventional lifestyle of 'all-night' illicit gambling, heavy drinking and general debauchery (Masondo, 1994d: 43, 57, 87). Both Koopman (1987) and Neethling (1994) hold the view that these nicknames are used in specific, intimate, social circles as is the case with the closed gambling party that Mamba holds.

The name Mamba is an intriguing example of Masondo's use of invented and meaningful nicknames. Conventionally the name is that of a deadly snake found in South Africa. In *Ingalo Yomthetho* the attributes of the snake are personified in the character bearing this name. *Mamba* is the son of *Nxumalo*, a rich milk farmer, who has hired *Makhosonke* to investigate his son's activities because they have resulted in heavy financial losses for the Maseru-based company which *Mamba* heads. Whilst *Nxumalo*'s description of his son suggests all the qualities of a venomous snake and *Makhosonke*'s initial assessment of this character attests to that description, *Makhosonke* soon discovers that it is a front that conceals his numerous weaknesses, including his lack of vision and foresight, his addiction to gambling, life of pleasure and debauchery. Masondo's naming strategy with regard to this name has created unrealised expectations as he has subverted its conventional meaning by showing that names do not always mean what they suggest. The structural paradox underscoring this name lies in the fact that *Mamba*, whose name carries associations of the most venomous snake, is actually killed by poisoning. The beverage which he takes on the spur of a moment is laced with poison. That he dies through poisoning can be read symbolically in two ways. Firstly, his poisonous qualities are seen in his treatment of his immediate family which he left for a younger model-like, Maseru beauty, Alicia. Secondly, they are seen in the way he bankrupts the family business through illicit gambling through the friends he keeps, and how his position as a businessman and role model to his community is misleading as his standing is compromised by the dark activities he engages in. His symbolically poisonous role is ironically undercut by the actual poisoning that leads to his death.

It is not only the name, *Mamba*, that exemplifies Masondo's style of de-stereotyping. Names like *Bhoyi* and *Sambo* also reflect this complexity. Both characters are law enforcers in *Ingwe Nengonyama*, yet ironically their names carry pejorative meanings in racial politics and racial discourses. Both names are derogatory within the racial politics of the South African, African and African American contexts. In the South African context the name *Bhoyi* is derived from the English noun 'boy'. During apartheid and possibly in the post-apartheid context this was a pejorative term for any black male in white domestic employment or was a marker of black male inferiority when used outside white employment. It is quite interesting, though, that the name *Bhoyi* has made it into the praises of *Cetshwayo* (Nyembezi, 1958).[9] Equally, the name *Sambo* was used to refer to slaves of African descent in Africa and in America. In areas of Musina, in the Limpopo Province, the name *Sambo* is prevalent as a surname of the Tsonga and Venda people.[10] The point being made is that the conventional meanings of the names emphasise inferiority, dehumanisation, mockery and derogation. However, in *Ingwe Nengonyama*, these names are devoid of these associations as the characters bearing these names are law enforcers. For instance, *Sambo* and *Bhoyi* form part of an investigative team in *Ingwe Nengonyama*, and *Themba* calls on them for backup when he intends to expose the culprits (Masondo, 1994a: 88–92).

Taga is central to the plot of *Ingwe Nengonyama*. Part of the mystery in the case which *Themba* investigates is unraveled by the clues that he slips out from time to time. Some of the clues he gives to *Themba* relate to the movements of *Duduzile*, *Kubheka*'s new wife (Masondo, 1994a: 6–8). *Taga* also informs *Themba* about the people who tried to kill him and later visited him in hospital to finish him off (Masondo, 1994a: 36–37). Later on in the novel, after *Taga* has been murdered, the letter he left with the police for *Themba* helps him solve the case (Masondo, 1994a: 60). Although his character is central to the development of the plot, the name assigned to his character does not have any meaning in this context. It could be that the name is a result of his involvement in the *Kabasa* gang in the secondary plane of the narrative. In the primary plane, where he is involved with the police and private investigators, the essence of the name is lost. However, the associations of the name link him to the gang, identifying him with the underworld. As pointed out before, the name has been bestowed on a character in *Iphisi Nezinyoka* and has migrated to *Ingwe Nengonyama*. In *Iphisi Nezinyoka* it structurally depicted a prime suspect and in the latter text a corpse. Although *Taga* eventually becomes a corpse in *Ingwe Nengonyama*, his centrality as opposed to his peripheral positioning in the former text has assisted in reading his character as a completely different entity. This is because in the latter text he has been endowed with personality traits, as a former gang member and eventually a vagabond, which the character bearing the same name in the other text did not have. Exploited in his depiction in the latter text is the interplay between reality and appearances. His appearance as a vagabond was a cover up for his illicit involvements in the past and as a decoy to avoid attention from *Vika Kubheka* who was on a spree to kill all his criminal associates from the underworld.

Linked to these names are those that are semantically meaningful but contextually meaningless. According to Ngonyani (2001) there are three sources of names: realistic names, invented names and mythological names. Realistic names are those that are common.

Masondo's employment of these names reflects, to a certain extent, the stock of names from which he has selected them. Quite interestingly, these are names commonly found in the urban areas and they do not reflect much ingenuity in their coinage. Even though the plots revolve around the characters of *Themba* and *S'fiso* in *Ingwe Nengonyama*, or *Popi* in *Ingalo Yomthetho*, their names do not have any thematic significance. Equally, the names of secretaries, like *Thandi*, *S'fiso Ngubane*'s secretary in *Ingwe Nengonyama* and *Zethu*, *Mamba*'s secretary in *Ingalo Yomthetho*, are common, realistic names reflecting the urban milieu of the narratives. The function in the texts of the latter two characters, beyond their secretarial jobs, is very minimal. In *Ingwe Nengonyama*, *Thandi*'s generosity in lending money to *Themba* is a pretext to get closer to him. Much later in the narrative, when she is married to *Themba*, *Themba* remarks that:

> *Suka lapha mkami! Ukuguga lokhu sekwenza ukuba nenhliziyo encane. Angithi wabe ulunge kakhulu ngalesiya sikhathi ngisahlupheka ngiboleka imali njalo. Nguwena kuphela owawunginika imali eningi* (Masondo, 1994a: 109).

> Oh put a sock on it, my wife! I think old age makes you too sensitive. You were too kind when I used to borrow money from you. You were the only one who gave me more money.

Equally, *Zethu*'s depiction in *Ingalo Yomthetho* is ambiguous. Although she has a lover, she indicates to *Makhosonke* that she wants to be involved with a man in his thirties, someone like *Makhosonke*. Her attraction to *Makhosonke* is also seen in her seductive behaviour whenever *Makhosonke* is around (Masondo, 1994d: 34, 63). Whilst Masondo might be faulted for stereotyping secretaries, his stereotyping derives from the presumed public view of secretaries and not from his naming practices.

Name-giving through which personality traits are indicated is a widely used stylistic device in isiZulu literature. Masondo also draws from this class of names and in illuminating some of the thematic concerns of his texts I will analyse the names of the characters *Magwegwe* (crooked legs) *Buthelezi* and *Vika* (to duck) *Kubheka* in *Ingwe*

Nengonyama. The underlying didacticism of this novel is captured in the axiom 'crime does not pay' and by the observation that an individual's innate goodness is subsumed by being in the company of evil people. These truisms are applicable to both *Magwegwe Buthelezi* and *Vika Kubheka. Magwegwe's* involvement with the *Kabasa* gang, led by *Vika Kubheka,* has tainted his good heart. His desire for wealth has clouded his judgment and damaged his morality. The name, *Magwegwe,* seems to highlight these defects in his moral being. In the narrative he is introduced as a failure who has resigned his life to living in the jungle. Out of reach of his enemies and the people he blackmails, he retreats, not into the inner self on a moral or psychological journey, but into a world that is underpinned by self-effacement (Masondo, 1994a: 4–21). His withdrawal stems from a penitent realisation of his complicity in the murder of Kubheka's wife. *Magwegwe* is one of the people who knew *Vika Kubheka's* history. Therefore he could have warned *Kubheka's* wife about his underworld affiliation or, better still, informed the police about his past shady dealings and his current intentions. Furthermore, *Kubheka's* wife whole-heartedly trusted *Magwegwe:*

> *wabemethembe kakhulu lo mlisa oboshiwe. Wayengakaze akhononde ngaye ngiso nangelilodwa ilanga. Okungenani wayeke amtuse* (Masondo, 1994a: 42).

> she trusted him immensely. She never complained about him, not even on a single day. Instead she praised him.

Another important observation regarding *Magwegwe's* ambiguity relates to the assistance he gives *Themba* in unraveling the case. He slips him clues but retains much of the information required for the arrest of the culprits. His assistance is marked by a fear of what *Vika Kubheka* will do to him (Masondo, 1994a: 27–30, 64–66) and a sense of anger because he believes that *Vika Kubheka's* unbounded gluttony and greed have failed him. He insists that his gang activities are not crime-related but driven by an ambition to become wealthy. Yet it is this very ambition that led to the murder of *Vika Kubheka's* wife.

Vika Kubheka, for his part, is a conniving, immoral and hypocritical gang lord. He waits two years before he hires investigators to find the person who killed his wife (Masondo, 1994a:3). However, it becomes apparent in his second meeting with *Themba* that his soliciting of private investigators has been 'to duck from the law', as his name suggests. He has been ducking from his gangster friends ever since striking it rich. His failure to share the loot equally with *Magwegwe* and *Taga* has compelled him to employ a hitman, *Bheki Nxumalo*, who eliminates all the people who knew him before. However, his ducking from the law is short-lived as *Themba* uncovers the secrets through his former contacts and he is arrested and indicted for the murder of his wife.

The naming of the character *Bhadi* (ill-luck) *Shongwe* in *Ingalo Yomthetho* also emphasises thematic issues. His involvement with a gambling party and its illegal activities and his presence when *Mamba* is poisoned make him a prime suspect for murder. His education, (he has a Doctor of Philosophy degree), misleads readers into thinking that he is the mastermind behind all the activities that eventually lead to *Mamba*'s death. Only after *Mamba*'s death is the semantic significance of the name highlighted. His name means bad luck or misfortune. However, what the author seems to be highlighting through the association of the name with this character, is the misfortune that occurs in society, through which intellectuals are reduced to illegal gambling in pursuit of wealth or as a recreational activity.

Meaningful names that have drawn on their contexts also include symbolic names. In *Ingalo Yomthetho*, *Makhosonke* and *Makhosazana* represent such names. Both names have to do with ancestral beliefs in African society and the positions of eldest sons and daughters. First-born male children stand to be heirs and benefactors of their fathers' assets while the first-born female children in families are the ones called upon in an oath. In *Ingalo Yomthetho* both characters so named are involved in relationships that, culturally, are regarded as abominable. *Makhosonke*, a private investigator, is in love with an old wealthy widow, *Popi Hadebe*, the wife of his deceased partner. *Makhosazana*, *Mamba*'s estranged wife, has an affair with *Jona*, a gambling friend of her husband. In the African tradition, a love affair with widows is a phenomenon that has emerged with the industrialisation and urbanisation of African people. Traditionally a widow would have been married off to one of the brothers of the husband. Culturally marriage is not simply an agreement between two parties but takes on a deeper symbolic significance that involves ancestors when two families are brought together. Therefore the continuity of the relationship is ensured by the widow being married off to a brother of the husband. *Makhosonke*'s involvement with *Popi* reflects practices of contemporary society, which is heavily influenced by a Western mode of life.

A similar reading is reached for the character of *Makhosazana*. Her involvement with *Jona*, (whose analogous reference to Jonah in the Bible should be emphasised) is unacceptable to both the African tradition and Christian belief. On the symbolic level both *Makhosazana* and *Makhosonke* are representative of the traditional value system. But there is tension and conflict in their names, which reflects the tension between an African view of life, on the one hand, and their actions, which are steeped in the practices of modern life, on the other. On the symbolic level, the clash between African tradition and the Western way of life are played out. Their end attests to African tradition's rejection of Western practices. *Makhosazana* and *Jona* are sentenced to death for their hand in the murder of *Mamba* (Masondo, 1994d: 166). *Makhosonke* and *Popi* are killed in an explosion at a party celebrating their success in resolving the case (Masondo, 1994d: 170). Not only *Makhosonke* and his lover, but all the major characters, are killed in the explosion (Masondo, 1994d: 168). Through this ending Masondo seems to suggest that these types of people, irrespective of the positive attributes they may have, are not fit to be part of society.

Regarding these culturally symbolic names, King's (cited in Ngonyani, 2001: 126) investigation of names in African-American naming traditions is very useful in illuminating Masondo's intention. King's concept of double-voiced signifying practice is of interest in explaining Masondo's conclusion of *Ingalo Yomthetho*. In this concept the names convey the narrator's or writer's message. *Makhosonke*'s name, actions, conquests and his involvement with a widow, a contemporary practice that is culturally abhorred, firstly draw attention to the symbolic significance of his position within society and the traditional belief system. Secondly, the author's message regarding such relationships is revealed as embedded in the ironical reading of the name and behaviour of this character. The same reading can be reached for the double-pronged names and love relationship between *Makhosazana* and *Jona*. There seems to be a notion that, according to both African traditional and Christian values, the relationship is frowned upon and that seems to be the reason why the author gives them no opportunity for repentance and they are sentenced to death.

There are certain names like *Sandile* (*Themba*'s only son, who is kidnapped and later killed by *oMashayabhuqe*) in *Ingwe Nengonyama* and that of *Jona* in *Ingalo Yomthetho* that are based on ironical reversal of things. In the former text, *Sandile*, which means 'we have multiplied', that is, the family has multiplied, works in sharp contrast with actual events in the text, for *Themba*'s family does not multiply: it is annihilated by *oMashayabhuqe* hit men. He is the only one of his family who survives (Masondo, 1994a: 53). In a similar manner *Jona* points to a double contradiction in the sense that in the Bible the ambiguity of the individual so named is highlighted, but eventually, in the context of the Bible, he repents and does as God has advised him to do. In the context of the novel, whilst the name alludes to this ambiguity, he is not given a chance to repent. On hearing the sentence *Jona* indicates to the group of hit men that he had arranged all along to carry out the explosion that kills everyone at the end of the text (Masondo, 1994d: 166).

Culture: Praises and naming in Masondo's novels

There are two key issues mentioned by Herbert (1995) that are relevant to this discussion. These relate to the private and public coinage of the name or names bestowal and to changes in forms of address. They are relevant to the practice typical in isiZulu culture of *izibongo* (praises) and *ukuthakazela* (to say a clan's praise phrase). The inclusion of *izibongo* and *izithakazelo* has been a dominant stylistic practice in the writings of the first generation of writers. However, the literature produced during the apartheid period was marked by a sharp decline in the use of this stylistic device. The re-emergence of the use of *izibongo* and *izithakazelo* in novels does not point to any newness in Masondo's application but to an existing practice that had been established by the first generation of writers. Masondo's characterisation through this device also reaffirms past applications, whereby the individual whose praises are recited is urged on. In *Ingwe Nengonyama*, *Themba* recites his praises:

> *Ngingumphikeleli ophikelela kumnyamakuluvindi!*
> *Umsusuluzi wenkanyamb' emakhandakhanda.*
> *Usilwa netshe ngob' amagabade ayazifela!*
> *Umkhukhuzi wenyama kusal' amathambo,*
> *Okhukhuz'imamb' emagilo!*
> *Nani bafazi baseNcenceni nofa nizilanda,*
> *Ngokuhamba nihefuz' ize,*
> *Nith' ekaXaba kayizalanga yazal' ivaka,*
> *Kodwa nisho ningabonanga!* (Masondo, 1994a: 16)

I am the forceful one, who forces his way even when it is dark and invisible!
I am the beheader of the great river snake that has many heads.
The one who fights with the stone because the mud stones break up!
The eater of meat until the bones remain,
The eater of the mamba of many throats!
You, women of Ncenceni you will die talking,
Because you go about talking nonsense,
Saying the daughter of Xaba did not give birth to anything but a coward,
When actually you have not seen anything!

Themba recites this praise during an incident in his investigation into the activities of *Kubheka* and his new wife *Duduzile*. These praises appear at the beginning of the text, alluding not only to *Themba*'s bravery but also to the fact that he is very forceful and not numbed into immobility easily. Thus, when a number of mishaps befall him, such as the kidnapping of his son and the killing of his family members, these events are anticipated and urge him to find a resolution to the case.

Linked to the use of *izibongo* in the narrative is that of *izithakazelo*. Masondo has explored traditional practices reflecting different situations. Surnames and *izithakazelo* in the narratives do not point to any underlying meaning but they add a cultural flair to the conversations in the narratives. *Zondi* is alternatively addressed as *Mthiyane, Dlamini* as *Lusibalukhulu,* and *Nxumalo* as *Ndwandwe.* Ngonyani (2001: 131) points out that the use of surnames locates an individual in a genealogy and in a society. In addition this practice establishes social or close personal relations. Quite interestingly, these social relations are what Masondo explores to show that they are not premised on old lore where people were good citizens who aimed to uphold the law. In the narratives the personal and social relations are a vehicle for deeply embedded social conflicts, tensions and intrigues where the ones shown respect are not actually deserving of the respect shown to them by the society at large. *Vika Kubheka* is interchangeably addressed by means of his clan name *Khathide* in *Ingwe Nengonyama* and as *Dr Shongwe* and *Mamba Nxumalo* or *Makhosonke Ndima* in *Ingalo Yomthetho.* Many female characters are also addressed respectfully whilst they are not deserving of that respect.

Also significant is the change in the form of address to the female characters in the texts. If their first names are not used they are named after their husbands. For instance, *Kubheka*'s wives are said to be *Nkosikazi Kubheka* and in the case of another character, *Nxumalo,* his wife is addressed as *Nkosikazi Nxumalo.* This naming practice acts contrary to the custom whereby women are addressed by the surnames of their fathers and where a gender marker /Ma-/ is prefixed to the surname. The usage in the narrative reflects western forms of address: *Mrs Kubheka* or *Mrs Nxumalo.*

Another striking occurrence in *Ingalo Yomthetho* is *Makhosonke*'s refusal to be addressed by his surname, *Ndima,* saying that the real *Ndima,* (his father) is still alive. The motives for his refusal are seemingly deep and largely informed by his relationship with *Popi.* He has always been self conscious about the affair with his partner's older wife. Could it be that the reason for his refusal to be located within his father's genealogy is to shield his family from this abominable behaviour or does it reflect urban forms of address, where genealogies have long lost their essence? Since all of Masondo's characters are drawn from an urban setting these changes, to a large extent, substantiate Herbert's (1995: 1–2) observation that the urban centres are marked by a decline, not only in traditional morality, but also in traditional naming practices.

Conclusion

Ntombela (1995), Makgamatha (1992) and Kunene (1994) have shown that characterisation through naming is a widely used narrative strategy in literature. Masondo introduces a technique in isiZulu literature in which characterisation does not necessarily proceed from the names assigned or selected for characters. In this way he de-stereotypes the act of naming as a stylistic device while acknowledging, as Neethling (1988) points out, that names are loaded with associations. While the paradox underpinning Masondo's acts of naming and characterisation is a fundamental aspect of de-stereotyping, he introduces a practice in which similar names are drawn from the store of realistic names and are then simply deployed and re-iterated in different texts to animate different personages, personalities, psychologies and emotional states. This migratory technique contributes towards the disruption of archetypes.

Endnotes

1   The first two *Isigcawu Senkantolo* (1990) and *Iphisi Nezinyoka* (1991) made it to the Department of Education prescribed set works for isiZulu matriculation in the early 1990s. The latter novel further prescribed for the grade elevens in the late 1990s. In 1994 alone he published five more detective stories. After this marathon he seems to have shifted focus and experimented with closet dramas, *Kungenxa Yakho Mama* (1996) and *Sixolele* published in (2004). He also wrote a radio/stage/TV drama, *Inkundlanye: A Collection of One-act Stage, Radio and TV Plays* (1997), which was translated with the collaboration of Rachelle Gauton into *One-act Plays: A Collection of One-act Stage, Radio and TV Plays* (1998). Masondo also collected folklore and published it as *Inkunzi Isematholeni* (1997).

2   In a telephone interview conducted in July 2005, he intimated that he completed a manuscript of each text within four weeks. He was referring

in particular to *Ingwe Nengonyama, Kanti Nawe, Ngaze Ngazenza* and *Ingalo Yomthetho, Kunjalo-ke Emhlabeni*, all published in 1994.

3   In the same interview, he intimated that he was attempting a trilogy and hoped to repeat that with subsequent publications. However, with subsequent publications the relationship between the texts is not as apparent and stylistically effective as with the first three texts.

4   During the apartheid period, law enforcement agencies were regarded with suspicion by the black majority and white progressives who lived under the repression of the apartheid regime and after elections this view of law enforcement agencies did not change much. The negative associations of law enforcers were further exacerbated by the upsurge in criminal activities in the country and their failure to combat this upsurge has since made their image a national crisis. See Mokwena, in Everrett and Sisulu (1992).

5   Formalists and Structuralists' stylistics entail the usage of ordinary familiar words in ways that are unfamiliar in order to bring about a heightened artistic effect.

6   Masondo informed the author in an interview that in his teen years and early adulthood he had been an ardent reader of detective stories. But that which kindled his interest had been the James Hardly Chase collections, which were readily available in paperback cover in many urban households. He also had access to the detective stories of Sherlock Holmes. Masondo has drawn from stylistics of these authors. His style of representing received reality, his use of unthought-of twists which invariably affect conventional social stereotypes about class, professions or the general society are some of the stylistic devices he uses in his naming practice as reading strategies of the psychologies of contemporary black South Africa.

7   Sholes and Kellog (1996), and Ogude (1996) discuss extensively issues of allegorical characterisation. They conclude that allegorical characterisation leads to considerations of characters as types stripped of all individuality but what is emphasised are the symbolic functions or discourses standing for a larger framework.

8   The name of Buthelezi brought up associations with the leader of the Inkatha Freedom Party, uMntwana uGatsha Mangosuthu Buthelezi. On the eve of the new political dispensation his controversial political stance

towards both mainstream politics and black national politics earned him and the organisation he led mistrust, animosity and marginalisation in the post-apartheid South Africa.

9   There is a line in Cetshwayo's praise which refers to the Zulu civil war of the late 1870s between his supporter, Usuthu, and Mandlakazi, under the leadership of Mbuyazi. When Cetshwayo received information that his regiments were winning against Mbuyazi and Mandlakazi's supporters, he is said to *'watakasa njengebhoyi'* (he was as happy and performed certain dancing steps like a boy (a male servant at the colonial place of employment). See Nyembezi, 1958. *Izibongo Zamakhosi.*

10 The ethnic mix that constituted the Tsonga and the Venda people because of migration and the Mfecane wars of the second and third decades of the nineteenth century makes it difficult to determine whether the surname is originally from the Tsonga or Venda or other ethnic group that could have migrated from neighbouring states like Mozambique or Zimbabwe.

'A world in creolisation': Inheritance politics and the ambiguities of a 'very modern tradition' in two black South African TV dramas

In the first three chapters I have drawn on a diverse collection of post-apartheid novels to illustrate the extent to which Barber's theoretical model of African popular arts and popular culture provides a solution to the aesthetic conundrum (Dhlomo, 1977) that has beset the African-language literary tradition for the past hundred years. Barber's model is helpful because it focuses on everyday African culture and draws extensively on Bakhtin's (1981) and Lefebvre's (1947) studies of ordinary people and their everyday experiences which is the domain to which African-language literature addresses itself. In these first three chapters I argued that the conditions created for the development of African writing in the past hundred years, and the inability of Eurocentric literary models to excavate the hermeneutic world, particularly of African-language poetics inherited from the oral and the modern worlds, exemplify the nature of the many challenges and issues that exist in current discourses about expressive forms in African languages.

In the next three chapters I intend to apply Barber's model to other artistic productions, particularly black South African television serials. This will allow me to illustrate how the themes of these newer art forms are sourced from earlier oral forms, making them resonate with the popular discourses that animate everyday African culture.

Broader questions relate to how Barber's model of African arts and culture is able to bring the oral and written forms and the elitist and popular genres into a relationship with each other and locate the resultant eclectic culture in its socio-historical context. Barber's paradigm of popular arts and culture goes beyond literary boundaries as it is able to explore a wide range of cultural products, all the while focusing on what matters or what is of interest to people of all classes and views. It explores a range of discourses at the disposal of the producers and recipients which are recreated to articulate the concerns of the people. According to Hannerz (1997: 16) the model considers artists, writers, and academics as engaged in a conversation. It helps reveal how global influences and cultures produce international meanings that flow into or interact with the national culture. In addition, it is capable of explaining how popular culture and popular arts are able to counter internationalising influences by being critical or by being self-appointed guardians of traditional cultures.

African-language literatures, right from its early years, were engaged in conversation with an international culture; European civilisation. African-language literatures projected themselves in elitist terms (Gerard, 1983, Grobbler, 1995, Kunene, 1992) and this elitism persisted and made invisible 'the loud and colourful outburst of creativity in music, oral lore, and the visual arts, emerging from the masses' (Fabian, 1997: 19). But over time the discourses in society became more creolised and pervasive and African-language literatures therefore engaged with them and became more elaborate until we can say that this literary tradition is shaped by these eclectic discourses: it largely draws from contexts shaped by them and it is produced by writers that cut across the African social fabric.

Many definitions of creolisation exist (see Sidbury, 2007; Flores, 2009; Cohen, 2007; Stewart, 2007 and Knepper, 2007), however, they all stress similar aspects. Creolisation has come to be associated with cultural mixtures of African, European and indigenous ancestry to form new cultures and new identities. The African-language arts tradition evinces diversity, complexity and fluidity and, as Hannerz (1997) points out, this should be seen as an invitation to look at systems of meaning which do not hide their connections with power and the material life.

This observation is supported by Fabian when he says that there is a need to make the vast and vigorous expressions of African experience visible.

We must stress that the emerging forms of expression, reflecting the life-like experiences and consciousness of the masses, deserve our fullest attention as evidence for cultural independence and creativity. From sterile fixations on the presumed disintegration of tradition and on the rare accomplishments of 'assimilated' elites we must proceed to a fuller appreciation of the new mass cultures (1978: 19–20).

In the next three chapters I will examine those art forms, such as film and TV productions, that have been made 'invisible' by a preoccupation with only oral or elitist written forms.

Moving into film with Barber's model

In their programming from the early 1990s, the South African Broadcasting Corporation (SABC) emphasised social engineering policies such as nation-building (Ives, 2007; Evans, 2010; Teer-Tomaselli, 1997) and neo-liberal policies (Kruger, 2010; Laden, 1997) that were in line with South Africa's new political economy. In this chapter I will demonstrate how two South African TV drama series, *Ifa LakwaMthethwa* (The inheritance of the Mthethwa people) and *Hlala Kwabafileyo* (Remain with the dead), draw from the neo-liberal policies and popular discourses found in contemporary creolised culture to construct 'aspirational' narratives (as defined by Vundla and McCarthy, producers of *Generations* and *Gaz' Lam II* respectively) that reflect changing economic patterns in post-apartheid African society. The changes explored in these TV dramas can be read against traditional inheritance conventions which, in both filmic narratives, are signalled by the pivotal use of genres from oral and popular discourse.

While the SABC's adoption of transformative policies like nation-building and neo-liberalism marked a significant shift from and provided alternative models to the apartheid past, the alteration of socio-economic and cultural contexts of production and reception have remained the most daunting task for transforming not only television productions but also South African film production (McClusky, 2009;

Dovey, 2009). South African film production, with its long history of colonial and apartheid controls as well as the post-apartheid mix of commercial and state-funded infrastructure, continued unabated, albeit reconfigured, in the post-apartheid political and cultural economies. Kruger, basing her arguments on Brecht's analysis of the relationship between theatre and social change, points out that:

> Changing dramatic form or the technical apparatus of theatre or other media does not automatically lead to the transformation of society. … only a full transformation of the social relations that determine who produces, finances and validates the dramatic form – whether in the theatre, radio or film, or in our day, in television, and an array of new media – will amount to a revolution (2010: 7, 8).

The white, male-dominated South African film industry (Tomaselli, 1989a; Kruger, 2010; Jacobs, 2011) and the tendencies towards racial collaboration within the South African television industry that began in the mid 1980s (and which, at that stage, were a ploy to produce material that masked and elided power relations in all spheres of South African life) persist into the present and continue to shape the post-apartheid national imaginary on television (Ives, 2007: 158–159).

Arguably, television production from the mid 1980s featured aspirational content for the black middle class as a logical response to the national identity encouraged by the co-option policy[1] (Tomaselli, 1986) which continued the preoccupation with black middle classness (Laden, 1997) that stretches back to the colonial, missionary enterprise (Posel, 2010). Post-apartheid, neo-liberal ideologies in television programmes, just like the co-option policy of the late apartheid era, focused on the black middle class and its patterns of conspicuous consumption to forge new ways of fashioning mainstream black identities. The aspirational narratives of *Ifa LakwaMthethwa* (The inheritance of the Mthethwa family) and *Hlala Kwabafileyo* (Remain with the dead), in the early 1990s, provided glimpses of how the post-apartheid African National Congress (ANC) wanted to 'shape, contest and reflect the popular national imaginary' (Ives, 2007: 161) to the African majority through television programming.

One question to ask is what created fertile ground for the reception of films that shifted radically from the hegemonising socialist discourses (which the current ruling party used to conscientise the African majority) to the neo-liberalist ideology espoused in the films under discussion? Both films employ African aesthetics as the pivotal axis through which these neo-liberal, post-apartheid ideologies and representations can be mediated. A follow-up question is whether these aesthetics allow for the visual reflexivity celebrated in black Film and African Cinema, or whether they have been used for false consciousness as Fabian (1997) observed about the deployment of popular discourses in mainstream cultural productions.

Artistic entanglements: The relationship between the

African-language literary tradition and South African black film

By the beginning of the twentieth century, the missionary enterprise had succeeded in creating a distinctive black middle class with distinctive class values (see Comaroff & Comaroff, 1997; Peterson, 1997; Cobley, 1990). These imperatives were articulated in many cultural areas, and fictional narratives became prominent spaces where these views were expressed. The migration of some of these narratives to radio broadcasts from the 1940s and again in the 1980s when black television was introduced, further circulated these black middle class imperatives. By now this class had assumed the position of key cultural broker and gatekeeper of African modernity (see Peterson, 1997, 2003, 2006). Right from the beginning African modernity evinced an eclectic admixture of traditional and European sensibilities. These mixed worldviews argued neither for a pre-colonial existence nor for a Eurocentric vision of the future, but illuminated the in-between state of being a modern African in spaces that were neither wholly traditional nor European.

African-language literatures, from their beginning, and black television dramas of the 1980s successfully created fertile ground for the reception of drama series such as *Ifa LaKwa-Mthethwa* and *Hlala Kwabafileyo*. They were broadcast to an audience who had definite tastes and expectations and responded well to the middle class sensibilities depicted in these dramas. It is apparent that these series draw not only from dominant Western film conventions, particularly Hollywood conventions, but also from sensibilities encapsulated in the literary tradition of African elites as may be seen in the adaptation of Shabangu's (1982) *Bamngcwaba Aphila* to *Hlala Kwabafileyo* and the turning of *Ifa LakwaMthethwa* into a novel. The conceptualisation of African-language literatures in elitist terms meant that its concerns reflected a class-consciousness that in most instances marginalised the interests of lower classes. Most often voices of the underclass were suppressed in favour of elitist perceptions and ideologies. This practice further fragmented black society along class lines. The impossibility of control over means of production by the lower classes ensured the dominance of middle class imperatives. Middle class sensibilities permeated all aspects of black life and became mainstream. Ever since the emergence of the black middle class during the late nineteenth and early twentieth century the sensibilities of this African class have reflected the aspirations of the upwardly mobile. This African middle class, because of its social standing and education, sought inclusion in white mainstream culture. However, the nature of racial politics of South Africa made this impossible.

By the 1980s there was tacit acknowledgement of the existence of this class as a separate, self-contained group. The state used the political strategy of incorporating the African middle class by acknowledging their socio-economic ambitions through the co-option policy (Tomaselli, 1986). This incorporation was achieved by creating illusions, through television programmes, that seemed to acknowledge their aspirations. It was hoped that these constructions would be interpreted as evidence not only of equality but also of acceptance into the white mainstream culture. Kruger (2010) also points out that the incorporation of blacks into film production was a ploy to foster a sense of identification that would encourage blacks to protect some of these values because they had been made to think that they had a stake in the system. From the 1980s onward numerous social development programmes, solely targeted at this class, were implemented. This was seen in the housing sector where Africans from this category were housed in structures similar to the ones seen in white suburbs; their salaries were also significantly improved and, for the first time, medical aid programmes were instituted for them (Tomaselli, 1989). These concessions by the apartheid state exploited black middle class imperatives instituted and modified over the last century. Its policy of incorporation exploited existing forms of social differentiation being carved from the existing social fragmentation, from patterns of solidarity and social organisation, and drew on social aspirations for the general improvement of black society. The elitist terms through which these changes were articulated in literature and the first television dramas resulted in a stultifying conservatism that yoked together both African traditional and Christian morality to depict a syncretic culture that typified contemporary society.

In such juxtapositions the traditional episteme is re-invoked to address pro-Western modern sensibilities with the scale tilting towards a model that exalted a mixture of cultures. Although earlier films proceeded from this model, those produced between 1990 and 1995 harnessed the popular urban perspectives that problematised conventional maxims. Simplistic dichotomies between good and evil, or moral and immoral, were under-emphasised in favour of heightened and relevant explorations of social specificities and particularities in popular black lifestyles. The construction of black characters in *Hlala Kwabafileyo* and *Ifa LakwaMthethwa* follows this new paradigm that brought new ways of analysing and interpreting black township and 'aristocratic' life. In these dramatic narratives issues are explored beyond simplistic Christian or African traditional morality, even though these seem to have been the basis of the filmic discourse. *Hlala Kwabafileyo* differs from *Ifa LaKwaMthethwa* because of its familiar, urban locale. *Hlala Kwabafileyo*, as Thackway (2003: 11) has pointed out about Senegalese Francophone films during the same period, is a 'hybrid, urban film that freely juxtaposes popular cultural forms of all origins with more specifically African cultural references'. *Hlala Kwabafileyo* and *Ifa LwakwaMthethwa* demonstrate what Teshome Gabriel (1982: 8) observes in Third World Cinema, that this Cinema is 'able to grasp and portray popular life in more profound authentic, human and concretely historical fashion'. These films portray the petit bourgeoisie within familiar and unfamiliar localities and give a cross-section of 'imagined' African communities in urban diversity in the case of *Hlala Kwabafileyo* or in a pure, traditional ethnicity in the case of *Ifa LakwaMthethwa*. In addition, as intimated by Imruh and Mbye (1996: 4), both films critically engage with certain aspects of African cultural beliefs and traditions and use the resources of these traditions to comment on the contemporary social, cultural, political, historical and personal realities, experiences and challenges faced by Africans. African lives were complicated by the tumultuous history of colonialism and racial capitalism which, by the early 1990s, had formed multilayered existences (Oguibe & Enwezor, 1999) that went beyond simple binaries and pointed to the complexity of contemporary identities.

The literary output of Sidney Shabangu bears testimony to such layering of contemporary experiences. Sidney Shabangu is amongst the few literary writers whose switch to television drama allowed him the space to further explore the complexities and intrigues of contemporary African lifestyles brought about by the interplay between tradition and modernity. Both Whener's (1994) *Hlala Kwabafileyo* and Shabangu and De Kock's (1995) *Ifa LakwaMthethwa*, simultaneously subvert and resist the rhetoric of colonial cultural imperialism and African authority and their parochial interpretations of what constitutes culture. Shabangu's stint as a creative writer began in the 1960s with the publication of *Imiyalezo* (Advices, 1966), which was followed by a second novel, *Imvu Yolahleko* (1977) (The lost sheep), a narrative exploring an incestuous relationship between two siblings. His third novel, *Bamngcwaba Aphila* (1982) (They buried him alive), translated into Siswati as *Bamngcwaba Ephila* (1989), became an experimental adaptation to a film, *Hlala Kwabafileyo* (1994). Significant in Shabangu's writing and the later adaptation of his novel into film is a preoccupation with capturing African life in multi-layered transitions where recent experiences continually inform the cultural choices that people make. Such transition is informed by a state of being in-between where old values are no longer fully relevant and where newer ones are adapted and infused with older values to make them comprehensible. Shabangu's exploration of silenced taboos and practices, both in the traditional and modern worlds, places him within a space where he can reflect on the passing of tradition and at the same time offer interpretations of the multi-layered mutations of modernity and tradition in localities where the discourse of survival takes prominence. Therefore his experimental film, *Hlala Kwabafileyo* and his later work, co-authored with John De Kock, *Ifa LakwaMthethwa* (1995), are sites for contesting, approximating, and expanding representations of African lifestyles in metropolitan zones where these interpenetrate rural ones. His later work, *Emzini Wezinsizwa* by Shambe Productions (2000), co-written with his brother, Pixley Shabangu, and not discussed in this chapter, offers expanded representations of ethnic identities in metropolitan localities.

Ifa LakwaMthethwa and *Hlala Kwabafileyo* offer fascinating constructions of contemporary African life and ways of thinking that continue to grow out of the interplay between tradition and modernity. These contemporary ways reflect an increasingly complex culture that defies a simple binary categorisation of modern versus traditional, or elite versus illiterate, or marginal versus central. In both films, the tensions between traditional and modern perspectives on the politics of inheritance are played out against Western influences and African aspirations. The treatment of these perspectives does not argue for either position, but at stake is the advancement of an eclectic view that, in certain instances, through the imposition of traditional or modern values, favours contemporary metropolitan culture(s). Fascinatingly, notions of what that social organisation ought to look like in popular media such as South African television do not conform to mainstream imperatives but rather to popular ideas of what is considered a 'good life' usually drawn from the lifestyles of the rich and famous.

The reading of the politics of inheritance in *Ifa LakwaMthethwa* and *Hlala Kwabafileyo* in this chapter draws on notions found in creolised cultures. Through this reading I interrogate how the filmic narratives reconstruct popular culture that not only derives from post-apartheid society but also interprets how post-apartheid African society wants to be seen, what its understandings are of how its place in the world may be perceived and what its fantasies are. I discuss inheritance politics in post-apartheid African society by evaluating how filmic narrative, through the use of popular discourse, makes space for the depiction of contexts that allow for cultural retention or cultural change.

Creolised cultures in former colonial countries

According to Hannerz (1997), theories on creolisation have moved beyond a parochial concern with racial identity and linguistic issues to encompass issues of social and cultural development. The films discussed in this chapter are constructed around popular concepts of what constitutes contemporary life in post-apartheid, African rural and cityscapes. Traces of the combined culture that developed over centuries are evident in the construction of these spaces, which have come to define contemporary, African society. As a point of departure, creolisation theories offer macro-ethnographic tools to explain plural societies that are characterised by a prior relationship between a dominant foreign culture and a subjugated culture and where cultural separation was institutionally enforced through broader social variables (Hannerz: 14). Hannerz also postulates that the foundational elements in such a heterogeneous society revolve around its social structure and how it is organised around the national culture, the overall organisation of cultural complexity and issues around restrictions to a society-wide flow of meaning (14). As seen in Drummond (1980) and Fabian (1997), the most important aspect regarding creolised cultures is the notion that the aftermath of colonial contact resulted in mixed, contact cultures that have since formed new, viable syntheses that are meaningful to people who experience and live by them. The extreme view propounds that there are now no distinct cultures, only one interconnected, creolising culture (Drummond, 1978 & 1980 cited in Hannerz, 1997: 14). Hannerz, in support of this assertion, comments that

> creole cultures like creole languages are those which draw in some way on two or more historical sources, often originally widely different. They have had some time to develop, and integrate, and to become elaborate and pervasive. People are informed from birth by these systems of meaning and largely live their lives in contexts shaped by them. There is that sense

of a continuous spectrum of interacting forms, in which the various contributing sources of culture are differentially visible and active. And, in relation to this, there is a built-in political economy of culture, as social power and material resources are matched with the spectrum of cultural forms (1997: 15).

Postcolonial and post-apartheid social organisation has not veered much from the cultural organisation established by the colonial powers. There is still a growing interaction with the world system in its political, economic and cultural dimensions. Postcolonial and post-apartheid social structures remain arranged in ways that allow for an international flow of cultures in varying combinations that synthesise with local cultures and thus create an international culture. The zone of contact for these international influences is numerous institutional and occupational subcultures which, in turn, form 'bridgeheads' from which metropolitan cultural influences can permeate the Third World national culture.

According to Hannerz (1997: 16) one other crucial contribution from creolisation theories regarding the flow of culture has to do with the arrangement of our world system as an international order integrated asymmetrically in terms of the 'centre' and 'margins'. This arrangement has been replicated internally within Third World states. In this arrangement, former colonial powers are a metropolis of the centre with the Third World states occupying the margins. In relation to the relative successes of the Third World in creating nation-like states this arrangement has been helpful because the national culture also flows, in spatial terms, from the centre, which is usually located in the cities, to the periphery, the rural villages in the hinterland.

The entanglements of the local ethnic mosaic with metropolitan centres of influence are crucial in understanding contemporary African lifestyles in city centres and in rural villages. There are other cultural organisers but perhaps key amongst them is the role played by education. Hannerz points out that education is one cultural apparatus in a context where relatively few control large currents of meaning for the great majority. What is fascinating about education is that it is spread across a formalised curriculum and a hidden one. This dual curriculum means that while education is poised to give culture and shape to individuals, it can also help generate an alternate culture that exists in-between being fully and semi developed. In Third World states there is a large category of people who occupy this position in the cultural spectrum. And this category comprises people for whom the term 'hidden curriculum' is intended. They are mainly school-leavers who have not completely mastered an elite culture. Their notions of cultural consumption have been mainly acquired through modelling; by exposure to the media and to the middle class or cultural elites with whom they have come into contact. Hannerz in this regard offers very valuable observations regarding this category:

> Observers of many Third World societies are familiar with 'the problem of school leavers', [...] They often form distinct subcultures – at times, of a disreputable sort [...] with the school leavers the world system in its cultural dimensions may reach the remote village; in their sunglasses and ragged T shirts they are at its tail end, as it were. But they are also pioneer customers of the products of another part of the cultural apparatus – popular culture [...] it has intense reflexive qualities, telling us how producers as well as consumers see themselves, and the directions in which they would like their lives to move. Clearly it also helps order the continuum of creole culture (Hannerz: 16).

The current central positioning of popular culture in post-apartheid cultural politics has assisted in shifting the cultural focus to privilege those life experiences that have always been shielded by the former preoccupation with mainstream culture. By and large, the change in the political dispensation has centralised marginalised life experiences and has brought into the light unexcavated sites of contemporary African lifestyles, offering nuanced and complex understandings of post-apartheid, plural societies. Even though that may be the case, the position of South African black, television dramas within the black film discourses, and debates on the black experience in the diaspora, reveal that black film in South Africa has always been tied up with the state's hegemonic discourses. As a result, there has been no clear advance made in terms of developing a national filmmaking practice which is independent of the state's control. If we consider the four distinctive eras of the evolution of black television drama (the apartheid era from 1981–1990, the transitional era from 1991–1994, the reconciliatory period from 1995–1999 and the sedimentation of democracy from 2000 to date) black television dramas emerged as articulating the predetermined political discourses of the time. The ideas informing the initial envisaged role of black television dramas have not altered with the change in political players. Black television, and particularly its dramas, remains strongly aligned to the different governments' attempts at winning the hearts and minds of black South Africans in the apartheid period and both black and white South Africans in the post-apartheid context. In view of Brecht's (2000) seminal observations regarding revolutionary forces and their absorption into capitalist institutions, my reading of these TV dramas will explore the capacity of these films to normalise capitalist and neo-liberal policies, highlighting those aspirational aspects that seek to normalise old power relations within new hands. As Kruger comments, the post-apartheid society is

> characterised by the normalisation of old power relations in new hands … as erstwhile activists and their formerly anti-government organisations enjoy positions of power while only intermittently addressing the majority excluded from the good life promised by transformation (2010: 78).

It is in view of such challenges that we perhaps need to take into cognizance Oguibe and Enwezor's (1999: 165) cautionary remarks regarding contemporary, visual culture in Africa. They maintain that readings of contemporary, visual culture should be underpinned by a commitment which does not privilege 'constructions and contestations of identity; identities fashioned by others and foisted on Africans; identities contested and rejected by Africans', but on self-reflexive, transient forms that continue to explore new layers of recent experiences.

Theories on creolisation are best suited for a reading that privileges the many layers of contemporary experience in *Hlala Kwabafileyo* and *Ifa LakwaMthethwa*. As pointed out by Abrahams (1983: xix), both these

TV dramas are generally conceived as African stories and dramas but although they draw from expressive resources that are limited in range and tied to recurrent occasions, they can achieve potency of meaning and subtlety of expression. Such expressive resources are archaic but are capable of inscribing themselves anew in practices that are foreign but performed in an African style. Also reflected in the TV series are current perspectives of culture; both dramas reveal a society that emphasises life-as-lived rather than revealing communities that are simply seeking order and organisation. In a sense, both these TV dramas illustrate how a post-apartheid community negotiates and derives meaning and value out of a random flow of accumulated modern experiences.

Summary of *Ifa LaKwaMthethwa*

Ifa LaKwaMthethwa revolves around the struggle for succession both in the Chiefdom of the Mthethwa clan and in their business empire. The Mthethwa Chieftaincy is an extremely wealthy entity with all its businesses listed on the international stock market. It is headed by two rival half brothers, Sizwe, a Westernised elite businessman and the rightful heir to the throne, and Nzobo, a traditional, backward, domineering regent. The struggle within the business empire is played out between Nana (Sizwe's niece), a ruthless and ambitious woman, and Bafana (Sizwe's son) who is a shrewd, arrogant, business mogul. Sizwe and his children have laid the foundation of a modern, Western-styled, business enterprise. The power struggles between his children are fuelled by the acquisition of shares. As a result they blackmail and sabotage one another. The business is structured around traditional familial relations that also include the extended family, allowing the children of the assassinated Chief, Mabandla, to be core partners and occupy positions of power in the business. Bafana eventually acquires the most shares, illegally, and Sizwe, acting on the advice of the family advocate, Xaba, resolves the matter using not the relevant Western business protocol but his traditional position as a head of the family and of the Mthethwa Chieftaincy.

In the second part of the drama series, Nzobo, one of the brothers from the non-throne-ascending Chiefly house, has overseen the assassination of Mabandla, who has been reigning in the Mthethwa Chiefdom. He has killed Mabandla knowing that Sizwe, the intended successor, is not interested in the throne, since his interests lie in the Mthethwa Empire. Initially Nzobo's assessment of Sizwe's interest in the business empire is correct. However, Nzobo's arrogance, stemming from this certainty, makes him a tyrannical ruler and he soon falls out of favour with the Mthethwa people. All his attempts to have Sizwe killed are foiled as his hit men and his witchdoctor defect and expose him to Sizwe and the grand council. Nzobo is dethroned and Sizwe is prevailed upon by the grand council to assume his rightful position as the ruler of the Mthethwa people.

Summary of *Hlala Kwabafileyo*

Hlala Kwabafileyo is about Zakhe Mhlongo, a rich businessman, and his family. It starts with Zakhe's illegitimate son, Zuzumuzi, and his attempt to murder Zakhe on the night before the wedding of his only daughter, Babazile. On the wedding day, Zakhe Mhlongo disappears while on his way to see his jealous young lover. He goes missing for several days until the family decides to search hospitals, prisons and mortuaries. A corpse is mistakenly identified by Jessie, Mhlongo's wife, and Bheseni, Mhlongo's brother. It is buried in a funeral of such splendour that it almost divides Jessie and her children. After almost a year has gone by, and after the lawyer has apportioned the inheritance as reflected in Mhlongo's will, Zakhe Mhlongo reappears, having been released from Sterkfontein, a mental hospital, to which he had been admitted. His reappearance shocks the community and particularly his wife, Jessie, who has conducted his mourning, burial and tombstone unveiling according to custom. She thinks this is a conspiracy by her enemies to swindle her and her family out of their inheritance, which by this time her illegitimate son, Zuzumuzi, has squandered. However, her real rejection of Zakhe is fuelled by her love affair with a local bankrupt and married taxi owner, Sgwili. Zakhe's presence is an obstacle as Sgwili is under pressure to repay his debtors. Both Jessie and Sgwili conspire to kill Zakhe whom she takes for an impostor and whom she strongly believes is solely interested in the inheritance left by Mhlongo. The plan goes awry and Zuzumuzi is killed instead. The night Zuzumuzi is killed is also the night on which Zakhe has planned to commit suicide having realised that no one but Babazile believes him. He writes a suicide note calling Jessie, 'Nomkhubulwana wami',[2] an affectionate term he normally uses when re-assuring her, and indicates that he should be buried in the grave in which Jessie 'buried' him and that she unveiled when he was still alive. Zakhe's suicide attempt fails as Babazile and her husband, Ben, a local policeman, save him. One morning, long after he has healed from the rope wounds around his neck, he meets Jessie at the graveyard and Jessie tells him that she now believes that he is who he claims to be as no impostor would call her Nomkhubulwana. The film closes with Jessie holding Zakhe's hand and going home, the home from which Zakhe was banished after his reappearance.

Residues of cultural elements in *Ifa LakwaMthethwa*

Ifa LakwaMthethwa demonstrates the prevailing view amongst creolisation theorists that the racial and cultural heritage of Africans that has been overlooked by the educated middle class can no longer be excluded from any artistic depiction of contemporary African life (see Noakes and Aub-Buscher, 2003: vii). For this school of thought, this cultural heritage is made up of diverse yet unifying cultures born of common experiences. These common experiences continue to form new layers of life-as-lived happenings that simultaneously display both a cultural melting pot and cultural residues drawn from the source cultures. *Ifa LakwaMthethwa's* discourse on economic order draws on two broad ideologies, an African and a Western economic philosophy, to reflect the changing political and cultural economy of South Africa in the 1990s. The overriding ideology in this series lobbies for an understanding of the symbiotic relationship between Western and African traditional modes of knowledge as the solution to South African economic problems. It seeks to show those values that are most beneficial to both modes of living, and how their transference will have mutual benefits for the traditionally-based Mthethwa people and the Western-oriented family of the chief. It achieves this through merging bourgeois economic sensibilities with the traditional ethos on an array of political, cultural and social issues.

The hybridised economy, which the series advocates, is depicted in the contradictory positioning of the chief's family in relation to the Mthethwa clan. The oppositional positioning of the two groups, which eventually experience a complex amalgamation as the narrative progresses, are the chief's family as representative of Western values and the Mthethwa clan as representing tradition. The initial class distinctions and mutual exclusiveness of these groups is signified by a river between KwaZulu, where the chiefdom is based, and *Esilungwini* (at the place of white people), accessible only by ferry. Sizwe, his children and his associates are ferried on numerous occasions on this unnamed river, the first occurrence being when they go for *ihlambo* (the cleansing ceremony) to mark the end of mourning and the recalling of the departed spirit into the homestead.

The historical symbolism of the river in folk memory recalls a similar river that demarcated Zululand and Natal during colonial times and the colonial discourses of civilisation and the darkness of Africa. According to Bartlet (1996: 3), Africa and its inhabitants were associated with darkness and evil, the forces of night and the underworld. The re-enactment of Sizwe's coming as a new, powerful, economic force echoes the colonial encroachment that resulted in the annexation of Natal and Zululand. In the series the symbolic annexation becomes Sizwe's coronation as chief of the Mthethwa people. The scenes in the drama play out the second conquest of Zululand where the black bourgeoisie has replaced the colonial players. The new, bourgeois, economic relations between social classes proceed from those established by white, economic and political relations which were marked by strong divisions between the classes of masters and servants.

The beginning of the TV series is marked by this bourgeois life. Sizwe's chiefly house is modelled on those of the super-affluent classes. Sizwe is woken from a nightmare to the scuttling of servants as they prepare for his journey to KwaZulu that day. The servant class is signified by their garb which marks them as being different from the other members of his family. A professional chauffeur drives Sizwe to all business commitments and takes him to the ferry that transports him across the river to KwaZulu. All of these activities betray a contemporary, aspirational discourse, a fantasy of deep-seated assimilation. The homogeneity of all belonging to one subclass, that which the apartheid ideologies assigned to black people, is reversed to reveal differences that follow the stratification observed in other capitalist societies. This reversal of monolithic perspectives about black people generally invites the construction of images that emphasise the betterment of black people as opposed to a depiction of their reality. While this kind of positivity in film imagery is generally denounced by high-art, African (Hondo, 1996) and black film makers in the diaspora (Guerroro,1996), within the South African context, especially in view of the sudden explosion of programmes with similar images that became popular after 1994, it seems that this self-adulatory image-making is the celebrated trope. These images seek to locate the South African black bourgeoisie within the international system and world culture. These representations go against the observations of high-art, African filmmakers, particularly from African cinema, that these positive depictions are farcical, unrealistic and misleading to the African masses (Bartlet, 1996: 10).

In *Ifa LakwaMthethwa*, the popular association of modernity, civilisation and sophistication with class mobility is revisited to celebrate the bourgeoisie. Yet at the same time the film includes a celebration of the African past. This is revealed in the interplay between the populist tendencies of the subalterns, which are normally associated with popular discourses, and the self-consciousness of the affluent middle class with its associated imagery of pomp, grandeur, affluence and power. The juxtaposition of Sizwe and the traditional populace marks this interplay. Sizwe's superiority is emphasised in all his encounters with members of the peasant class. Sizwe compares best with Nzobo, a despotic tyrant ruling on his behalf. His stature is that of a cultured man and he is placed in a dialectical relation to Nzobo, a barbaric despot whose rule is marked by fear, violence and brutality.

Nzobo's depiction crystallises the decadent morality within the traditional mode of life so that it is exposed for its destructiveness. His actions are reflective of moral intrigues informed by self-centred and individualistic intentions that are not merely destructive to himself and the people around him, but are unable to bring change and prosperity. Nzobo's reign is one of fear with all the trappings of the anachronistic past the contemporary society would rather leave behind. By conspiring with witches and hit men in his attempt to remove all those who are a threat to his newly acquired position, he re-invokes the menace of such kings and is a reminder of those stereotypes about the tyranny of African leaders whose reigns are marked by brutality, physical and psychological violence and inhumanity. His destiny is thus predetermined since there is no place for retrogressive rulers and, in this manner, Sizwe's decision is predicted. Sizwe's decision to dethrone him stems from Nzobo's inhumanity and cruelty.

The film's strategic use of the ethnographic gaze[3] not only points to vestiges of the tribal past but also highlights certain cultural retentions that are vital for the maintenance of expressive traditions. The depiction of the rural landscape and the construction of the rural people in *Ifa LakwaMthethwa* conform to ethnographic film techniques and the documenting of past traditions in this film betrays an ethnographic gaze, as it seeks to recreate the spaces and focus on practices that are characteristic of the African past. The setting of the Mthethwa royal house is depicted as a site for happy and merry Mthethwa people singing, dancing, and ululating while the men sing praises. The men who have come to visit the chief are seated in a circle with the calabash making its round. As they drink beer with the king, the grand council scuttles about, soliciting affirmation and support as they negotiate and deliberate in preparation for the rightful chief to be enthroned.

According to Bartlet (1996: 10), 'the return to the roots' film genre, including ethnographic films, operates in two significant ways. It either solicits authenticity in drawing on past traditions or, alternatively, makes it 'possible to ask how things stand in the here and now: what part is this authority to play in contemporary Africa'. Drawing from past traditions and performative elements in black expressive art is the cornerstone of twentieth-century, modern literature and general arts that employed African, oral and popular discourse as the metatext. In black film criticism, drawing from past traditions is also a necessary undertaking. Not only do such presentations buttress the resilience of black, cultural traditions, but, as Lardner (1972: 80) comments, they also 'proceed from a point of view located within the black experience as opposed to a pre-determined use of the dominant society's point of view'. The creative act of drawing from past traditions foregrounds a cultural framework that has its own autonomous systems of values, behaviour, attitudes, sentiments and beliefs as in the conflicts and tensions besetting succession politics in *Ifa LakwaMthethwa*. These are projected within a traditional, culturally autonomous framework that reflects old methods for resolving succession feuds.

As Abrahams (1983: ix) points out, in African folklore the play and replay of traditional expressive events has predetermined meanings, and it is through repetitions that meaning is negotiated all the time. For example, during the preparations for *ihlambo* 'the cleansing ritual' Nzobo's selection of the cows for the ceremony is framed by two songs: *Uqhatha abantu* and *Selokhu yakhulum' iNkosi*, (to be interpreted below), which allude to the tensions brewing between him and the old members of the grand council. The sound images also reveal Nzobo's precarious position as an interloper. The names of the cows that he selects: *itsobe* (one who slips in unnoticed), *ithathilunga* (the taker of a body part/of membership/officialdom) and *inhlavukazi* (pellets/grain/bullet) are highly suspect. They do not refer to known oxen types and thus connote his intentions and his refusal to hand back the throne. The images in the song thus act in counterpoint to Nzobo's plans. They act as moral censors; embedded in the inferences of the songs are age-old maxims regarding transgressions and deviations from the norm in matters relating to the enthroning of traditional leaders. Fundamentally, the songs point to the general disaffection of the populace with him as their ruler and to his Machiavellian connivance as he plots to usurp the Mthethwa throne:

Song 1

Call: Uyambona elokhu eqhatha abantu?

Do you see he is setting up people to fight?

Response: Ukhulum' amanga yona zifa ngayo

He lies to them but they love him to bits

Call: Ye mama, khona lapho

Oh mother, just there

Response: Wo ha ho ha ho zonke ma

Wo ha ho ha ho all of them mother

Song 2

Call: Iyakhalis'

There are complaints

Response: Selokhu yakhulum' inkosi

The king had said it all along

All: Nansi

There he is

Following cultural directions in such matters, traditional authority has long-established mechanisms to be used when appointing the rightful heir to the Mthethwa throne. However, both these songs reveal Nzobo's corrupt and self-serving tendencies and the manner in which he divides the chiefdom unnecessarily.

The other example of cultural retention mechanisms which links to the inferences in the song, is the myth associated with a hunting ritual for the *ihlambo* (cleansing ceremony). The myth points to the deep philosophical and religious convictions of the Mthethwa community regarding ancestral approbation of a successor. This myth is an important part of the succession ritual, and the success of the hunt is highly prized and is called *inkatha yabaphansi* (the choice of the ancestors).[4] As in the series, instances that necessitate the hunt-ritual are sparked by the different factions that result from the princes' conflicting claims to the throne. In such instances, the feuding princes are sent out on an *inqina* (hunting expedition). During the hunt, one prince must be killed by the wild beast; the ancestors would then be said to have identified the survivor, who will receive the approbation of the nation and be the ruler. Significantly, the beast that has killed the prince must be overpowered, slaughtered and brought back to the palace. Normally the corpse of the prince is not returned; however the carcass of the beast must be brought back. Although the film does not exploit the first phase of this ritual, where feuding princes are sent out on the hunting expedition, there is a depiction of warriors returning to the palace with the carcass of the kill. This symbolism is further substantiated by a council member who points out the age-old tradition of enthroning the rightful king, saying,

> *Kusemqoka ukuba kungenzeki iphutha kubekwe ikhohlo libe inkosi.*
> *Ukwenza kanjalo kungaba nomphumela omubi esizweni sonke kanye*
> *nabasebukhosi imbala.*

> It is important that mistakes do not happen and a non-throne-ascending royalty is installed; should that be the case, it will have negative consequences in the nation and in the royal house as well.

The inclusion of these oral discourses in the film establishes that Sizwe is not appointed to the position of leadership by his birth status alone but by the ancestors as well. The implication, in relation to Sizwe's bourgeois status, lies in the underlying interpretation of this symbolism. The filmic narrative seems to suggest that the bourgeoisie represent a logical solution to leadership problems and that they have been sanctioned by the traditional, ancestral institution to be in that position.

The bourgeois Sizwe's claim to traditional leadership is couched within a filmic language that denigrates the backward and barbaric manner in which Nzobo claims the throne. His belief in witchcraft and sorcery is mocked. The witch, Zembe, to whom he entrusted his ambition, is confused regarding the particulars of the role he plays in the traditional institution of divination. In a scene where Nzobo threatens him because of his failure to kill Sizwe, Zembe points to the possibility of Sizwe's supernatural power. Zembe's philosophical views about his trade are confused: he fails to distinguish between witchcraft and the traditional institution of divination and healing. In addition, Zembe's characterisation seems at odds with his nature and he professes that he is confused about the role he must play. He dresses in a fashionable style wearing trendy trousers, flamboyant, colourful shirts and a hairstyle based on African American hairdos that were introduced to South African black popular culture in the 1980s.[5] This dress code is very unusual for a person with his role and is different from the regalia of traditional healers or the received notions of witches as represented in the film. On the surface his characterisation displays cultural inaccuracies with the series showing his failures in the way he presents prescribed rituals. However, on another level, his difference marks his practice as being different from the traditional healing practice which remains untainted by the evil and diabolic activities with which he is concerned. Most significantly, Zembe's taste in fashion attests to the progressive nature of contemporary society where even witches refuse to be outpaced by change, and this depiction is the crystallisation of creolisation in this series.

According to Thackway (2003), there is a new development in the way in which the film interrogates Africa's past to inform and reflect upon the present and the future whereby African knowledge systems are not systematically condemned in the pursuit of Western values that are thought to be 'clean and sophisticated'. This is a reversal of past conceptualisations of tradition, the significance and values of which, under Western tutelage and African views of modernity, were often rejected as obstacles to progress. In *Ifa LakwaMthethwa*, the symbolic juxtaposition of traditional African and Western symbols points to a powerful call for the utilisation of African knowledge systems as part of the practices of modern, Western rationality. Zembe's plotting illuminates this view. His failure to kill Sizwe incurs Nzobo's wrath and Nzobo gives instructions to have him burnt alive in his hut. Sizwe intervenes and he is taken instead to a Western medical institution where he recovers with the help of a combination of traditional and Western medicine.

It seems that the study of cultural control mechanisms in *Ifa LakwaMthethwa* should not be confined to those of succession politics only and that its interpretation should be extended to post-apartheid political organisation and society. The film's depiction of these divergent discourses on the socio-economic positioning of the bourgeoisie in the post-apartheid context is contradictory, as is expected, but there is also concern with the manner in which the film silences certain sectors of the community. The peasant community in the film who, according to Ngugi (1986), conserve, preserve and keep alive the traditional culture and the African vernaculars, are marginalised and shown negatively as the faceless throng that regards leaders as idols. Although they can discern Nzobo's actions, as reflected in their songs, they are incapable of taking a stand. Similarly, their voice, which could have been heard through their elected councillors, is subsumed within the articulations of the ambiguous grand council members who are dressed in Western suits. Despite these problematic depictions, *Ifa LakwaMthethwa* cannot be summarily dismissed as pure escapism because it engages in debates about economic development and the position of women and it raises issues about the construction of blackness in film. Its treatment of these issues follows a trend started in black-themed filmmaking. The practice in this film genre has been the construction of positive black images. According to scholars of black film such as Smith (1997: 1–2), many problems exist in the positive/negative debate about the construction of blackness because

> [i]t presupposes consensus about what a positive or negative image actually is. To some viewers, images of hardworking, middle class, heterogeneous African Americans are inherently positive and to be celebrated wherever they are found, because they replace models of African American pathology with signs of the fact 'we are like everyone else'.

Smith (1998: 65) further points out that this kind of criticism encourages an uncritical acceptance of this equation and allows the hegemony of mainstream, representational strategies to go unchallenged. Such criticism also overlooks the ideological impact these films will have, and may lead to essentialism. The exclusive preoccupation with images, whether positive or negative, can lead to a kind of essentialism which generates in its wake a certain ahistoricism; the analysis tends to be static, not allowing for mutations, metamorphoses, or altered functions. According to Shohat and Stam, (2003) it seems, however, that black film criticism has moved beyond this preoccupation and is now concerned more with the diversity than with the homogeneity of the black experience. The construction of positive images as synonymous with the bourgeoisie and negative images with the traditionalist in *Ifa LakwaMthethwa* provides an example of the issue that Smith (1997 & 1998) and Shohat and Stam (2003) raise. The film's engagement with the debates of authenticity presents Sizwe's class as representative of the authentic black identity that occupies the interregnum between traditional and contemporary African identities, and as sanctioned by the ancestors to inherit the political leadership of the Mthethwa chieftaincy and, by implication, of the post apartheid dispensation.

Finding the limits of a creolised middle ground

Although Sizwe occupies the creolised middle ground between the traditional African and Western modes of life (being both a traditional leader and the head of a successful, Western-model, business empire) traditional values can restrict this creolisation while, at the same time, allowing the flow of certain international, cultural meanings. The view that traditionalism can be used to limit the appropriation of Westernised and syncretic values is demonstrated in the depictions of Sizwe's children who each represent specific aspects of the bourgeoisie. His son, Bafana, the child of a Western marriage and director of a business empire, represents extremes of excess. Bafana is depicted as a wastrel whose unbridled sexuality is manifested in his sexual transgression with an ex-girlfriend who is now his father's favourite wife. In spite of his being a business mogul directing the day-to-day running of the Mthethwa business, his disposition is far removed from one that would provide the economic lift needed for the development of the Mthethwa people. His hunger for power and his greed and alcoholism are inherent flaws that exclude him from playing any part in the economic development advocated in the film's narrative.

Bafana differs greatly from Sizwe's other children from his traditional marriage. Through these children, the tensions existing in Sizwe's polygamous marriage are played out.

The first limit regarding the creolised culture opted for by Sizwe's class, is seen in the lack of influence Sizwe's matrimonial bonds have in relation to the inheritance politics of the Mthethwa dynasty. On the one hand, Bafana's claim to his father's inheritance stems from the Western, legal system that only recognises matrimonial relationships bound by legal documents. The claims of Muzi, Sabelo and Mumsy, on the other hand, are recognised by traditional laws. In the film Bafana does not deserve greater claim than the other children to the family's inheritance because of the legal, Western marriage of his parents; instead certain traditional laws take precedence to protect the rights of all Sizwe's children.

Another mediating aspect that may diffuse the hostilities brought about by inheritance politics, are the unlimited number of career paths that can be followed by members of this class. All Sizwe's children from his first marriage provide examples of the positions available to this class. The career paths they follow (politics, commercial farming and business economics), firmly place members of this class within the international, corporate world, as the focus is no longer on the traditional throne and a local business empire but on the international networks that form part of local political and economic organisation. In the traditional world populated by ordinary peasants, as in *Ifa LakwaMthethwa*, Sizwe's children by his first set of wives serve as models of metropolitanism and this is reflected in their culture and patterns of consumption. All are deeply enmeshed within a Western lifestyle and are in turn emulated by the ordinary people, as reflected in Zembe's fashion tastes and the servants in Sizwe's royal home.

The other limit on the creolised culture adopted by this class revolves around familial responsibilities vis-à-vis economic evolution. It is through Bhekifa, Sizwe's illegitimate son, that the narrative suggests a model for economic leadership. The narrative revolves around Bhekifa and his relationship with his father, his siblings and the imperatives of his father's class and thus seems to be carrying the central moral of the series. Bhekifa is portrayed as a better leader than

Sizwe. This is shown in his philosophy about family which is informed by the value he places on and the responsibility he feels for his long lost daughter and the woman he lost during his youth. Bhekifa, unlike Sizwe who denied any responsibility towards him and his mother, is a believer in monogamy and values a single unit family, a philosophy that Sizwe does not follow. This contrast is explored in matters relating to Sizwe's traditional marriages. Sizwe's selection of a set of new, young wives after his coronation is his second marriage, the first set of wives being those that gave birth to his older sons and a daughter. The generation gap between him and his new wives, who realistically are similar in age to his children by his first wives, not only suggests he is as gross as Nzobo, but also marks the moral distance that exists between him and his son, Bhekifa. Bhekifa's emotional worth is seen in his search until adulthood for a lover he lost in his teens and what his character also reveals is consistency and cultural continuity in the values relating to familial responsibility that are transposed from vestiges of the past to the contemporary world.

Ifa LakwaMthethwa attempts to indicate two ways of thinking about contemporary economic politics. The first reflects a conservative approach that looks into what can be achieved through an exploration of past, cultural values and how these can be used in pursuing economic ideals that advance individual, capitalist objectives. The second makes us think about the multi-embeddings of foreign contemporariness, nonetheless fashioned by Africans themselves and reflecting popular views on how they wish to be understood as they move into a new political dispensation. The way the film is constructed echoes Cripps' (cited in Bartlet, 1996: vii) call for the black film movement to 'instil a sense of the past and acknowledge its own traditions as part of its self-consciousness'. *Ifa LakwaMthethwa's* traditional background is infused with Western, economic zeal, so that the modern values of prosperity are understood within the values of traditionalism. The narrative of *Ifa LakwaMthethwa* presents a new class of highly affluent Africans who use a pre-colonial economy to create, advance and succeed in a Westernised stock market economy from which they were formerly excluded. It achieves this through the projection of self-sufficient and independent Africans that behave and decide independently. The film has seemingly moved 'beyond social paradigms that foster a victor-victim, power-subordinate mentality to develop alternative modes of knowledge and social organisation' (Yearwood, 2000: 9–10).

Black TV colonised: Adapting film conventions to accommodate orality

Hlala Kwabafileyo, like *Ifa LakwaMthethwa*, is an 'all-black spectacle' that has its own internal forms of reflection and critique confined within the realities of an up-beat, urban lifestyle. Its selection of traditional elements is in tandem with the popular, township cultural practice of picking certain traditional systems to reflect on both the functionality and the extent to which these traditional systems have been grafted onto modern influences of other cultures. This is evident in the opening scene of the expository sequences of *Hlala Kwabafileyo*, a riveting drama about love, betrayal, family infighting, hatred and forgiveness in a rich, urban family in Soweto. The wedding preparations, combining township elements with traditional flair, are indicative of popular culture. Mhlongo's house is teeming with neighbours, both inside and out, who have come to help. Cows have been slaughtered and men are scuttling about as they prepare a customary festive meal. These activities take place in front of a yellow and white tent, a symbol in township culture proclaiming that an *umsebenzi* (imminent occasion) is to be held in the household. Included in this opening scene is a group of hired dancers who perform traditional dances, complementing the festive atmosphere of the moment. Inside, women from the neighbourhood are preparing food for the following day. Significantly, Mhlongo's daughter, Babazile, is inducted into marriage by local women. Although included, most of these traditional practices have only a superficial function as they will be pushed to the background when the Western wedding is celebrated the following day. The Western-style wedding celebration includes a helicopter and open convertibles that take the bride and the groom to the church, and a brass band to whose accompaniment the general populace sing popular, township, wedding and religious songs. A choral, wedding song, popularised by a Zulu radio station, marks the conclusion of the church wedding service.

This admixture of the traditional and the popular in *Hlala Kwabafileyo* is foregrounded by drawing from the genre of oral praise and praising, and it provides a base for the sequence of events located within the nebulous and ever-shifting imperatives of township culture. Mhlongo's surname is a symbol: both his disappearance and reappearance are encapsulated and foregrounded in his extended surname, which is revealed in the clan praises that his lawyer friend, Ntshalintshali, recites at the wedding:

> *AbakwaMhlongo kaNdaba*
>
> The people of Mhlongo, son of Ndaba
>
> *AbakwaNjomane kaMgabi*
>
> The people of Njomane of Mgabi
>
> *Eyaduka iminyakanyaka*
>
> Who disappeared many years ago
>
> *Yatholakala kowesine*
>
> And was found on the fourth one

Mhlongo's praises are a signifying practice, alluding to the conflicts that are caused by inheritance politics. These praises point to significant events that occur outside the story line in the series which, within the context of the film's narrative, are aligned with imperatives and signifiers underpinning the plot. Not only does Zakhe disappear and reappear in the film narrative, but his brother, Bheseni also disappears and reappears. Bheseni's reappearance takes place long after their father's death, and after Zakhe has been bequeathed all assets as the only surviving son. Zakhe eventually used the inheritance as seed money for the establishment of a modern business enterprise. The symbolic significance of the praises quoted above is that they project a traditional, cultural ethos that has been imprinted with numerous influences. Furthermore, Zakhe's praises are set against Zuzumuzi's search for identity and a sense of belonging as the praises provide histories of lineage and of relations that can either be exclusionary or inclusionary. Obviously Zuzumuzi, as an outsider in Zakhe's family, feels excluded both psychologically and culturally from Zakhe Mhlongo's family unit. This is revealed in one of his outbursts. He informs his mother that *'Mina angishongo ukuthi ngifuna ukukhuliswa uMhlongo. Mina nginabo abakithi kwaZungu, koManzini, koGwabela. Nguwe ongilethe kulomuzi'* (I did not say I wanted to be reared by Mhlongo. I do have my family at the Zungus, people of Manzini, people of Gwabela). Zuzumuzi's rebellious nature is enhanced by the physical violence he suffers at the hands of both his parents. As his name suggests,[6] Zuzumuzi's definition of his identity, which resists the one that his mother has procured for him, points to deeply embedded traditional views governing a patriarchal sense of identity in Zulu culture. These patriarchal vestiges within the context of inheritance politics not only allude to complexities resulting from these arrangements, but also resuscitate traditional sanctions regarding illegitimacy. Zuzumuzi's illegitimate status is foregrounded in the respect he shows to his parents but particularly to his father, and in the politics of inheritance after Zakhe's disappearance.

The traditional, cultural values underlying Zuzumuzi's depiction are further manifested during the family's search for Zakhe. Zuzumuzi fails to identify Zakhe after he is pointed out by a nurse who has seen him only once before at the wedding. On the surface, Zuzumuzi's failure to identify Zakhe stems from his callousness and his hatred for him; he has attempted to kill him before. On a deeper level, however, the link that exists between Mkhonto Magwaza, the only representative of the traditional institution of divination and healing, and Zuzumuzi in their failure to 'see' Zakhe, is indicative of the limits the traditional philosophy has within contemporary forms of self-identity or contemporary lifestyles, norms, values and so on. The divination ritual performed in the search reflects this.

Mkhonto: *Makhosi! Makhosi! Makhosi! Vumani bo!*
Makhosi! Makhosi! Makhosi! Do you agree with me?

Jessie and Babazile: *Siyavuma!*
We do!

Mkhonto: *Ngibona isithunzi sikaMhlongo phakathi kwe … Vumani bo!*
I see Mhlongo's shadow amongst … Do you agree with me?

Jessie and Babazile: *Siyavuma!*
We do!

Mkhonto: *Kumnyama, Nkosikazi! Kubi! Vumani bo!*
It is difficult Madam! It is bad! Do you agree with me?

Jessie: *Makhosi, amazwi akho ayangithusa*
Makhosi, your utterances are scaring me.

Mkhonto: *Kunjalo, Nkozikazi. Kumnyama.*
It is so, Madam. It is bad.

Jessie: *Pho, kusho ukuthi …*
So it means …

Mkhonto: *Angisho nokuthi ningabe nisafuna, kodwa kumnyama.*
I am not saying that you should stop searching, but it is difficult.

Jessie: *Usho ukuthi njengoba elahlekile, asiyobuye siphinde simthole?*
Are you saying that just as he is missing, we will never find him?

Mkhonto: *Makhosi! Uzotholakala / Makhosi!*
He will be found!

Jessie: *Pho-ke?*
Now then?

Mkhonto: *Okunye-ke lokho. Uzotholakala. Mina sengiqedile. Makhosi! Angifuni ukuthi ungikhokhele. Yena uzotholakala. Makhosi! Thokoza!*
That is a different case altogether. He will be found. I am done now. *Makhosi.* I do not want any payment. But he will be found. *Makhosi Thokoza!*

The diviner sees only *isithunzi* (shadow or dignity) of Zakhe within a dark, ominous presence that he does not explain. The diviner's analysis either points to his inability to locate Zakhe's spiritual essence in the spiritual world or alludes to his compromised dignity. In either interpretation the analysis is befitting of Zakhe's disposition. He disappears on his way to a secret rendezvous with his lover who is the age of his daughter. His behaviour compromises his standing within his community.

The other technique through which orality has colonised *Hlala Kwabafileyo* is through the use of the social gaze, a form of collective consciousness and memory responsible for sanctioning private affairs and rendering them as belonging to the public domain. The tensions existing between the community and Mhlongo's family are alluded to in the expository scenes of the film. The Mhlongo family is subjected to a running commentary, a constant social gaze that reflects on the difficulties experienced by the family. The social gaze is a deeply embedded traditional form of social surveillance. According to Yanga (1999), the social gaze functions as a source of criticism in African societies although underpinned by the philosophical views of *ubuntu* (humanity). The excesses of individuals in the society are what bring about disequilibrium. In essence, *ubuntu* is a social mechanism that guards against and curbs excesses in individuals subjected to similar forms of social organisation.

In the film narrative, the social gaze presents a cross-section of the society. The streets, shebeens, print media, train station and private homes are localities where codes of behaviour and the social outlook or orientation of the township are negotiated and proclaimed. The social view appropriated by these spaces exerts pressure and completely overwhelms the Mhlongo family, as rumours, truths and half-truths are generated about them. Their private lives become public knowledge and aspects of their private lives influence the inheritance politics. *Hlala Kwabafileyo* exploits tensions existing within the social consciousness which functions as a moral censor on the individual's right to an independent life. In the film, Jessie's individuality is constantly pitted against the social gaze represented by a comic character, MaMgobhozi, a local gossip.

Female sexuality and inheritance politics in *Hlala Kwabafileyo*

The film is set in a township where the traditional hold on female gender has been defied and undermined to such an extent that traditional claims are acknowledged only shyly. Green and Kahn (1985) and Bhavnani, Foran and Kurian (2003) are of the opinion that there are certain cultural practices that are observed only by females who have been conditioned by tradition to control their sexuality. In *Hlala Kwabafileyo* one such cultural observance is that of *ukungena* (the right of surviving brothers of the deceased husband to claim his wife). This cultural practice not only controls female sexuality but also ensures that the assets accumulated are returned and placed under the control of the deceased husband's family. The film narrative has introduced this custom as a base for the exploration of gender and inheritance. In the film Bheseni is sceptical about asking for Jessie's hand in marriage after his brother's 'death' because of the numerous changes that have influenced people's lifestyles, especially those who live in the urban centres. However, according to cultural norms, Bheseni has a legitimate claim to his brother's wealth and assets. His claim to his brother's inheritance stems from the fact that Zakhe established his businesses using their father's livestock. Acting on this knowledge, he informs his friends that he will take back '*izinkomo zikababa*' (my father's cows). He vows that '*zobuya izinkomo zikababa, zobuya emasisweni*' (my father's cows will be back, they will be back from whence they have been used as seed for wealth). His observation regarding the claim that each member of the family, except Babazile, has on Zakhe's inheritance, points to deepseated reservations about Zulu tradition and culture in Zakhe's family set-up. He points out that '*uZuzumuzi akayena wakwaMhlongo, umlanjwana owafika nonina. Angadla kanjani ifa lwakwaMhlongo?*' (Zuzumuzi is not Mhlongo's offspring. He is a bastard that came along with his mother. How can he be apportioned Mhlongo's inheritance?) As for Jessie, '*wathengwa ngezinkomo, uyefana negrosa*' (she was bought with cattle, she is like groceries). However, Bheseni is afraid to confront them about his reservations in respect of Zakhe's inheritance. Moreover, his claim to both the inheritance and

Jessie as custom expects, is problematised by changing circumstances and a female consciousness that has become popular in the townships.

Changing gender roles in contemporary African societies are reflected in the depiction of Bheseni. He comes across in the narrative as a compromised patriarch. His powerlessness is pitted against Jessie's assertiveness and incisiveness. She prevails as she subverts the custom of *ukungena*, throwing into disarray the old tradition of keeping the assets of the deceased within the family to be dispensed by the surviving patriarch. When Jessie realises that Zakhe's brother, Bheseni, might ask for her hand in marriage as custom expects, she arranges for her spinster sister to come from KwaZulu to Soweto. She takes her to her trusted diviner, Mkhonto Magwaza, to be prepared for Bheseni. This scheme succeeds as Bheseni is attracted to Jessie's sister and Bheseni's claim is narrowed to that part of their father's assets that Zakhe used for starting his business. Bheseni functions as a symbol: he represents a dying tradition which Jessie manipulates to strive for further independence. Thus, in the will that Zakhe left with his lawyer, Bheseni is given the cows and the house in the rural area to which he returns. Zakhe's will accords financial power to Jessie. She inherits the chain of stores and a considerable sum of money. Within the context of the novel from which the film is adapted, her inheritance marked a significant move away from past conventions for apportioning wealth in which the in-laws had the upper hand in bestowing the wealth of the deceased.

Hlala Kwabafileyo's depiction of female independence is built upon the dominant stereotypes of such women. Their independence becomes associated with wanton expressions of sexuality. Jessie's defiance of tradition is juxtaposed with her illicit involvement with Sgwili, a married man, which has disastrous consequences for Sgwili's wife and makes a mockery of the family as a site for the instilling of traditional values, albeit modified. Jessie and Sgwili's affair creates tensions and conflicts in Sgwili's home and, as a result, Sgwili's wife is battered when she attempts to assert her influence as the wife and mother in her home. The dramatisation of the violence and brutality she suffers at the hands of her adulterous and criminal husband is an indictment against societal tolerance of women like Jessie who, because of their financial standing, infringe on other women's rights and emotional well-being. The film's discourse seems to suggest that the cause of the abuse of women is the promiscuity of their gender, because Sgwili's wife points out that Sgwili's violent behaviour started after his extra-marital affair. While Sgwili is in dialectical opposition to Zakhe, they nonetheless share commonalties in their infidelity. Jessie's fight against patriarchal members of her family in claiming the inheritance that her husband left her is subverted by her involvement with Sgwili, whose intention is to siphon off her wealth and settle his financial debts.

Jessie's character is contrasted with other female characters in the film. MaNdlovu, her friend, Babazile, Jessie's daughter, and Mafakude, Bheseni's landlady, all represent women who invariably conform to tradition. Perhaps Zuzumuzi articulates the most accurate view of Jessie's questionable sexuality when, in a drunken state, he poignantly says to her,

Hhayi mama izono zakho lezo. Mina angizange ngisho kuwe ukuthi thanda laba ubuye ubashiye uyogana labaya. Ngangingekho ebusheni bakho.

No Mother, those are your sins. I never said to you fall in love with these ones and leave them, and marry elsewhere. I did not live in your youth.

Zuzumuzi's indictment of his mother's sexuality is prompted by his search for identity. He is raised as Mhlongo yet he knows that he belongs biologically to the Zungu family. He thus suffers an identity crisis as, on the one hand he feels he has a stake in Mhlongo's inheritance and thus demands more of the inheritance from his mother, while on the other hand he colludes with his biological father, Zungu, for him to reunite with Jessie. Zuzumuzi's greed, shown in his involvement with a woman old enough to be his mother, functions on the same level as that of Zungu. Zungu uses his son as a route to Jessie's wealth.

Unlike other women characters in the film, Thembeni, Jessie's younger sister, is a personification of pure womanhood. Like Babazile, her symbolism is concretised visually in a traditional

Zulu conceptualisation of womanhood. Their innocence and purity are virtues that the filmic narrative foregrounds. In addition, their positive attributes are further enhanced by the men folk with whom they are associated. Ben, Babazile's husband, is a representation of a true patriarch. Babazile does not use her part of the inheritance to live a life of sheer opulence and luxury. Ben is cautious regarding money that one has not earned, somehow prefiguring Zakhe's return when they have to return what is left, as opposed to Zuzumuzi who squanders his share within six months.

The narrative signifiers and the representation of prominent characters in the series reveal complexities that neither a simple Christian nor a traditional African philosophy can solve. Instead, the human psyche is explored in a capitalistic and hedonistic society and innate human goodness is shown to emerge as the victor. *Hlala Kwabafileyo* shows both Christian and traditional African philosophies as irrelevant to the events represented; these philosophies are peripheral. Christianity serves as a facilitator of weddings, burials and tombstone-unveiling ceremonies and the symbols associated with African traditions are used to highlight certain values. They facilitate the desires and aspirations of those who conform to tradition and they are rendered impotent for those seeking a break from tradition. This is demonstrated during the divination ritual for Zakhe when his family searches for him and when Magwaza Mkhonto dies before he can explain and interpret the bone throwing ritual he performs for Zakhe's search.

It is however ironic that the film's solution to the confusing changes besetting the urbanised community is to suggest a back-to-the-homeland move. After Bheseni has been given his father's cows, he marries Thembeni and both return to KwaZulu. Their return to eMabedlana, a rural area in KwaZulu, serves as a symbolic break with the urban and decadent morality saturating its inhabitants and can also be interpreted as going back to African tradition. This ending points to the problem raised when merging two traditions: the literary and black television drama traditions.

The 'back-to-the-homelands' theme betrays the conventions in the isiZulu literary tradition from which the drama series was adapted.[7]

Although the drama series was aired in the mid-1990s and included a range of different political sensibilities, the novel was written in the late 1980s when apartheid was still a reality in South Africa. Both Tomaselli (1986, 1989b) and Davis (1994) point out that the theme was propagated earlier in the last century by the Afrikaner government's policies, which were intended to control the African influx into the cities. This propaganda was achieved by projecting the city as an evil place not suitable for Africans. However, there was a reversal of this policy by the beginning of the 1980s, which was highlighted in the television dramas of the period as the government raced to win the hearts and minds of Africans (as seen in the discussion of *Ifa Lwakwa Mthethwa*).

Conclusion

What I wanted to illustrate in this chapter was the way the post-apartheid ruling elite used mainstream media, including broadcast media, to propagate neo-liberal ideologies to an African public formerly conscientised by Marxist ideologies. This was done in response to pressure from the global capitalists (Kruger, 2010; Ives, 2007) for a free market system to which they had consented during the liberation negotiations. Kruger maintains that this ideological shift was achieved by transmitting images of individualistic success which are passed on as national success and are mediated by a popular discourse steeped in traditional culture. By adopting an African aesthetic with its pivotal connections to popular views, these television dramas were able to slide into the rhetoric of nation-building and the neo-liberal policies, ideologies that sanctioned the new, black, middle class identities. Furthermore, for these liberal ideologies to remain imperceptible and natural, the film practices presented an all-black spectacle that foregrounded sensibilities parallel to those of the white middle class by absenting this racial category. Furthermore, the adaptation of *Ifa LwakwaMthethwa* into a novel drew on the African-language literary conventions that also normalised black middle class sensibilities in a manner similar to the way in which the interplay between *Hlala Kwabafileyo* and its prose form has done.

Both these films present images of black people who successfully gained entry into the business world. These representations of a black bourgeoisie have 'image uplifting effects' and do not necessarily reflect or represent the socio-political realities of Africans. Debates abound in film discourses about whether films reflect the national culture that already exists or whether they produce a fantasy of their own that eventually is accepted as real. This observation is true for the depiction of 'glamorised Dallas-Dynasty-style black images' in *Ifa LaKwaMthethwa* and of *Hlala Kwabafileyo*. Nonetheless, these images reflect the myriad-layered experiences of contemporary Africans and are reflective of their negotiations with global systems of meaning.

Endnotes

1   In the 1980s, the South African government responding to political pressures introduced the co-option policy. This policy was aimed at co-opting Indian and coloured communities into a tripartite government with the white government. The implications of this policy were broader as the African middle class' material life was also positively affected by this policy.

2   Nomkhubulwane is a Zulu rain goddess associated with fertility, celebrated every spring, by the young female folk. During this ceremony, girls dress up in male regalia, herd cattle towards an enclave where they will partake of traditional beer and howl obscenities and vulgarity to passersby, particularly male passersby. See Berglund (1889).

3   Ethnographic film is a documentary film related to the methods of the study of ethnology. It has come to be used for the study of ethnic cultures. Ethnographic gaze is the term used in photography where images of people that are studied in a photograph have been taken by photographers who are outside the cultures of the subjects in the photograph.

4   There is an intriguing treatment of this ritual in Gcumisa's (1978) play *Inkatha Yabaphansi*.

5   The popularity of the permed hair is also illustrated in the film Coming to America, which depicted an African American family whose business has to do with the new fashion of wet looking curly hair.

6   His name implies 'the one who has acquired marriage or a home'. For his
     mother the name points to her acquiring marriage and for Zuzumuzi, it
     implies 'for whom a home has been acquired'. Therefore his mother has
     acquired a home for him and he is a benefactor of the assets of that home.

7   The discursive practices of isiZulu literature have always been implicated
     in the dominant discourses of the hegemon. Subtle ideological shifts in the
     hegemonic mainstream discourses were not immediately observed in the
     latest artistic productions, thus by the end of the 1980s when the apartheid
     government had distanced itself from the 'back to the homelands' policy,
     some isiZulu narratives still saw the move as a viable alternative.

5

Thematic re-engagements in the television drama series *Gaz' Lam* and isiZulu literature

Certain epochs, key historical moments, and currents in the culture of contemporary society are the sources from which texts draw to construct seminal narratives, initiating a 'vast progeny of literary and filmic descendants' that are further recycled in an infinite number of renditions (Stam, 2005: 1). With every recycling, new twists and turns are introduced that reveal changing discursive practices and the ideologies prevailing at the moment of reinterpretation. By considering artistic expressions as an endless permutation of textual cross referencing, a comparison of seemingly diverse artistic traditions, such as isiZulu literature with a television drama series, is made possible. The drama series, *Gaz' Lam* (Cousins/Friends) I, II, III and IV by Yazbek, flighted on the South African Broadcasting Corporation's, Channel One (SABC 1) in 2002, 2003, 2004 and 2005 respectively, provides an instance of intertextual dialogism with isiZulu literature. These films, though addressing a post-apartheid, African society, return to well-established themes in isiZulu literature such as culture and change, urbanisation, modernity and popular culture that provide prisms of refraction of present day actualities. Key to the film narratives, however, is how certain conventional, partisan, parochial and hegemonic discourses are reworked so that they resonate with evolving, post-apartheid, urban experiences.

In this chapter I focus on three of these thematic re-engagements in *Gaz' Lam*. These themes are common to isiZulu literature and demonstrate how the drama series in the post-apartheid context not only retrospectively reviews and dispels received meanings, but also offers fresh, new readings in line with the socio-economic and political realities of post-apartheid, African society. These themes are forced marriage, youth migration and music. Within these broad, thematic categories are other sub-themes such as love triangles, economic marginalisation and popular culture that underscore this intertextuality and at the same time help generate a freshness and newness. I will focus on *Gaz' Lam I* since the themes developed in subsequent seasons of the series were further explorations of those introduced in this first series.

Narrating a mosaic

According to theories of intertextuality 'a text cannot exist as a hermetic or self-sufficient whole, and so does not function as a closed system' (Worton and Still, 1990: 1). This theory, as propounded by Bakhtin's dialogism and Kristeva's (1967) intertextuality, holds that any text is read through its relation to other texts (Bakhtin, 1981: 272). In particular, Kristeva (1967) believes that a work of art is shot through with references, quotations and influences of every kind. Her source is Bakhtin's views regarding human discourses in general. Bakhtin holds that human language is a mixture of appropriated discourses. When people speak they use a specific mix of discourses which they have appropriated in an attempt to communicate. However, they inevitably suffer interference from two sources: the pre-existing meanings of words and the alien intentions of a real interlocutor. Bakhtin (1981: 272) maintains that every concrete utterance is intersected by both centrifugal (unifying) and centripetal (disunifying) sources. Although these theories have both a linguistic and literary (particularly relating to the novel) origin, Barthes (1985), Genette (1999) and other scholars have since broadened the applicability of dialogic and intertextual theory to other spheres of artistic expression.

Central to this theory is that texts are cultural interventions and therefore their meaning is conditioned because they are dependent on existing social reference systems or social knowledge to make meaning. According to Childers and Hentzi (1995: 195) the hidden associations that are invoked during reading impact on readers' expectations about the content and form of the writing as well as its meaning. According to Kristeva (in Worton & Still, 1990: 2) the meaning in the text is attributable both to the life experiences, associations and other influences brought into the text by the reader, and to the fact that the writer of texts is the reader and consumer of other texts. She refers to this pre-existing knowledge as 'the cross-fertilization of packed textual material' and further points out that:

> A delicate allusion to a work unknown to the reader, which therefore goes unnoticed, will have a dormant existence in that reading, on the other hand, the reader's experience of some practice or theory unknown to the author may lead to a fresh interpretation (Kristeva cited in Worton & Still, 1990: 2).

The whole web of interconnectivity and referencing is realised through imitation, allusions, influences, translations, quotations, parody and other literary or fictional tropes (Worton and Still, 1990). There are conflicting views amongst scholars regarding the use of these fictional techniques and whether their application leads to fresh interpretations, or to generalisations as Genette in the *Palmpsestes* (cited in Worton and Still, 1990: 14) argues. However, a key notion is that instances of references, allusions, quotations, imitation, parody and so forth combine to create popular stereotypes (Horace, cited in Worton and Still, 1990: 5) which affect the meaning of a text.

In spite of discordant views on what constitutes intertextuality there is a point at which these divergent views find commonality and it relates to what Kristeva initially surfaced in relation to intertextuality. This is that texts are dependent on outside influences and that the role of the reader or audience or perceiver of an artistic form is significant in creating meaning from the text. Walton (1990) demonstrates in the introduction to *Mimesis*, that the perceivers' associations form the largest sector of the frame of reference and that these associations come into the text as an intertextual network or a collage of ideas or a mingled mosaic of quotations.

There are other definitions of intertextuality. Leon S. Roudiez (cited in Hawthorn, 1992: 86) views it as the transference or transposition of one or more systems of signs into another. And Barthes (cited in Hawthorn, 1992: 86) perceives intertextuality as consisting of a text that is a 'new tissue of past citations. Bits of code, formulae, rhythmic models, fragments of social languages etc. pass into the text and are redistributed within it, for there is always language before and around the text.' However, Caminero-Santangelo (2005) offers a fascinating advance on this theory. He explores the notion of the rewriting or revising of history through inserting oneself into that history. Citing earlier formulations, he points out that 'Bakhtin situates the text within history and society, which are seen as texts read by the writer, and into which he inserts himself by rewriting them' (2005: 11). He maintains that the connections between literary texts and the broader cultural or social texts not only suggest a notion of parodic revision, but also point to the transformative dialogue that occurs between the literary texts and the variety of texts they appropriate. His notion of appropriation explores the idea that re-inscription can carry the intention to revise and rewrite. This is of interest to the discussion in this chapter as the themes I examine from *Gaz' Lam* are not entirely new: they have been a constant feature over the past century in isiZulu literature. However, their treatment in the series offers new interpretations, while their re-inscription in a post-apartheid period offers refreshed readings of the complex interplay of competing vantage points and languages.

According to Fuery (2000: 109), there are three interrelated tiers in the production of meaning in film. These are the film's social order, the social order it is derived from and the spectator's social order. Regarding the first tier, Fuery points out that it is normally set up in the diegetics of the film, most often paralleling in some way, the historical and ideological order which produced it. The second tier is constituted by the familiar landscapes, over-familiar social settings, overly-familiar positioning of characters in ordinary and everyday experiences which can be established through intertextuality, connotative reading, or how the contexts operate in the social domain. The cultural orderings of things, since they are familiar, are crucial for the establishment of certain readings as legitimate or true to the realities depicted (2000: 111). In the last tier he points out that 'the spectator's own position within different, but ultimately interconnected, cultural contexts has a bearing on filmic textual productions' (2000: 113).' In addition, he says that even though interpretations are heavily influenced by other social and textual contexts, there must be a point where

> [w]hat the spectator sees, and how he or she reacts, is derived from the unique position of their subjectivity [...] These unique positions allow deviation and difference, rather than the sense of identity figured in the Grand Narrative. These meta-narratives' unique positions challenge all narrating positions in their production of a multiplicity of positions and perspectives (2000: 113).

Despite Fuery's new trajectories the intertextual links between him, Bakhtin and Kristeva are obvious. His ideas on the social contexts making up a film's reality, on the multiple positionings of the spectators and on their role in challenging mainstream ideologies in the filmic text are useful in considering the intertextual links between *Gaz'Lam* and Zulu fiction.

Summary of *Gaz' Lam*

Gaz' Lam explores a love triangle between S'fiso and Khethiwe, both childhood sweethearts, and an old Chief. The youngsters' romantic relationship and dreams are disrupted by the polygamous Chief's request for Khethiwe's hand in marriage. Khethiwe, a young, respectful, innocent girl, is bound by tradition and compelled by her patriarchal father to accept the Chief's request. At the same time she is torn apart because of the feelings she has for S'fiso. Upon learning of Khethiwe's dilemma, S'fiso asks her to move to Johannesburg with him to avoid this arranged marriage. Khethiwe refuses. S'fiso leaves for Johannesburg alone to live with his cousin, Welile, a migrant from rural KwaZulu, and his wife, where he is introduced to the world of music and a life of women and alcohol. S'fiso's life experiences in the city intersect with a newly found community of friends related to his cousin. He also makes new friends and one of his friendships with an aspirant singer, Lerato, develops quickly into an illicit romance: Lerato is involved with a nightclub proprietor who is also her music patron and sponsor. One day Khethiwe decides to leave her rural home and reappear in S'fiso's life in the city. She discovers to her shock and disappointment that S'fiso has changed and, more significantly, she is no longer sure of his love for her.

Arranged marriages

Although isiZulu fiction is conservative, with strong links to Christian morality and African traditionalism, one of the dominant practices most persistently disparaged by authors throughout the century, is the custom of arranged marriages between chiefs and young maidens from the commoners' class. *Gaz' Lam's* appropriation of this theme not only joins the chorus of disapproval of the practice but also includes issues of female sexuality, teenage rebellion, unemployment, HIV/AIDS and other challenges affecting post-apartheid African society. *Gaz' Lam* plays out the theme of arranged marriages by exploring the tensions between the rural areas, as localities of unbending traditionalism, and the urban centres, as paradoxically progressive or retrogressively liberal areas where individuals can either discover themselves anew or bring destruction upon themselves. In addition, it draws on known gender relations in Zulu patriarchal society, placing emphasis on popular stereotypes about Zulu patriarchy which is generally viewed as intransigent in its ideas about the position of women in the Zulu community. Furthermore, as in isiZulu fiction, it also explores internalised customs such as that, just as the divine right of traditional leaders cannot be questioned, they also can never be called to account for decisions they take affecting their subjects. The underlying running commentary on this theme is based on the traditional observance that *inkosi, umlomo ongathethi manga* (the king or Chief's commandments are law). *Gaz' Lam,* while exploiting this theme to dramatise the absoluteness of this view, simultaneously explores various forms of women's resistance to arranged or forced marriages.[1] Both the filmic and the literary narratives seem to have as a basis the proverbial maxim of women's resistance, *ucu aluhlangani entanyeni* (the necklace does not fit), a saying normally ascribed to women resisting unwanted love.

In the series, resistance to an arranged marriage is depicted through Khethiwe's eventual rebellious relocation to Johannesburg and her rejection of the Chief's proposal. Furthermore, her being in Johannesburg alone, outside the direct supervision of her parents, her status as a 'pure Zulu maiden,' fit to be married to the Chief, can no longer be validated. As in isiZulu fiction, her pre-arranged marriage to the Chief emphasises the traditionally accepted custom as well as the predictable turn of events when the bride-to-be rebels. In the film, however, unlike in isiZulu fiction, her refusal to be part of the Chief's polygamous marriage setup allows for feminist discourses to creep into the filmic discourse. Her adoption of feminist sensibilities regarding her gender and sexuality allows her the liberty to shape and control her destiny and, eventually, to realise her dreams. In the light of the changing cultural context, her desire to pursue tertiary education and her aspirations to be a writer are read sympathetically and the Chief's intentions towards her are viewed with suspicion and justifiably abhorred.

The first novel in the isiZulu literary tradition to explore arranged and forced marriages between chiefs and commoners was Dube's (1929) *Insila KaShaka* (The bodyservant of Shaka). The theme was later returned to Bhengu (1965) in *UNyambose noZinitha* (Nyambose and Zinitha) with its strikingly similar structure to Dube's *Insila KaShaka*. The novels' emphasis is on the ridiculousness and callousness of the practice. Equally, Vilakazi's (1944) *Nje nempela* (Really), whilst exploring the Bhambatha rebellion, introduces conflict and intrigue into the narrative by drawing in the theme of arranged and forced marriages. His displeasure with the practice is revealed in the annihilation of the chiefly house into which the heroine of the narrative would have been married. Perhaps the most heart-wrenching and emotionally stirring renditions of this theme are to be found in Mncwango's *Manhla iyokwendela egodini* (1951) (The day she marries the grave) and *Ngenzeni* (1959) (What have I done). In these plays resistance to the practice is registered through the heroine's suicide or when the hero or heroine's resistance is countered by their gruesome murder by the fiercely angry chief or his right-hand men. The fact that this theme is still revisited with enthusiasm in the 1990s points to its resilience. Molefe (1991), in *Ngiwafunge AmaBomvu* (I swear by my AmaBomvu ancestors) and Xulu (1994), in *Udwendwe lukaKoto* (Koto's wedding party), re-explore the issue but their renditions do not result in any notable innovations in the treatment of the theme.

Gaz' Lam's exploration of the theme, by contrast, takes on new levels of meaning through the depiction of contradictions such as the visual vestiges of tradition set against post modernity, for example where the Chief, as the symbol of this tradition, engages with the modern. The Chief displays a preference for 'European' middle class ways, which signals that he is progressive, and yet he intrudes into the life of Khethiwe who is, in turn, a progressive teenager. He resuscitates an abhorred cultural practice that belongs to primordial times. In the scene of the only public sighting of Khethiwe and the Chief together, the ill-suitedness of the couple not only evokes sympathy for the teenaged Khethiwe, who is expected to give up the best years of her youth to an old man, but the Chief's pretension of being a 'cultured gentleman' is ridiculed and subverted by his depiction as a 'tradition-aided,' sexual predator. His polygamy is sanctioned by tradition but the continual intake of wives, even among young, teenaged girls who are supposed to be in school, is one of the key ways in which the series underscores this sexual predatoriness. That women are psychologically tormented by this practice and have to suppress their unhappiness and protests is shown by the orders the Chief barks into his mobile phone regarding his latest wife. He states that this young wife at home, who is jealous of Khethiwe as the new, incoming wife, only gets sick if and when she wants to and he orders her to take pills to suppress her outbursts.

The ridiculousness of Khethiwe and the Chief as a couple is brought under further scrutiny through its juxtaposition with a well-matched young couple seated in the background in this scene as well as when the film cuts to a scene in Johannesburg where other young people at a party are living out their youthful experiences. The contrasting images emphasise the activities and interests of youngsters in postmodern times, as opposed to those customs which compel young people to live out their futures and destinies through questionable practices that have lost relevance.

It seems that *Gaz' Lam*'s criticism of arranged marriages is informed by contradictions between the cultural norms governing youth sexuality and the infringement by traditional authority on the private lives of individuals. In particular, the culturally permitted practice that gives certain persons with traditional authority the right to interfere with the sexuality of young people comes under sharp criticism. The apparent sexual promiscuity associated with youth is equated with that of lascivious Chiefs who take girls in their teens from school and keep them as wives for their sexual pleasure. The Chiefs are supported in this by an equally misguided cultural setup steeped in a patriarchal system that, at heart, gives tacit permission for the abuse, suppression, humiliation and manipulation of women. Despite a loving father-daughter relationship between Khethiwe and her father (as seen in episode one), when the marriage proposal is put to him as a patriarch, he does not decline, despite its effect on his daughter and his wife's protestations. As far as Khethiwe's father is concerned, the proposed marriage will elevate his status considerably in his community and that is the perspective from which he prefers to see his daughter's marriage to the Chief, regardless of Khethiwe's age and the fact that this is the umpteenth time this polygamous Chief is taking a wife. He allows his daughter to undergo a most questionable ritual, virginity testing, to please and appease the Chief whose uncontrolled lecherousness contrasts with S'fiso, who has promised to wait for the consummation of their love relationship. S'fiso's promise not only embodies the underlying HIV/AIDS message embedded in the series, but also follows the older, customary practice of *ukusoma* (thigh sex), hence allowing an alternative model for safer sex. This model places the onus on both lovers for their protection against sexually transmitted diseases compared to the gendered virginity testing that places the onus on the girl child for protecting a future husband against venereal diseases. Despite the objections of both Khethiwe and her mother to the virginity testing, it is pointed out that Khethiwe must go through with it to protect the Chief against *umkhonyovu okhona* (the sexual disease scare) implying HIV/AIDS, that is currently affecting all age groups.

This reading of *Gaz' Lam* suggests that the cultural code that governs girls' sexuality is insisted upon to privilege the powerful and influential individuals in society that subscribe to these cultural practices. In many instances, such individuals become ill-suited suitors who are not loved, while the true lovers are pining with unconsummated passion, as in the case of S'fiso. In this series, S'fiso's grief and anger over his loss of Khethiwe is brought into the filmic narrative through flashbacks, in black and white, of the romantic moments in the serenity and purity of the countryside, as both innocently and curiously explore their sexuality. It is also brought in through the nightmarish, recurrent dreams that leave him sweating profusely as his subconscious taunts him with the illusion of a consummated, sexual relationship.

Re-evaluation of youth migration

In view of the inability of youth to change tradition and traditional authority, *Gaz' Lam* seems to suggest that youth migration is inevitable. The filmic narrative seems to suggest that reasons for migration to the cities cannot be confined to conventional notions revolving around land dispossessions, adventure, searching for greener pastures and aspirations to social mobility. Through S'fiso's characterisation there is a reading that suggests that emotional estrangement and despair resulting from inconsiderate traditional practices and stereotypes can lead to relocation, which is tantamount to dislocation. S'fiso's symbolic dislocation is accentuated by the loss, not only of Khethiwe, but also of his father, a great Maskandi musician, who would have been his symbolic link to this rural place. As it is, this rural location has nothing to offer him and has drained and emptied him of his zeal for continued existence in it. In spite of being ill-prepared for the harshness of the city, and fuelled only by his love and deep understanding of music, he journeys to it hoping that it might change his destiny.

S'fiso's journey recreates numerous social problems that are legacies of the past government. The most glaring of these social problems are structural unemployment and the economic marginalisation of Africans. Through the narratives of each friend in this community a number of conventional discourses and counter-discourses regarding

Africans in the city are replayed. One such dominant socio-political discourse created the impression that Africans are temporary sojourners in the cities. This perception contributed to the lack of key social infrastructure and amenities that would cater for their urban accommodation and existence. In the filmic narrative S'fiso's accommodation crisis is reflective of this. He gets temporary accommodation with his cousin, Welile, and his family, and he is given a couch in the living room to sleep on. Equally, his later relocation to an overcrowded flat where his unemployed community of friends lives, is also indicative of the crises that Africans experience in the city. Lack of employment, squalid living conditions, overcrowding and lack of privacy, in particular, have made life difficult for Africans, and have often been persuasive reasons to discourage them from entering the city.

Gaz' Lam's depiction of these colonial and apartheid legacies and the social experiences of Africans in the city, are juxtaposed with counter-discourses fashioned by Africans about their experiences. These counter-discourses become progressively clearer as S'fiso gets to know and understand each friend. His friends are representative of the underclass and their perceptions about the city reflect the popular imagination regarding city life. Counter-discourses that surface with the depiction of each of S'fiso's friends not only attest to the defiant view that Africans are permanent dwellers in the city, but to the fact that they can eke out a living in the margins of the mainstream economy (Hooks, 1994). The latter perception is another area in which *Gaz' Lam* differs from the conventional treatments of the theme of migration in isiZulu literature. *Gaz Lam*, rather than affirming received notions of the city as a decadent, evil, crime-infested location, questions these perceptions by presenting characters whose psychological outlook has been informed by city life. For example, Welile's outlook on life is affected by his retrenchment. S'fiso's lower class friends with whom he later squats, Ghetto Professor and Menzo are involved in crime because of unemployment.

The re-inscription of the village/city dialectic begins with the stance the film takes on the issue of migration, which varies radically from the established views created by isiZulu fiction. *Gaz' Lam* seems to support youth migration to the city by suggesting that as long as the impact of cultural practices such as arranged marriages is not fully understood, and their consequences seen for what they are, blame should not be apportioned to the youth who find the city and city life a viable alternative. Generally, isiZulu fiction seems to find it difficult to suggest that young people, let alone maidens seeking to escape traditional entrapment, should migrate to the cities. *Gaz' Lam* adopts this stance despite the fact that S'fiso and Khethiwe's initial encounters with city life border on shattered dreams. The uncertainty of city life is an aspect that *Gaz' Lam* fully explores, with the depictions of Khethiwe and S'fiso as new migrants being precisely the imagery that influences isiZulu literature to take a stance against youth migration.

The treatment of the migration theme in isiZulu literatures has altered with the hegemonic ideals of different segregationist governments. The initial phases of migration in colonial times, caused by the diamond and gold rush, have been seemingly celebrated in isiZulu fiction although the literature produced through missionary presses noted with displeasure the behavioural changes amongst some migrants. During colonialism migration to the city supplanted or substituted for numerous traditional practices such as the rites of passage for young boys to adulthood or the heroic adventures provided by military expeditions. Numerous isiZulu texts that espoused modernity celebrated the exposure of young men to other cultures, after which they returned home and established a viable business or raised enough money to take a wife or care for the polygamous family institutions. According to Welsh (1971), this initial phase was supported by the colonial government as more unskilled labourers were recruited to work in the dangerous diamond and gold fields.[2] But subsequent white administrations, such as the Pact government (unity government of the Afrikaans and English speaking whites) attempted to stem the tide of mass migration to the city from the mid-1930s. IsiZulu literature added its own ideological discourse to this political bickering, lambasting young people for leaving the serene, morally-upright countryside for the violent, morally-decadent, crime-infested cities.

According to Coplan (1985), the emergence of youth subcultures around the second decade of the last century and the political instability

(Walshe, 1970) towards the close of that decade created white hysteria about 'the Black Peril'. In response the Pact government instituted controls that aimed at preventing massive influx into the cities. These measures took a repressive turn from the 1950s when it was made illegal for Africans to be in the city unless they had permission. IsiZulu literature, which has conventionalised dominant ideologies, added its voice to this mainstream discourse through one-sided dramatisations that intimated that the young migrants eventually fall prey to crime due to endemic unemployment in the city. This orchestrated a view that emphasised the unsuitability of Africans for urban existence: Africans did not belong in the cities. Some of the texts that allude to this view are Dhlomo's (1935) *Indlela yababi* (The ways of the wicked), Nyembezi's (1950) *Mntanami Mntanami* (My child, my child), *Ngavele ngasho* (I said so) by Mkhize (1965), Nxumalo's (1969) *Ngisinga Empumalanga* (I look towards the east) and many other titles published between the 1950s and the late 1980s. The experiences of several characters in the series, such as Welile and Foxy, a woman with whom both Welile and S'fiso have a sexual relationship, betray such undertones. Both are migrants from rural KwaZulu-Natal whose dreams are shattered, and who are subsequently forced into the underworld.

Welile's migration, employment, marriage and other exploits occur outside the main story-line of the series. His introduction in the film is as a retrenched, disappointed, lower class member, who is embarrassed by his state of unemployment to the extent that no one at home in the rural areas knows about this. He has continued living large in order to create an impression of his success in the city. However, the reality of his unemployment is discovered by S'fiso shortly after his arrival in the city when he sees him exchanging dagga money with Foxy. His fall from a responsible father to a dagga trader not only depicts how uncertain city life is but also how its day-to-day demands slowly erode all moral values until individuals swim in a sea of disillusionment, despair and deprivation. Welile's state, like that of his friends Ghetto Professor, Menzo and Foxy, eventually becomes a pretext for engaging in criminal activities, an outlet for pent-up frustrations.

Welile's fall also emasculates him: the reversal of gender roles resulting from his retrenchment deprives him of his status as a provider and reduces him to dependence on his acid-tongued wife for survival. Taking over wifely chores such as child-minding, running errands, taking instructions from his wife, as well as other experiences such as being called derogatory names, takes its toll on his sense of manhood, as a Zulu man. However, key to Welile's crisis of masculinity is the 'ghetto survival syndrome', a state of inertia justified by a self-deluding sense of economic injustice, the internalisation of debased lifestyles as a result of squalid conditions, and a newly emerging practice among black men of preferring to remain at home whilst their womenfolk work for them. This view is arrived at after scrutinising Welile's so-called 'domesticity' – there is an episode when his wife, Thuli, phones him about her promotion and the possibility, now that she is going to earn more, of moving to Morningside, an up-market suburb. All that Welile can do, on the other side of the phone, is mock her in the presence of Foxy with whom he is having an extra-marital affair, dismissing any suggestion that he ought to seek work.

Foxy's characterisation can equally be read as postulating that Africans do not belong in the city. Foxy's migration is also located outside the primary filmic narrative and her reasons for being in the city are peripherally alluded to towards the climax of the series. She has come to the city in search of an elusive dream: to become a full woman by being married and 'given a surname.' In her search for suitable partners, she indulges in indiscreet sex activities, including being involved with Welile, the husband of one of her friends. In isiZulu literature representations of Foxy's archetype are prominent and intended to dissuade women from deviance and socially deplorable behaviour.

Whilst *Gaz' Lam* does not negate the established meanings of the city and the personalities that it helps create, the series proceeds to explore how debased lifestyles in the city become, in themselves, survival strategies for individuals who choose a permanent abode there. The city provides a refuge from parental control where the youth can create a world that exists and functions without the authority of parents and the confines of traditions or religion. According to Watkins (1998: 178), this rezoning of the existing cultural order is a common aspect in post-industrial societies where a 'new popular cultural landscape gave rise to the formation of an enlarged youth marketplace that further enabled youth to create and maintain a separate social world that existed outside immediate adult supervision.' This world, according to Jeffries (1992: 160), offers opportunities to 'pursue many avenues to erase the pain associated with the elusive urban good life, and it has created its own profound and sometimes feeble semblances of good life.'

Perhaps the part of the series that best illustrates the search for the elusive, urban, good life is that of S'fiso's metamorphosis. His metamorphosis, accompanied by Ghetto Ruff's kwaito sound, *Abobani abakhumul' izinja la* (a localised version of the African American popular rap song 'Who let the dogs out'), goes beyond the physical adoption of city fashions to the adoption of a psychological outlook which is marked by a loss of traditional morality. As far as he is concerned this change is for the better as it places him firmly on a route to the good life. This is the life that his friends lead and that is introduced to him in the first scene. He has been urged to 'walk like you have money to impress girls … buy beer, dagga and smokes, then the guys will like you'. This becomes the life S'fiso adopts after his transformation. The values he closely guarded in his early days in the city, symbolised by a worn out suitcase and Khethiwe's photo, worn at the edges and corners from constant handling, are discarded in favour of a life that consists of narcissistic behaviour, urban fashion trends and a new urbanised identity. It is after this transformation that he loses his innocence to Foxy, a deed that is celebrated by his new-found friends and interpreted as if he were coming of age, a ritual that introduces him to a life of women, sex and alcohol. In isiZulu literature, the adoption of a city identity and the attendant loss of cultural values are associated with a slide into a criminal life. One post-apartheid novel with a character closely resembling S'fiso's characterisation is Sibiya's (2002) *Kuxolelwa abanjani* (What type of people are forgiven). In this narrative the character's adoption of urban behaviour and identity does push him into a life of crime.

The depictions of Ghetto Professor and Menzo reveal deep-seated convictions about the good, city life. Both are quasi-criminals whose lifestyles consist of loud music accompanied by shouts of merriment in the evenings and days spent hanging out on the veranda of the flat, puffing away at their dagga and sizing up passers-by. Their libertine behaviour, stylish fashion and substance abuse are far from being perceived as compensating for the lack of a sound social base grounded in a sound family life, but are misconstrued as success and freedom. Ghetto Professor's dress style becomes a magnet for many women including materialistic, adventurous women such as Portia, and innocent girls, whom he infects with the HIV virus. Equally, Welile and Foxy's life experiences in the city, their illicit activities and secret affair, create the illusion of a good, meaningful life for them.

Gaz' Lam's dramatisation of migration and city life offers a balanced perspective, contrary to that of isiZulu literature which instils a one-sided view in line with the Nationalist government's influx control policies. IsiZulu fiction is seemingly unable to move beyond presenting the countryside and the city as mutually exclusive binaries. The post-apartheid novel that reflects this is Mathenjwa's (1994) *Ithemba lami* (My hope). This novel explores HIV/AIDS within the context of the city versus countryside opposition. In this novel, the city is not only crime-infested but also a domain where innocent 'country bumpkins' are infected with life-threatening diseases that traditional knowledge cannot even begin to comprehend, let alone cure. In Mathenjwa's text, there is a perception that the promiscuity of rural and urban dwellers is different. The indiscreet sexual behaviour of rural dwellers (in Mathenjwa's case, in KwaZulu), since it feeds into the traditional perceptions of *ubusoka* (a traditional practice where a young man courts numerous maidens), is regarded as a lesser evil than the practices of urban dwellers.

However, there is commonality about the perceptions of the spiritual significance of rural places in both *Gaz' Lam* and isiZulu fiction. Both the TV series and isiZulu fiction regard the rural area as a site of perfection and human completion. Both maintain that a protracted sojourn in the city corrupts human morality and leads to a life of criminality and hedonism. In the series, there is a sense in which this view is embraced. In all *Gaz' Lam*'s series, the rural areas have a special symbolism. It is not only Foxy who returns to the rural areas when she realises that her search for a husband who will give her a surname is futile. Similarly, after Welile's death in the opening episodes of the second series, his rural family comes to claim his corpse and to take it back to Natal. Furthermore S'fiso, after his fall from stardom in the third series, also returns home to rediscover his music and reconnect with traditional sounds. In the last series, the rural areas are where S'fiso and Khethiwe romantically reconnect after a long period of separation and misunderstanding.

Perhaps epitomising the place of the rural in the life of black people are Ghetto Professor's utterances when he is about to die from full-blown AIDS: he points out to S'fiso that at least he (S'fiso) has a rural home to return to when things have gone bad, unlike himself who has been 'born, bred and buttered' in the urban centres and who has nowhere to turn to. Despite his penitence and the forgiveness he begs from each and every woman he has unwittingly infected with HIV, he finds no solace as they are either already dead, or bitterly vengeful and unforgiving. The reading of the countryside as the only place for moral and cultural regeneration of Africans after horrible spells in the city, prompts critics like Gugler (2003: 76) to point out that the notion that Africans belong in the countryside and that the city is destructive and flawed, fails to acknowledge that Africans have worked in the mines, in the industries and in domestic service for generations, and that Africans are well-established in the cities.

Jim comes to Jo'burg: celebrating a dream in the city through music

Gugler's views are echoed in the motif 'Jim comes to Jo'burg.' This motif establishes counter-hegemonic discourses in that it recreates and reaffirms the ability of Africans to carve out an economic niche, through the arts, in an environment that was designed to exclude them from all cultural and socio-economic participation. The theme of 'Jim comes to Jo'burg' was introduced in the late 1940s with the film *Africa Jim*. S'fiso's character is modelled after the character of Dan Odemwah, who left the rural areas to look for employment in the city. His job as a sweeper at a social club exposed him to music talent scouts who noted his beautiful voice when he sang a duet with Dolly Rathebe, another leading character. Both were eventually given a recording contract.

Like in *Africa Jim*, S'fiso gets a job as a sweeper at Ziyawa Night Club, owned by Jerome, who initially treats him with contempt and disdain. S'fiso's work is regarded as a dead-end job by his cousin and his friends and he has to withstand constant mockery and abuse from them. It is through his work at this club that he meets Lerato, a beautiful young singer, who is looking for a break in the music industry. Lerato's character is played by Thembi Seete of Boom Shaka fame, a local kwaito music group whose dance style (a West African popular dance move known as Kwasa Kwasa) took South Africa by storm in the early 1990s. Thembi Seete's casting, as Watkins (1998) observes with African American films' use of the hip hop musical genre and hip hop stars, is an intervention aimed at harnessing the commercial viability of these music genres, and it positions these films at the crossroads of the youth markets.

Gaz' Lam's incorporation of this musical form transposes all its underlying concerns. Kwaito emerged during the early 1990s and presents an admixture of local, bubblegum music and international music sounds including hip hop, d'gong, house, reggae and elements such as clothing and language that negotiate youth identities. In particular, it is a reaction to the material conditions of the underclass of black youth in post-apartheid, democratic South Africa. Numerous definitions exist of kwaito. Impey defines kwaito as

> the hottest contemporary music of black urban South Africa [...] mediated by a complex music industry, the mass media, and by state-of-the-art and modeled images derived from South African and African American inner-city rap/hip hop styles. Furthermore, it is an encompassing term for a popular dance music that is associated with contemporary urban black youth style and identity (cited in Chrispo, 2003: 94).

Fred Khumalo (1998: 17) points out that kwaito 'is angry, in-your-face music rooted in urban angst: it speaks of violence, drugs and sex through pared-down, repeated lyrics.' He further points out that over and above the violence, drugs and sex, it also features songs and music that talk of development and positive issues, for example, urging 'the youth to get up and do it for themselves.' According to Watkins (1998), authorities in the United States view the intensification of sexual and violent imagery in popular culture as largely responsible for what is broadly perceived as an erosion of traditional values and escalating youth crime and drug use. Like its rap and hip hop counterparts, as brilliantly demonstrated by Peterson (2003), kwaito has been singled out as an example of how popular culture allegedly promotes anti-social values and youth nihilism.

In *Gaz' Lam*, the exploitation of this musical genre is devoid of this negativity. Instead, this musical genre is presented as an imaginative solution to problems of unemployment, youth idleness and low youth self-esteem. Significantly, the accessibility of the equipment used for its production not only provides the youth with a chance to participate actively in a cultural form that gives expression to their worldviews, but also gives them a sense of purpose in life. Watkins (1998) points out that their initial breakthrough, like that of hip hop and gangsta rap music, took place in the underground music culture through the entrepreneurial attempts of poor ghetto and working-class black and Latino youth. It is music associated with the 'studio gangsta'. Relying on new technology for its production, it is capable of changing musical tastes and youth trends; it is grounded in the spirit of entrepreneurship and it is produced by small, independent rap labels. There are more commonalities to be found when comparing Watkins' observation with Simon Stephens's (2000) treatise on kwaito, its production and its depiction in the series. Stephens is also of the view that the accessibility of the equipment and the favourable conditions for the production of kwaito music encourage the entrepreneurial spirit. In the series, kwaito music is depicted as related to the underground music culture associated with clubbing and with informal, independent music studios. Boloka (2003) points out that the processes of its production – reliance on music technologies, a small inexperienced production team, its manipulation and eventual commodification by the greater music industry – reflect the appropriation of global practices and are reproduced in the series.

In the series, the introduction of kwaito music happens as early as episode two, when Lerato visits a club manager, Jerome, in connection with the demo tape she had given him earlier. She wants a gig in

Jerome's bar. Eventually she gets the opportunity but on condition that she becomes Jerome's lover. Lerato's characterisation explores a number of issues affecting women in show business: their exploitation, and how they also exploit and play influential people against one another in order to realise their aspirations. As soon as she discovers that S'fiso is a talented music producer, she develops feelings for him. These feelings are not given immediate expression while she remains dependent on Jerome, her sponsor and benefactor. She acts on her feelings once S'fiso has helped her record her first album, financed by Jerome.

The series gives room for women to make conscious decisions regarding their exposure to exploitation. Lerato is dialectically juxtaposed with Maduvha, a local kwaito idol who, within the context of the series, needs a breakthrough. Maduvha's resolve and principled behaviour throughout the period when she seeks S'fiso's help, contrast sharply with Lerato's pretence of firmness and principled behaviour with Jerome. When Lerato realises the nature of the business and that her development depends on human and capital resources that she does not possess but which Jerome, as an experienced and well-connected bar proprietor, has, she changes radically. She even convinces her morally upright mother to allow her to move in with Jerome. Ironically, her smash hit underpins the contradictions of her character. The song's message emphasises honesty and fidelity, attributes that she fails to display as she changes her affections in accordance with her musical needs and career development.

Kwaito, as portrayed in the series, also provides aesthetic solutions. The working class origins of kwaito invariably affect the aesthetics of this musical genre. According to Peterson (2003: 197) 'the accolades are for the intricate mix of players that produce and consume kwaito music in ways that ensure that its "ridim an tings" [rhythm and things] continue to rule the swing in townships across South Africa'. Lerato's music exemplifies the aesthetic appeal of incorporating not only international but also traditional sounds that reflect what has been achieved through the Maskandi music genre. S'fiso's refining of Lerato's song is heavily dependent on the Maskandi music sounds that he has been socialised into by his late father. By drawing on

Maskandi music, S'fiso seems to affirm the versatility of earlier, urban identities that can still be seen in the construction of kwaito-lubricated contemporary identities. According to Boloka (2003) the musical evolution from the Maskandi genre to kwaito indicates that kwaito is a manifestation of a changing society.

Maskandi (also called Mazkande and Maskanda), according to Coplan (1985) and Nhlapho (1998), is a musical form which comprises traditional tunes performed on Western instruments by working class guitarists. Nhlapho defines Maskandi music as a 'Zulu musical genre that is the domain of Zulu, strolling musicians' (16). Crozier (cited in Nhlapho, 1998: 17) defines it as 'musicians most often seen wandering along the road, plucking at the strings of the guitar and singing in a low mournful voice to no-one in particular.' Maskandi remains true to its working class origins, despite the incorporation of modern Western instruments. It has a broad popular base amongst a variety of language groups and reaffirms a specifically African, cultural identity and expressive mode. S'fiso's incorporation of the Maskandi musical form is both acknowledging the journey made by black, urban music, as well as anchoring kwaito, seen as a highly fluid musical form susceptible to various international influences, to an Afrocentric identity. Kwaito, like Maskandi music, is presented in the series as a means for constructing an urban, African identity because through its own narratives and images, kwaito addresses itself to the squalid, harsh and hostile urban landscapes.

Despite the fact that the Maskandi musical genre can be traced to the early years of African urbanisation, isiZulu literature has given recognition to this art form only since after the 1994 democratic elections. IsiZulu literature has been indisposed to realise the centrality and the role of popular musical forms which, in composition and presentation, are cultural innovations by urbanised Africans as well as legitimate mouthpieces of the broader African society for its protests against socio-political and economic injustices. In isiZulu literature, throughout the cultural evolution of black modernity, this musical genre, like Marabi, was associated with the underclass and therefore dismissed as holding no cultural value, in spite of its connection with the oral art form of traditional praise poetry.

It is ironic that, in isiZulu literature, the absence of narrative recreation of the relevance of Maskandi in the society of the last century occurred in a context where contemporary extensions of praise poetry received attention and where many folklorists and culturalists remarked on the resilience with which oral art forms continued to find expression in contemporary art forms. The dismissive attitude of earlier isiZulu fiction towards Maskandi explains the failure of this literary tradition to engage with the cultural significance of musical forms such as kwaito in post-apartheid novels. IsiZulu literature acts as a self-appointed guardian of society, and kwaito, which gives vent to the 'rough-sides of popular, black, youth culture' (Boyd cited in Peterson, 2003: 200), definitely does not qualify as a virtuous, cultural phenomenon for the instruction of African youth.

As mentioned earlier, the treatment of Maskandi as an imaginative and cultural solution that addresses itself to social disparities occurred only well into the democratic period. Both *Usumenyezelwe-ke Umcebo* (The wealth has been announced) by Mngadi (2005) and Sibiya's (2006) *Ngidedele ngife* (Let me die) explore different aspects of Maskandi music ranging from composition to recording and performance. These are novels by seasoned, progressive and budding Zulu authors who have been exposed to current debates about the role of oral art forms in contemporary African society and have thus introduced these debates into their work. Although Sibiya's *Ngidedele ngife* makes a peripheral mention of the kwaito genre, the text's focus is on the Maskandi genre. This occurs in spite of the fact that kwaito music is more realistic and inclusive of the experiences of black people than Maskandi's focus on individual composers as it uses the self-adulatory practice of the praise poetry tradition. The elitist celebration of Maskandi music in isiZulu fiction prevents the capture of the diverse, black, social experiences often invoked in kwaito lyrics and imagery. This celebration ironically glorifies the individual experiences refracted in Maskandi music, often expanding them to be representative of the whole African experience. In view of this, *Gaz' Lam*'s inclusion of kwaito as an evolving musical genre, incorporating both modern and traditional styles, marks it as different. *Gaz' Lam*'s view of kwaito as expressing some of the social and aesthetic dilemmas of black culture, reveals how this musical genre can be salvaged from its earlier associations with the underworld and menacing youth subcultures.

Articulating re-marginalisation through tsotsitaal

Another black, cultural expression regarded in mainstream debates as a menace of youth subcultures is tsotsitaal. The use of tsotsitaal in *Gaz' Lam*, as is the case with kwaito music, underscores where the counter-discourses of the re-marginalised youth in post-1994 society are located. Tsotsitaal is also a vehicle for identity construction, and is representative of social classes and cultural spaces. *Gaz' Lam*'s inclusion of this language variety as a language of choice for its youthful characters reflects its dominance in black, urban, cultural identity construction. Like kwaito, this linguistic variety has, in the past, been associated with the underworld, the rebellious, the uncouth and the black youth. Both Ntshangase (1995) and Makhudu (1995) point out that tsotsitaal developed as an argot, a criminal language. Although tsotsitaal's origins denote resistance and defiance, over time this perspective changed to reflect a 'spontaneous in-group outcome of social and linguistic interaction among equals or those sharing similar socio-cultural values and perspectives' (Makhudu, 1995: 298). The past, South African, socio-political order created perceptions of a shared, black, social experience and tsotsitaal transcended linguistic, political and ethnic boundaries. Glaser (1990, cited in Ntshangase, 1995: 292–293) adds that young, black children growing up in Gauteng identified more with criminals than with professionals. This resulted in the increased use of languages associated with criminals. Thereafter tsotsitaal and *iscamtho* no longer reflected 'the life of the underworld but that of the young and urban-wise, assuming an urban identity, which distinguished itself from the rural identity of migrant workers' (Makhudu, 1995: 301). Makhudu shares this opinion and emphasises the popular perceptions of its users; that they definitely associate themselves with urban life and that they are superior to non-users, who are stigmatised as 'country bumpkins'.

The use of tsotsitaal in *Gaz' Lam* not only underpins the street conscious identity of the characters, but, as Jeffries (1992) and Hall

(1997) note with kwaito music, its popular style is also capable of describing more fully the emotions and circumstances that black, urban residents encounter, as well as being a site that defines what is contemporary. According to Jeffries (1992: 159), the language is spoken for the black, popular ear. Tsotsitaal in *Gaz' Lam* is no longer a language variety reflecting resistance to the hegemonic mainstream, but speaks fundamentally of the post-apartheid, urban, youth experience of re-marginalisation and their disillusionment with the realities that force them out of the economic mainstream. There have been attempts in isiZulu literature to incorporate this language variety. Novels like Sibiya's (2002) *Kuxolelwa abanjani*, Ngubo's (1996) *Yekanini ukuzenza* and a number of Masondo's post-1994 detective stories incorporate tsotsitaal, but in all these texts the original dominant views regarding its users prevail. The characters are fixed in the underworld.

The stigma with which tsotsitaal and its speakers are associated generally and in the isiZulu literary tradition in particular, operates on a gross oversight. Earlier research into tsotsitaal fuelled certain stereotypes which later remained associated with this language. Despite the fact that tsotsitaal is an old form that can be traced to the turn of the twentieth century, interest in this language phenomenon only emerged from the 1980s. Around this time Language Boards tasked to oversee the linguistic and literary issues of African languages created stultifying views regarding formal and standard languages. The exclusionist tendencies that resulted from the isiZulu standardisation process and the outcry about the purity of the language that saw the ambiguous status of isiZulu spoken in the cities, particularly in Johannesburg, were equally responsible for the rejection of other urban, linguistic varieties like *iscamtho* and tsotsitaal.

The linguistic elements that make up this language variety were initially of no interest as it was seen as an urban language mix which was limited to a few speakers, mainly from the underworld. Both Slabbert (1994) and Makhudu (1995) were initially of the opinion that this language variety relied on Afrikaans for structure. However, by the early 2000s some fascinating features of tsotsitaal were discovered by Mulaudzi and Poulos (2001). In their study of the Venda variety of tsotsitaal, they discovered that it developed from the isiZulu lexical structures used in tsotsitaal. Their conclusion suggested that isiZulu is the base and Afrikaans is the upper layer. Perhaps the most illuminating finding about this is the contribution of Rudwick (2005). She unravelled some of the intriguing dynamics at work regarding the relationship between standard South African languages and their urban variations. Her findings refute earlier perceptions about the linguistic attributes of tsotsitaal and prove that in spite of the ambiguous status of tsotsitaal among isiZulu speakers, 'isiZulu is the matrix language and main lexifier of the tsotsi variety and hence the language is lexically more similar to what Ntshangase (1995) previously referred to as *iscamtho*'(Rudwick, 2005: 307).

Recent findings regarding the position and status of tsotsitaal help in situating films like *Gaz' Lam* within the isiZulu literary domain. The interchangeable use of isiZulu and tsotsitaal is reflective of linguistic trends in contemporary African society. This interchangeable use of language not only captures key moments in the social development of urbanised, African society but is also a frank and honest depiction of the realities of their everyday existence in the post-apartheid period, an existence which can be best articulated in a form that has come through history as non-mainstream.

Conclusion

The intertextual reading of thematic concerns in *Gaz' Lam* and isiZulu literature reveals certain ways of thinking in the public domain. The common popular discourses which these artistic forms have incorporated into their narratives reveal the topicality of the issues raised but the responses of these artistic forms to black experiences in post-apartheid South Africa reveal differing standpoints. The TV series reflects sensitivity to the contradictions that animated and shaped the history of South African cinema and thus endeavours, in its representations, to correct and redirect public debates about issues affecting black South Africans. IsiZulu literature, on the other hand, follows the terrain already laid down by its literary conventions regarding similar issues. Even though isiZulu fiction treads carefully on established routes, it does, in its own peculiar way, introduce other ways of seeing, by bringing into sharp focus certain moral sanctions that pertain more to individual morality than to a collective one which might or might not have been occasioned by social variables. This aspect will be shown in the next chapter when a comparative study of *Yizo Yizo* and Mngadi's *Kuyoqhuma Nhlamvana* is made.

In isiZulu fiction, just as in black television practice, the historical emergence of change, which was a consequence of a clash of civilisations, remains a remarkable source of inspiration for the composition of modern day narratives. The theatrical recasting of the clash of civilizations in both film and literature is intended to explore a variety of aspects of cultural change or resistance or resilience in contemporary African society. The treatment of arranged marriages, migration and urban music in both the TV series and numerous isiZulu novels dramatises this aspect, and its treatment in the post-apartheid context reveals numerous transitions that black society has undergone. This transition is more aptly captured in *Gaz' Lam* than in isiZulu fiction. In isiZulu fiction, the recasting of these themes is limited to old associations which often overlooked cultural issues; particularly frustrations with traditions.

This conservatism noted in isiZulu fiction is amongst the most important bulwarks guarding against the dilution of African discourses. Yet when considering the broader social variables affecting African lives, such conservatism prevents a proper exploration of the macro political and socio-economic realities that contributed to the wrecked lives of Africans in the first place. For example, certain cultural innovations have become key in dealing with economic marginalisation and political exclusion suffered by contemporary Africans. As *Gaz'Lam* has shown, the structural use of the musical motif to explore emerging musical forms such as kwaito, is a significant cultural form that holds key solutions to post-apartheid crises such as the youth problem, masculinity, employment and the aesthetics of black expressive art. It is also a significant area of the filmic narrative that gives credence to the role of black cultural innovations. However, isiZulu fiction shyly takes up this cultural form as the views espoused by kwaito are not considered to be properly traditional, but a mixture of all urban trends and fashions that have been faulted by the literary tradition for the disappearance of an African ethos.

Endnotes

1   The most celebrated resistance by women to forced marriages was the one carried out by the *Ngcungce* female regiment against King Cetshwayo who had attempted to force a mismatched marriage between an old male regiment and a younger female one. The female regiment resisted and sent word to the King telling him '*ucu aluhlangani entanyeni*' (the necklace [normally mutually exchanged by lovers as token of their love] does not fit). The infuriated King Cetshwayo ordered their execution; however, their resistance is still celebrated and it contributed to the view that no-one can dictate to a woman's heart.

2   Welsh (1971) explores in considerable length the colonial administration's orchestration of massive migration to the city through the Shepstonian system. The Shepstonian system is a colonial administrative policy introduced by Sir Theopholus Shepstone that gave him control over African affairs.

6

'It is not crime in the way you see it': *Kuyoqhuma Nhlamvana's* rewriting of *Yizo Yizo's* crime discourse and outlaw culture

A major threat to democracy in post-apartheid South Africa has been the rising tide of crime in the public domain, overriding other key socio-historical transformations. Anti-crime discourses have begun to build an increasingly detailed picture of this phenomenon. Factors such as endemic poverty, accelerated urbanisation, blurred morality, 'arriviste' lifestyles, youth subculture as a counter-culture, (dis)continuities between the politics of the 1980s and 1990s, past animosities between political authorities and youth and the disquieting relationship between politics and crime in South Africa have become dominant subjects, generating a myopic, though persistently adhered-to, understanding of crime in South Africa.

A glance at the literature produced in response to post-1994 crime offers mainly conventional frameworks for the understanding of social deviancy, delinquency, crime and violence; frameworks which hobble intervention strategies as they attempt to keep up with the growth of crime in South Africa. While these theoretical understandings have some value and may even lead to breakthroughs in understanding the causes and nature of crime, there needs to be a paradigm shift in the way in which crime and violence are perceived and investigated. This assertion is supported by the observation that conventional paradigms generated in privileged environments have, in many instances, failed to explain the social deviancy occurring in less privileged societies. Mainstream paradigms based on conventional modes of understanding will not be of much use in explaining the nature and causes of crime if they ignore the specifics of particular and possibly unfamiliar contexts. In contrast, the drama series *Yizo Yizo* (1999) and the Zulu novel by Mngadi (2004), *Kuyoqhuma Nhlamvana* (Concealed things will be revealed), as part of the public discourse, are insightful in examining this phenomenon in post-apartheid South African society. These texts enter into a dialogue with the existing scholarship and the public domain concerning the vantage points from which to explore and explain crime in the first ten years after the 1994 democratic elections. Significantly, it is not only new understandings of crime that are excavated from these texts but contrasting the film and the novel makes possible new departures in crime writing in isiZulu fiction. The isiZulu novel advances the treatment of this theme and exposes the multi-layered networks of crime.

Altbeker highlights the tensions between locality-based discourses on crime and conventional, 'one-size-fits-all' approaches. One of his most important observations relates to moral responsibilities vis-à-vis the law and an understanding of what constitutes legality in relation to outlaw states of mind and cultures. His insights bring an important dimension to the debate about crime in South Africa and underscore the need for a paradigm shift:

> The institutions of law ... are rooted so shallowly in the consciousness of some of the citizens of South Africa ... In such a context, society in general, the police in particular are not so much dealing with criminals, they are dealing with outlaws – people who are outside of the reach of the law, and whose identities have not been shaped by the law; people whose relationship with the world is not mediated by the social relations which the law is both premised on, and seeks to guarantee and uphold (2001a: 25).

It is against the backdrop of claims such as these that I will investigate representations of crime in the South African government-commissioned drama series, *Yizo Yizo,* and the novel, *Kuyoqhuma*

Nhlamvana, which extrapolated most of its crime discourse from the dramatic representations in *Yizo Yizo*. Both texts, as they unfold, offer a cluster of arguments concerning crime and violence in post-apartheid South Africa. The interventionist strategies depicted in these texts contrast with conventional approaches that are shown to be ineffective. Also important is the way the texts highlight that permeable and shifting frontier between law-abiding citizens and anti-social miscreants. I shall use *Yizo Yizo's* and *Kuyoqhuma Nhlamvana's* characterisation to investigate the tensions between crime discourses and their cinematographic representations and illustrate the intricate interplay between consciousness of the law and the outlaw culture. Linked to the latter aspect is an assessment of how *Yizo Yizo* influences and sets a trend for treatment of crime in *Kuyoqhuma Nhlamvana*.

Summary of *Yizo Yizo*

Yizo Yizo is about the experiences of the school community of Supatsela High School and the general community of Daveyton where Supatsela High is located. Both the school and the general community are besieged by gangsters who sell drugs to local school-going youth and subject the community in general to acts of violence. *Yizo Yizo* presents two types of gangsters: hardcore, ruthless gangsters and soft gangsters, the Robin Hood-type bandits who mediate between hardcore gangsters and the community. Zakes, Thiza's brother, falls into this category. On the first day of school, which is ghettoised in keeping with the township, the atmosphere of a crime-infested community is recreated by showing that the school boys, Javas, Bobo and Sticks, have painted graffiti on the classrooms walls on the eve of the school's re-opening. In addition, during the course of that day the gangsters, Chester and Papa Action, drop in and harass little girls in full view of the school. Papa Action is a school-going youth and Chester is a former student who has just returned from jail. The gangsters baptise Bobo in the toilet, an act that crystallises the 'criminogenetic' (Gordon, 2006) atmosphere in this school. All of the gangsters' activities occur despite the sternness of the principal, Mr Mthembu, and some morally concerned teachers, like Edwin.

This black television series also depicts the hopes, histories, romantic entanglements and aspirations of a cross-section of youth, both female and male. Young boys and girls such as Thiza, Javas, Nomsa and Hazel have dreams of successful careers and yet some, like Mantwa, Bobo and Sticks, because of the influence of a truncated township life, are without dreams. Others, like Gunman and Thulas, attempt to atone for the youthful years lost in political activism by ingratiating themselves into schools, despite being aware that their dreams have been shattered by politics. Unemployment also forces such militarised youth back to school in fear of the idleness in the township that can propel them towards crime. Not only has politics destroyed the future of youths in the context of *Yizo Yizo*, but unscrupulous and morally dubious teachers are responsible for destroying the future of girl children like Snowy, Hazel's sister, who has been impregnated and dumped by Ken, a teacher.

The private lives of both teachers and students intermingle with school life. Javas, who has been paying undue attention to Nomsa, steals her bag and gives it to a local hobo, Scavenger. Nomsa tries in vain to get it back from Scavenger and is late for school. She is severely punished by Mthembu. Mthembu's strict, disciplinarian approach to education proves to be no match for the increasingly libertarian attitudes of the students, his subordinates and the parents. Once he gets embroiled in a case of heavy-handedness towards the students and some teachers and, instead of apologising and assuring both the parents and the departmental officials that he will desist from corporal punishment, he offers to resign from his post. His departure marks the beginning of uncontrollable chaos in the school.

An unfit, gangster-aligned teacher is appointed to act as principal. Dedicated teachers such as Edwin, who would have been a better choice are overlooked. The new acting principal, Ken, is heavily indebted to Bra Gibbs, the mafia king for whom Chester and Papa Action work. Gang activities intensify at the school, leading to the disruption of classes, destruction of the school building and the sexual molestation of Dudu by Papa Action. The school takes collective action and these gangsters are banished from school. Ken is dismissed and a new principal, Grace Letsatsi is employed. However, the gangsters strike back with impunity. They initially concentrate their activities outside the school premises – such as selling drugs through the school fence – but then engage in sporadic disruption of classes. Grace uses an approach that involves the whole community to address the problem of gangsterism and drugs in the school. Eventually the community is spurred to act and these gangsters are apprehended and handed over to the police.

Summary of *Kuyoqhuma Nhlamvana*

The story paints the life of Nyathi who, after being retrenched and subsequently divorced, is forced to give up his middle class lifestyle for an underclass life in a township called Sobantu in Pietermaritzburg. He gets an RDP[1] house and befriends his neighbours, the Sokheles, who strongly advise him to start a transportation business in order to survive. Together they transport school children with their vans. Nyathi's wife finds out about his new source of income and files for child maintenance. The maintenance of his two children becomes a problem: he is left with half of what he makes from the transportation business after paying maintenance. In order to augment his earnings he gets involved with a gangster group transporting dagga (marijuana) from the rural areas to the city. He gets substantial sums from this deal and starts to extend his house. He invites Sokhele to join in. Sokhele, however, is arrested on the very first day he transports dagga back to the city, and is sentenced to twenty years in jail.

Sokhele's arrest and imprisonment does not dissuade Nyathi from carrying on with these deals. Instead, he and his Indian dealer, Moodley, decide to transport different types of chemical drugs such as Mandrax, cocaine and ecstasy. These drugs are from Colombia. Nyathi's mandate is to transport them from the harbour to the rural areas where they are to be stashed until buyers from all over the continent come to buy them in bulk. Because of the nature of this new deal he invites Sokhele's son, Jabulani, to be both a peddler to school boys and the transporter of these drugs. Jabulani, who is no novice to criminal activities since he previously stole his father's dagga to sell to his school friends, executes his job to perfection.

The availability of drugs to schoolchildren brings crime into the area. With the establishment of a gang culture that operates from street corners and gang hide-outs, the escalation of drug-related problems compels the school, the community and the local councillors to invite social workers to address students about the problem of drugs and drug addiction in the society. The crime rate soars further, and local police fail to deal with this problem since Nyathi has corrupted the station commander. The community, through their local councillors, writes to the National Prosecuting Authority and the Scorpions[2] are called in. They are able to uncover Nyathi's syndicate and he is arrested along with all the other members of his criminal chain.

Racialised crime control strategies in *Yizo Yizo*

The discourse of *Yizo Yizo* is concerned with social control, mainly of African youth, with a focus on the involvement of youth in crime and violence. An initial impression is created that crime and violence are an 'African problem' that can be explained by appealing to the 'one-size-fits-all' model mentioned above. Yet, in a strange twist, the cinematographic representations of crime in *Yizo Yizo* point to shared, and (un)spoken signifying systems that run counter to the officially sanctioned ideology of control. For example, images of tsotsi culture, delinquent culture, Mafia culture and youth militarism are presented – images that figure in the black, popular imagination as legitimate ways of resisting white hegemony. These images cut across and rupture categories of legality and illegality.[3] The cinematography brings into view long-standing socio-political and economic problems to which certain sectors of African communities have reacted by establishing modes of survival incorporating forms of criminal behaviour. At the same time, the script tends to operate within conventional theoretical paradigms, so that while, on the one hand, it follows this orbit, on the other the cinematographic images speak of a different world, animated by local specifics that have shaped its psychological states. In many instances these psychological states have existed alongside mainstream culture.

I argue that the crime situation reveals that the present crisis is an outcome of shared criminal culpability spanning centuries in a racially divided South Africa, where the dominant, white world and the marginalised, black world have remained mutually exclusive culturally. My argument is in accord with Diana Gordon's (2006) view that the seeds of our criminogenetic past were sown at the beginning of the colonial period, and produced fruit such as the tot system, land theft and the destruction of indigenous cultures. All of these, whilst viewed as non-criminal by the colonial mainstream community and the colonial administration, in fact laid the foundations of the criminal culture which now prevails in many black communities. Injustices to which Africans were long subjected have produced a culture of retribution accompanied by a diminished respect for the law. Gordon's views imply that Western law, since its inception, has never been perceived by black people as an apparatus for dispensing justice in an equitable manner, and that post-apartheid crime and violence are the result of centuries of unjust discrimination entrenched and enforced by law.

The colonially-rooted causes of the criminal lifestyle of Africans and the Africans' responses to these causes underpin the cinematographic representations in the world of *Yizo Yizo*. For example, the effects of land dispossession are depicted in the abnormally crowded housing conditions which Africans were compelled by law to accept, or to which they resorted in order to circumvent the racially-based residential policies. These images form a background against which harrowing details of black lives are recreated. Daveyton, the setting for the series, is a poverty-stricken and sprawling African township in Gauteng. Like numerous other African townships, it is a product of the 1913 Land Act, the Group Areas Act and other segregationist policies. Although the effects of this legislation were felt most keenly during the apartheid period because of the routine use of coercion, the policies themselves evolved during the era of colonial rule (Welsh, 1971).

Linked to the rise of the racialised, capitalist economy was the evolution of the migrant labour system. This movement of multitudes of Africans from traditional villages to urban slums, shanty towns, townships or compounds or anything that resembled some form of shelter brought a host of challenges for the white economy. This economy was not prepared to make any meaningful provisions for Africans who were to help amass wealth for successive white governments and their benefactors in the international economy. All these factors proved to be damaging to social and family cohesion. Bhekizizwe Peterson (2000), commenting on the deleterious effects of the migrant system, points out that Father Huss, a Trappist Father stationed at Marianhill, wrote a series of chapters in the early twentieth century describing the impact of industrialisation and urbanisation on African households. One significant institution that was seriously damaged was the African family, in both its traditional and Christian forms. This is supported by Mamphele Ramphele (1992) whose studies of African families at the dawn of the twenty first century reveal how the migrant labour system weakened African families through poverty, overcrowding, and a sense of worthlessness experienced by some adults. Migrant labour resulted in parents being separated from their children and youngsters being swallowed up by the cities.

Yizo Yizo provides this historical background through its use of Daveyton as a setting and through its depiction of the life experiences of young people bereft of parental authority. The historical background, as depicted in the film, is crucial to an understanding of African urban settlement. It also explains the absence of the white world and whiteness from the film, the effect of which is to create the impression that crime is an African problem, in particular, a problem of African youth. This 'take', involving as it does the exclusion of certain social orders (Fuery, 2000) and the portrayal of crime as a black aberration in the post-apartheid era, appears to be rooted in a sense of political betrayal by the African National Congress (ANC). This once-heroic liberation movement has engendered disillusionment and apathy in South Africa. The post-apartheid social order appears to have veered towards a middle class outlook on crime, as on other matters. Still, despite the middle class yardstick in terms of which crime seems to be judged in *Yizo Yizo*, the film is energised by shocking revelations of post-apartheid realities as they affect young people. The depiction of these realities has been successful in ruffling consciences regarding the multitude of black youth whose lives were disrupted in the service of the armed struggle and who were then re-marginalised after the democratic dispensation was inaugurated.

This re-marginalisation also generated concern about who should assume responsibility for the state of African youth. After the 1994 political revolution young people were excluded from the rush to self-enrichment by those in the higher echelons whose wealth now gives rise to the phrase 'black diamond.' At the same time, politicians anxious to divert attention from their own failings blamed white middle class South Africa for its support for the colonial, segregationist and apartheid policies designed to keep the majority of Africans undereducated and under-skilled. The truth is that no proper acknowledgement of the roots of our social ills has occurred, nor has there been recognition that the current political leadership has failed the country. These issues are foregrounded in *Yizo Yizo* by having the school act as a container for large numbers of marginalised, forgotten youth and as an arena for inculcating conventional 'middle class' attitudes to crime and lawlessness. The school has representative status as a site for the dramatisation of our social ills on the one hand and, on the other, for the testing of individual and collective responsibility.

Historically, in the education of African children, the school does not carry any sense of prestige as it has been the site where, through the Bantu Education Act, the hopes and futures of these children were legislatively guillotined. During the politics of resistance the school provided a terrain where these children were enthusiastically used as political buffers or shields and were also ideologically channelled by liberation movements to resist the state's repressive policies with nihilism. *Yizo Yizo*'s preference for the school as a microcosm to re-enact current social ills evokes these historical memories. Its representation of South Africa's collective responsibility and the depiction of youth psychology points to perturbing realities: the lack of a collective ethic which affects the manner in which the African youth perceive the law. However, what the filmic narrative overlooks, as was pointed out earlier, are parallel existences, parallel (counter)cultures, preferred hierarchies of social power and prioritising of survival techniques that have informed the social order it portrays.

The law and the outlaw culture in *Yizo Yizo*

As for the issue of scant respect for the law by many Africans – a theme prominent in *Yizo Yizo* – a key point to bear in mind is that the protracted effort, through colonial policies, to extract from Africans their total obedience to the British and Dutch laws had unforeseen effects: it gave rise to mistrust of the 'white man's laws' and to the conviction that they should be subverted whenever and wherever possible. This is a plausible explanation of the African tendency to political insurgency, labour unrest and religious cynicism. David Coplan (1985) and Tim Couzens (1985) point out that it was during widespread social disaffection that the Industrial Commercial Workers' Union (ICU) gained popularity, that separatist churches sprang up, and that the gang culture, the *amalaita*, which evolved into *tsotsi* culture, emerged in the 1920s. Throughout the last century *tsotsi* culture was ambivalent: on the one hand its criminal activities were geared towards self-aggrandisement and a lifestyle of over-indulgence; on the other, strong political consciousness pervaded most of its criminal operations. By the post-apartheid period this counterculture was entrenched and had extensive systems which appealed to vast numbers of people, blurring divisions between law-abiding citizens and outlaws. The transfer of power to an African government in 1994 did not wean criminally-minded people from their contempt for the law or their willingness to flout it with impunity. At the level of governance the crime situation in South Africa revealed what Ergang (1967) noted about French society during the French Revolution: that lack of proper political structure allows forces of disruption and dissolution to gain strength while those of order and progress grow steadily weaker. Now considering that South Africa had been (un)lawfully (mis)managing a state of confusion which bordered on anarchy since the colonial administration, one should not wonder at the enormity of misrule, corruption and administrative confusion besetting the post-apartheid state. The currents noted above – youth marginalisation, diminished respect for the law, crime as a way of life – are dramatised in *Yizo Yizo*, but selectively. For example, the television series seeks to valorise a mainstream attitude to crime and lawlessness while choosing not to investigate too closely the hierarchies of social power.

The spotlight in *Yizo Yizo* often falls on the criminal career of Zakes, who practices a Robin Hood kind of banditry which is seen as the logical outcome of marginalisation and deprivation. Zake's influence over Thiza, his younger brother, who is still attending Supatsela High, contrasts sharply with their grandmother's influence. Thiza's brief spell with Chester and his gang attests to the hold the gangster lifestyle has over him because of the influence of his elder brother. Thiza's experience reflects that of not a few African youth: their close proximity to festering cesspools of criminality in their social space, their dependence on criminal earnings for their daily 'legal' survival, the perception of social inclusion and success in mainstream culture seem to be intricately woven into a criminal way of life. For his part Zakes is presented as a 'good' gangster. Most of his criminal activities are portrayed as survival strategies necessary for his family and community. However, his connection to the underworld and his chosen lifestyle is the magnet for his younger brother and the other youth in the film, despite the responsibility he feels towards his family, and his community.

The film allows his criminal lifestyle to be read as a product of historical conditions and long spells of deprivation. The implications of such a reading are rejected by Holland (2010: 12) who remarks that 'South Africa's crime crisis represents indulgence of behaviour that ought not to be tolerated on the grounds of a violent past, former suffering, poverty, fatherlessness or anything else that perpetuates it.' She adds that the post-apartheid aftermath has produced a 'psychopathic society where hardly anybody takes responsibility for anything.'

Despite being a 'good' gangster, Zakes's criminal behaviour is problematic: first, because it represents destructive temptation for his younger brother and other youths and second, because even though Zakes possesses a certain level of self-reflection, his behaviour has the potential to become chaotic and ruthless. Another character, Chester, and his gang, actually embody that possibility and represent the most extreme aspects of the outlaw culture and the attraction it holds for school-going youth. Chester and his criminal associates' relationship with the younger generation, especially parentless and homeless youngsters such as Bobo and Sticks, speaks of the re-marginalisation experienced by youth in the post-apartheid period. Both these youngsters are moral castaways and social pariahs: Bobo's misogyny in episode one (my discussion will return to this later), his veneration of the underworld, as well as Sticks' delinquency, rebelliousness and attraction to Chester's lifestyle are all indications of alienation, while their vacillations between the gangster culture and youth militancy (episode 13) indicate an aspiration to experience a home life and a sense of belonging. At first glance, Bobo and Sticks's ideas seem to allude to certain post-apartheid discussions about the avoidance of responsibilities by youth like them because their tragic lives are closely linked to personal choices and decisions. But on a deeper level, questions around their social position as parentless children point to social disintegration and the many other failed social systems regulating African lives. Bobo's dilemma is evident from the scene (episode one) where he is torn between a life as a drug pusher and going to school. His refusal to be Chester's drug pusher earns him a humiliating baptism in the toilet, where his soul is consecrated to Satan, forming a diabolic connection that dogs him throughout the series. His vacillation between drug addiction and a yearning to be a 'better' person, splashing out money on fast cars, beautiful 'babes' and expensive food, blurs his perceptions of what constitutes a worthy lifestyle. Thus, while Bobo is part of Javas's group of morally upright boys who vow never to commit crime, his background as an AIDS orphan undermines this vow as he is not subject to the moral authority a parent would have provided.

Similar observations can be made in relation to Sticks, a teenager enmeshed in a delinquent culture. According to Albert Cohen (1955), delinquency is a collective, immediate and practical solution to structurally imposed problems. In the South African context, the exclusion of Africans from the mainstream political economy intensified from the beginning of the twentieth century. Amongst the majority of Africans, whose presence in the cities has been criminalised by discriminatory legislation, an immediate response, especially among working class youth, was the formation of a gang culture. *Yizo Yizo* alludes to the long existence of this culture through the representation of Stick and Chester's gang, whose activities dramatise the harrowing findings of Segal et. al.(2001) about youth subcultures: their desensitisation to violence, their self-consciously fashioned criminal careers, their materialism and indifference to the consequences of crime.

The gang's attitude to women in the series reflects the shifting attitudes that have come to define modern, African, gender relations. The colonial reconfiguration of African gender relations along European lines at the beginning of the nineteenth century contributed significantly to an erosion of respect for African womanhood (Comaroff and Comaroff, 1997) and by the post-apartheid period, at the time of *Yizo Yizo*'s production, the position of African women had worsened. During the rapid urbanisation of the twentieth century, labour in the major industries was reserved for males and the activities the women engaged in to support themselves were denounced and criminalised. The presence of women in urban areas gave rise to survival behaviour, or what Musila (2009) terms 'gynocratic transgressions,' that were soon to alienate and disempower them in the racist, political economy of South Africa. Patriarchal discourses from official pronouncements and un-official declarations by the African elite and African traditionalists were laden with moralising denunciations such as

> ... it may be said that as a rule the male native does not give rise to any difficulty ... The real difficulty centres around the native woman, who is the root of most location disturbances. Where she is a woman not in permanent service or living with her husband [...] her main occupation is immorality and liquor selling (Pienaar Commission Report (1925) cited in Cobley, 1997: 100).

Such 'phallocratic anxieties' (Musila, 2009) contributed significantly to twisted perceptions of African women in the cities. Colonial patterns of paternal authority over Africans resonated with traditional African paternalism over women as infantilised members of society. By the post-apartheid period, with the collapse of most forms of adult authority in African society, misogynistic discourses became commonplace with some males, whether young or adult, in private or public spaces, drawing freely on 'phallocratic grammars' of power in an endeavour to silence all women, including women in positions of responsibility.

Bobo's misogynistic discourse, Chester and the gang's stance on their female school mates and the history teacher, Ken's, sexually predatory behaviour towards schoolgirls underscore this attitude. Papa Action's demeanour towards Louisa provides another example. In two of Louisa's infrequent teaching sessions, Papa Action flies a paper plane with sexually loaded inscriptions at her: 'I want to have you for breakfast, lunch and supper'. To which she replies: 'Some filthy ghetto rat is dreaming. I say to you, you better wake up and go relieve yourself in the toilet', a recommendation on which Papa Action menacingly acts (episode three). Much later in the narrative (episode eight), when the gang has established itself, Papa Action suddenly jumps on top of the desks and forces everyone to sing, claiming in the process that they have to respect him. He then takes a girl by force, intending to rape her. Brandishing a condom at the helpless Louisa, he menacingly asks her if she wants it too. He nearly succeeds in raping the school girl but Thulas, the militarised youth, saves her. Papa Action's tyranny outside the classroom, from his disruption of the netball game (episode three) to the disruption of classes because of party preparations (episode six) and his rape of Dudu in the chicken coop (episode seven) while Chester crows, claiming that Dudu should die because of her sins, is part of a pattern of behaviour that exemplifies the gang's disregard for social codes. They see women and women's bodies as sites where male power is enacted, as objects and commodities to be consumed by males for their sexual pleasure and for the re-affirmation of lost African manhood.

Girls' subcultures: The girl child dilemma in *Yizo Yizo*

Another disturbing aftermath of colonial, gender reconfigurations takes the form of (sometimes illegal) sexual relationships across the generation gap. The liaison between Hazel and Sonnyboy, the sugar-daddy taxi driver, dramatises this issue within the context of the precarious, socio-economic situation of many of the minors involved. While pre-colonial Africa sanctioned relationships between older men and younger women, there were cultural safeguards against women's sexual exploitation. With the damage caused to African cultures, chiefly by industrialisation and urbanisation, certain cultural prohibitions fell away and by degrees women fell prey to sexual exploitation through prostitution, economic dependency, and unsanctioned cohabitation practices. By the 1980s transactional relationships had became common. Among the regulations that the apartheid government relaxed in a bid to co-opt the black middle class were those governing permit procurement in the Taxi Industry. This resulted in a sudden boom of minibus taxis operated by males, many of whom dropped out of school because of the general instability in schools during this decade and because of other restrictions, such as age, a policy advocated by the Department of Education and Training. The easy money made by ferrying passengers created an impression that taxi drivers and owners were loaded with cash and this proved to be a magnet for school girls (Mabena, 1996). Their liaison with taxi-drivers outraged most adults in the community. However, the socio-economic situations of many of the girls involved in these relationships ensured their continuance. *Yizo Yizo*'s treatment of this topic is significant because it highlights the persistence of such liaisons and because it shows how this remains an alluring alternative for girls, just as gangsterism does for boys.

Yizo Yizo depicts this reality through an exploration of girls' subcultures. It also throws into sharp relief the influential role played by such relationships within the context of the girls' quest for youthful experience. Girls' subcultures, according to Duck (1983) and Kutnick (1988), are based on trust, loyalty and the confiding of secrets and problems. Although there are positive elements in such friendships, they are apt to be marred by jealousy, conflict and emotional tension, as Orbach and Eichenbaum (1987) point out. In *Yizo Yizo*, these tendencies in the girls' subcultural formations are explored within the politics of family structures. The polarities are between the family structures of Nomsa and Hazel and the kinds of friends girls from these families attract. On Hazel's side the friends she attracts are Mantwa, a girl experienced in the ways of the world and Dudu, an innocent dreamer. As in the case of some of the boys, the parents and family backgrounds of Mantwa and Dudu are not represented, even at the times of Hazel's and Dudu's rape crises. Hazel represents the phenomenon of children as heads of households being susceptible to abuse and exploitation, as is the case with her sister Snowy and later herself when she is abused by her sugar daddy, Sonnyboy. Hazel's relationship with Sonnyboy lays bare one of the most devastating aspects of these girls' subcultures: such relationships do not emancipate them from the prescribed roles of women in the society, but locate them somewhere between prostitution and dependence on the adult male.

Hazel's relationship with Sonnyboy acts as a peg on which to hang the narrative of the girls' private yearnings for, and public manifestations of, their aspirations for the future, their love lives, disappointments, fears and moments of triumph. The relationship also exposes the deficiencies in their perceptions of males, romantic relationships, sexuality and, more generally, the trappings of Western affluence. Whilst Nomsa holds views that are consistent with social morality, Mantwa, Dudu and, to a lesser extent, Hazel, foreground the vulnerability of young black females to exploitation.

Hazel's story demonstrates two aspects regarding the world of girls attracted to the sugar daddy culture: their self-delusion in expecting respectful treatment from the sugar daddies who provide materially for them, and their failure to perceive the moral objections to such relationships. Before her rape, Hazel is dropped at school and collected after school, taken to eat at restaurants (episode four) and taken shopping for clothes (episode five). These attentions presuppose that she understands the nature of the sugar daddy game, and what is expected of her in return for all the gifts showered on her (episode four). However, her private recollections, which she confides to Mantwa, indicate that she and Sonnyboy do not share a common understanding. Hers is a girlish delusion and so, when boys of her age and stage in life approach her, she dismisses them because, like Thiza, they lack material possessions and glamour (episode five). When Sonnyboy demands sex from her in return for all the gifts he has given to her, she is not ready for a sexual relationship. Her resolve to abstain from sex becomes stronger after her rape, when she grows closer to Thiza. His humble position elicits feelings of mutual respect unconnected to material motives; this is far removed from the attitude of the gang members who refer to her contemptuously as *'is'theshana'* (a girl of no consequence) or *'le nto'* (this thing) who can be possessed by anyone who has the will and power as shown in Papa Action's retort, 'take her; she is yours' (episode three) or in Sonnyboy's attitude, which is most visible during the rape scene.

Hazel's relationship with Sonnyboy opens a window onto the fantasy lives of girls like Dudu and Mantwa, and onto the latter's reckless pursuit of her fantasies. The girls' talk in the first episode is about their dream lovers and leisure activities during the vacations, about fashions and house parties. Fantasy underpins their view of gangsters and of their delinquency. Hence Mantwa's failure to make a connection between her sexual desire for these anti-social and misogynistic men and the harm they cause to those closest to her. After Dudu's rape, she does not make the link between her sexual yearnings and their implication in Dudu's trauma. Her lusting after Zakes and his possessions (episode 12) is structurally symmetrical to her lusting after Chester, crystallised in her retort *'ngiyamrhalela yazi'* (I yearn for him you know), a statement that carries connotations of sexual devouring. Because of her sound values, Nomsa sees through Chester's glamour, exposing its falsity. But for Mantwa, Chester's badness holds allure: if he is 'rotten' she 'must have a bite' (episode one), and this comment links with her literally taking a bite out of Chester's apple later on (episode six). According to Andersson (2004), certain items associated with Chester, such as guns, apples, the BMW convertible and clothes, function on a symbolic level as his identity markers, and sharing these with him lays bare a desire to identify with him. Accordingly, Mantwa's biting of Chester's apple functions in a similar way to Thiza's getting into Chester's BMW or carrying his gun: these actions point to a narrowing of the distance between their values and his.

(Un)lawfulness and youth militarism

The militancy displayed by post-apartheid youth in *Yizo Yizo* descends from historical patterns of resistance. African, political radicalism and violent rejoinders to oppressive policies constitute a complex area, as there is an overlap between legitimate, political resistance and the propensity of such resistance to include violent, criminal acts. The portrayal of militarised youth in *Yizo Yizo* reflects this dual inheritance.

The militarised youth is represented in *Yizo Yizo* by Thulas and Gunman who are depicted as a counterpoint to the gangsters and the corrupt teachers in the school. But even Thulas and Gunman use excessive violence to bring about change. Their temporary hold over the school is characterised by chaos and unlawfulness which almost brings it down. But their use of violence seems justifiable in view of the brutality of the gangsters' violence and the teachers' unethical attitude and their relationship with the criminal underworld. The militarised youth present a formidable opposition to the ravages of Chester and Papa Action and are significant in turning the school around, though their methods are open to question. This is observed in an episode where Papa Action and Chester sexually assault Dudu. Gunman's nihilistic response to her rape, symbolised by an AK47 tattooed on his head, brings mayhem in its wake, reminiscent of the students' revolt that began with the Soweto Uprising and continued into the eighties. Questionable as his methods are, he is able to evict the corrupt deputy principal and the gangsters from the school, initiating a series of events that ends with Thulas taking the deputy principal hostage, thereby forcing the district commissioner to intervene on the side of the community at large.

Following the banishment of Chester's gang from the school, they carry out their criminal activities within the community, which finds ways to apprehend the culprits and hand them over to the police. Chester, who by this time has maimed Zakes, is cornered, stripped naked, paraded in public in the most humiliating way and eventually handed over to the police by the vigilantes. So it is through the initiatives and intervention of the militarised youth that the school

community and the community at large are restored to some semblance
of normality.

Representations of organised crime in *Kuyoqhuma Nhlamvana*

By contrasting and comparing the gangster narratives in *Kuyoqhuma
Nhlamvana* with those of *Yizo Yizo*, it is apparent that the former text's
narrativisation is influenced by the latter. Although this may be the
case, *Kuyoqhuma Nhlamvana* has gone a step further and provided
a broader contextual background that introduces new insights not
present in *Yizo Yizo*. This context provides other layers to the reading of
the crime situation in South Africa and does not reduce its complexity
to the youth problem. The additional layers include specific, post-
apartheid social orders that may or may not have antecedents in the
past. Issues such as the rise of criminality perceived as an aftermath of
the economic restructuring of the early 1990s, endemic corruption and
the complete disregard for the law by some government officials are
some that *Kuyoqhuma Nhlamvana* highlight as crucial to understanding
crime in post-apartheid South Africa. By this period these social
groupings have assumed particular characteristics that could not
justifiably be tied to the colonial or apartheid past; they were mostly
to do with greed and with a lifestyle of indulgence and the emerging
consumer culture in black society.

Furthermore, *Kuyoqhuma Nhlamvana*, unlike *Yizo Yizo*, has as part
of its major focus, the parent-generation that is not circumscribed
by indirect adult authority such as teachers or the drug kingpin
or education officials as in the case of *Yizo Yizo*. Rather, it has
foregrounded the family unit and through it has explored how its
dysfunctionality is not attributable to social conditions but to the
value systems the family has come to embrace. This is a significant
move away from the film as the values upheld by the family as a unit
are revealed as also complicit in the perpetuation of crime. Thus the
spotlight falls on the influence that parents and family acquaintances
have on the younger generation.

Whereas *Yizo Yizo* does not emphasise drug syndicates and
organised crime, *Kuyoqhuma Nhlamvana* represents a broad spectrum of

these activities. The novel explores how these organisations and their success are dependent on the corruption that criss-crosses local and the international criminal networks. Furthermore, certain central concerns such as structural unemployment, social fragmentation, family disintegration, economic dislocation and general social decadence are some of the themes of *Kuyoqhuma Nhlamvana* which seem to derive from *Yizo Yizo*. However, the manner in which the novel approaches these issues is different. There is a sense in which it attempts to correct the ambiguous reading of the crime culture in *Yizo Yizo*.

The transboundary factors and criminal families

Kuyoqhuma Nhlamvana's view of crime goes beyond the parochial view that postulates dysfunctionality in families as the root source of youth problems and the crime crisis in South Africa. This novel not only ruptures received ideas about the source and location of crime in South African society but also situates the crime question within a broader framework. The novel suggests that there are transboundary factors that contribute to the upsurge in crime that cannot be explained by simply attributing it to family dysfunctionality. Mngadi, in fact, looks at a fully functional family and situates it in socio-economic conditions that the family, like most families, cannot manipulate to their advantage. Even if this is the case, for Mngadi, it seems, there are fundamental values that form the moral fibre of society. The families of both Sokhele and Nyathi are looked at in relation to this and their activities are positioned against a social conscience, within a social gaze that serves as a moral censure. This moral prism is bound to the African value system which assesses how far these families have veered from social morality.

Ironically, this social gaze also socialises individuals to have certain expectations with regard to social mobility or the trappings of a Western lifestyle. For example, before being retrenched Nyathi's lifestyle was nested in middle class comforts, privileges and affluence. His family lived in the suburbs. His children attended mixed race schools. He owned expensive vehicles and had a middle class wife with a successful career. His retrenchment and subsequent loss of family and social status not only drives him to eke out a lower class living, but he interprets this as a 'great fall' from which he needs to rise again (Mngadi, 27, 32). Obviously, Nyathi's change of fortunes has been brought about by circumstances that are beyond his control. Seemingly, for Mngadi, that is not the burning issue; rather, at the core of the depiction of Nyathi's morality are the strategies he uses as he attempts to deal with unemployment, survival and parental responsibilities.

Equally, the Sokheles, Nyathi's new neighbours and partners in crime, are a functional family. Sokhele's family is traditional and, therefore, patriarchal. It seems stable in spite of its lower class living standards. Sokhele's entrepreneurial job of transporting school children from the township of Sobantu to town schools in Pietermaritzburg sees them through financially and he is able to keep his over-aged son, Jabulani, in school. However, key to the depiction of Sokhele is the simplicity of his mind. Together with his family, he immediately befriends Nyathi when he comes to live amongst them in the RDP section of Sobantu. Because of their concern for Nyathi's economic hardships, Sokhele introduces him to the business of transporting school children. Mngadi's juxtaposition of Sokhele and Nyathi, initially on the basis of differing class positions and later on as members of the same class, allows him to cover the breadth of black society and to reveal those aspects that force families into a tacit understanding of crime. A basic cause that is revealed is genuine economic hardship that reduces people to poverty, a lifestyle that emasculates and dehumanises them as in the case of Nyathi. As for Sokhele he seems to have internalised his class position and has devised strategies to deal with it.

Another reason some families tolerate crime revolves around ambition and a desire for immediate gratification (Mngadi, 27). For example, Nyathi's entrepreneurial venture of transporting schoolchildren is shown to be adequate for his subsistence but as he has to pay maintenance for his children (a demand he considers unfair and spurred by his wife's greed) he finds that he needs to augment the money he makes. He believes becoming involved in crime can help him amass wealth in a short space of time. The issue of child support is used as a pretext for engaging in crime (Mngadi, 7). Nyathi's views of child support reflect the trends seen amongst many men where child support is seen not as their duty but as that of mothers or the state. He is contrasted with Sokhele who, in spite of economic hardships, maintains his over-aged son and puts him through school. Nyathi's shedding of his responsibilities is the first indication of his self-centredness. He laments paying maintenance for his children because he wants to extend his two-roomed RDP home. He would rather spend money on traditional doctors whom he believes can strengthen him against his enemies such as his ex-wife. His view of child maintenance as irksome is not only misplaced but also reflects the deep-seated resentment and alienation caused by the government's economic policies that led to the downsizing of companies, as well as by its inability to create employment. He blames the courts and the government for unfulfilled electoral promises:

> *Kanti isondlo sifuneka nasebanwtini abangasebenzi? Inkantolo iyadakwa phela ngoba yona kufanele ibuze Hulumeni ukuthi maphi lawa mathuba omsebenzi athi uyowavula uma eseqhoqhobele izintambo zombuso* (Mngadi, 6).

> How can the court demand maintenance from people who are unemployed? The court is inconsiderate because it has to ask the government about the job opportunities it promised to create for the people once it gets into power.

Nyathi's remark feigns ignorance as he attempts to avoid his responsibilities. The outburst exposes a self-delusional psychology that justifies inertia through apportioning blame for his predicament to distant entities.

His justification for adopting a life of crime reflects changing social values where traditional notions of good citizenship, honesty and the Protestant values of hard work are no longer positively viewed but, ironically, are perceived to contribute to a life of poverty, humiliation and exclusion. Nyathi's views speak of an emerging culture that celebrates anti-social lifestyles where subversive behaviour is a magnet that draws criminals together in a 'criminal brotherhood' typical of the Mafioso culture. '*Sengifundile ukuthi ukugaba ngezandla ezihlanzekile ube uphilisa okwengulube. Awusikazali'* (I have learned that keeping to clean work leads to an inconsequential life, like that of a pig, and you cannot be helped (Mngadi, 13). He considers this criminal culture to be one of brotherly acts of mutual assistance where the criminal that has acquired most materially is bound by the 'criminal fraternity' to help a fellow criminal seeking a quick break.

Killings as part of the process of getting rich are not new phenomena; before the new political dispensation this crime was linked to ritual murders for 'wealth making medicine', popularly known as '*muthi* murders'. The first novel to explore this phenomenon was Kenneth Bhengu's *Uphuya WaseMshwathi* in the 1940s and RRR Dhlomo also explores the phenomenon in *Izwi Nesithunzi*. According to such beliefs, the individual for whom medicine is made must murder continually for the ritual sacrifice and for his wealth to continue expanding otherwise his blood, or that of his family members, will be demanded as a substitute, failing which the individual will suddenly become bankrupt. Maake, in his article 'Murder they cried,' explores this phenomenon in Lesotho during political transitions when new Chiefs are to be installed. His conclusion suggests that people with specific characteristics and attributes were murdered to help make medicines to strengthen the Chief. While medicine murders continue in the post-apartheid society[4] crimes dealing with international drug syndicates, car theft syndicates and human trafficking syndicates have taken centre stage.

The belief in, and role of, medicine in crime also comes under the spotlight in this novel. In the novel, Nyathi's syndicate believes in traditional medicine, although the novel does not delve into the procurement and the type of medicine Nyathi and his syndicate use. It is, however, so potent that they believe it protects them against arrest (Mngadi, 14, 17, 34–36, 58) and, once they are arrested, can also swing the court of law in their favour during the trial (Mngadi, 77). This belief in medicine is presented as going beyond racial boundaries. One of Nyathi's syndicate members, Moodley, is an Indian who places just as much trust in the power of medicine as his black counterparts in the syndicate (Mngadi, 34). The novel's reading of the use of medicine seems to suggest that this belief is not only far-fetched but also based on ignorance and gullibility. Two instances are shown where their medicine is overpowered by the law; Nyathi loses his case contesting child maintenance despite having consulted a traditional doctor, (Mngadi, 8), and Sokhele is arrested on the first day of transporting dagga despite having consulted an even 'better' and more 'effective' medicine man (Mngadi, 54).

Sokhele's involvement in crime is spurred on by Nyathi's sudden success. Although both believe that their criminal involvement will stop as soon as they have realised their dreams (Mngadi, 44–45), the narrative intimates that leaving criminal life is not easy. The first syndicated crime they deal with is the transportation of dagga in coffins. The centrality of dagga in black South Africa has a historical dimension. Traditionally, it was an accepted stimulant that was not only used on a daily basis by menfolk in the society but was also central in a ritual for preparing regiments on the eve of battle. With modernity and urbanisation, it became criminalised and this is the view on the use of dagga and the centrality of the dagga trade that is taken in the novel. Sokhele not only smokes it, but also keeps large quantities of it in his house and this is secretly stolen by his son, Jabulani, to sell to his school friends and local boys. The narrative hints that Sokhele is unaware of the trouble he courts,

Naye uyise wayenganakile ukuthi ukwenza kwakhe kunomthelela omubi enganeni yakhe. Wayengazi ukuthi uzigwaza ngowakhe. Futhi-ke lo ayezigwaza ngawo unesihlungu esimbi (Mngadi, 43).

His father did not know that his actions had a bad influence on his son. He did not know that he was killing himself with his own spear. In addition the spear that he used was laced with a fatal poison.

The depiction of Sokhele's family points to consciously or unconsciously overlooked activities and values that provide fertile ground for complicated and serious criminal activities later on. As the head of the family, he is blissfully ignorant of the culture of crime he helps establish by setting a bad example to his own offspring. Not only is Sokhele at fault but so is his wife who, though morally upright, is tolerant of and understands Sokhele's habit. This is shown the moment Sokhele is arrested. As soon as she finds out he is being arrested for dagga-related crimes she attempts to hide the stock that Sokhele keeps in the house (Mngadi, 66) and, interestingly, she does not call it dagga but 'Sokhele's tobacco' (*ugwayi kaSokhele*) in an effort to hide its presence from her son. Jabulani is equally tolerant of his father's habits and therefore is part of the criminal culture in this family. As soon as he gathers from a radio news bulletin that his father is in jail for possession of large quantities of dagga, he removes the evidence of his father's misdemeanours and hides it with one of his delinquent friends. Jabulani's act is indicative of how the culture of crime, especially withholding incriminating evidence, permeates from a close private family unit to the society, (Mngadi, 63).

Defeating the ends of justice becomes problematic when brutish, violent criminals are protected from the law, as Sokhele protects them. His testimony during the trial conceals the syndicate's operation and the identity of its members (Mngadi, 77, 88–89). Sokhele, together with the members of the syndicate, are true to their pledge to keep the activities of the syndicate secret. More significantly, Sokhele's act of protecting the syndicate allows for the emergence of more complex and sophisticated crimes which inevitably become harder to solve. Sokhele's syndicate progresses to international drug trafficking with its wider connections and deep secrecy with regard to the identities of the criminals in the chain (Mngadi, 96–115). The syndicate deals with an assortment of chemical drugs from Colombia and these are transported to the rural areas where they are kept safe until bulk buyers come to fetch them.

Criminal exploitation of delinquent youth

Sokhele's imprisonment creates a vacuum in his family and exposes his son, who already indicates that a criminal life is an alluring prospect, to exploitation by Nyathi and his criminal gang. In his absence, Nyathi lures Jabulani into a life of hardcore and organised crime (Mngadi, 119). He creates an illusion of equality between himself and Jabulani, where the generation gap between them and the responsibilities each has toward the other are non-existent (Mngadi, 104, 119–126). For Jabulani, this symbolic rite of passage establishes him as a full adult who can participate in all adult activities including keeping an under-aged, live-in partner in his out-room. Yet this creates confusion because, as a school-going youth, he is still subject both to school authority and that of his mother, yet as an adult he is answerable to no one. This confusion is played out in the resentment and contempt he shows towards a lady teacher, Miss Mthiya, a disciplinarian who does not regard Jabulani as an adult but as a schoolchild who should be subjected to strict disciplinary measures for his misdemeanours. Jabulani's interpretation of her actions reveals his twisted notions about being persecuted and he vows revenge of the most brutal kind. He waylays her with the intention of murdering her in cold blood but is eventually dissuaded by Nyathi who refocuses him on his criminal duties that promise even better rewards than the murder of a lady schoolteacher (Mngadi, 178–181).

Through Jabulani's criminal activities as a drug transporter and middleman, he acquires quick cash and gives large sums to his mother for the upkeep of the family (Mngadi, 129), while he also makes purchases for the home (Mngadi, 146). Some of the most embarrassing outcomes of his father's imprisonment have been the repossession of furniture and kitchen appliances which, in the township gossip mongering culture, have not gone unnoticed. For Jabulani and his mother, the shame of being the talk of the neighbourhood had to be reversed, thus he makes these purchases with the money he has earned from Nyathi's criminal activities (Mngadi, 146). However, he does not reveal the source of his income to his mother. He lies about it, claiming that it is the money he saved from his Saturday part-time work as a gardener (Mngadi, 129). Jabulani, just like the gangsters studied by Segal et al (2001), displays a dual identity – that of provider for his destitute family and that of a ruthless criminal. Jabulani's psychology reveals similarities to those investigated by Segal et. (2001) in more ways than one. Both Jabulani and these youth display gross desensitisation to violence, they have self-consciously fashioned criminal careers for themselves, and they are dedicated consumers, easily swayed by nihilism and indifference to the consequences of crime. Jabulani's continued participation in crime supports a hedonistic, fashionista lifestyle (Mngadi, 98, 104). Although he sells the drugs and teaches his customers how to take these drugs, he does not take drugs himself, as Nyathi has sternly warned him never to do so (Mngadi, 139, 143, 62). All this underscores Steinberg's view (2001: 4), which could apply equally to Jabulani and Nyathi, that crime is 'animated by far more than the exigencies of earning a living'.

Jabulani's participation in criminal activities indicates that he has been 'seduced into crime by a richly imagined world of masculine virtues: fearlessness, bravery, the capacity to wield power' (Altbeker, 2001: 9). As a middleman he protects Nyathi's hierarchy of criminals from the law and his operational title is 'dog'. As a 'dog', he is an inconsequential individual in the hierarchy of the gang; he may be murdered if the activities of the syndicate are threatened (Mngadi: 108). Jabulani's operational name is also symbolic; as a dog he becomes non-human in terms of his ruthless activities at school and in the community. His activities as an 'unleashed dog' are symbolic of the power he wields: intimidation, harassment, murder, induction of school boys into hardcore drugs (which usually occurs in the boys' toilet), womanising, statutory rape and rebellion. All these become his criminal signature in his community in Sobantu (Mngadi, 138–181). Despite Jabulani's notoriety in his community, he evades arrest for a long time.

A consequence of Jabulani's power is a deep loss of innocent, youthful experiences which he cannot realise because of the world he has fashioned for himself with Nyathi's assistance. His school work suffers because he is called at odd hours to perform his duties and he eventually fails his matriculation examinations (Mngadi, 177). He is constantly exposed to violence in the streets as he pushes drugs for Nyathi, who is forever lounging in his expensively remade home with a new pregnant wife while Jabulani, in turn, gets a pittance for his labour – all of which, unbeknown to him, is a form of exploitation. His mother gets to know about the activities that he is involved in and suffers a stroke resulting in her being taken away to a frail care home (Mngadi, 166–167). His mother's sickness, caused by a deep feeling of shame at her family's complicity in destroying the Sobantu youth and community, attests to the weight of the social conscience and its constant gaze on individual actions. Although Nyathi is subjected to this social sanction, he hides behind the high walls of his lavishly decorated home, closing himself off from prying eyes and keeping all rumours at bay. For Jabulani, however, who has to walk the streets of Sobantu as he runs errands for Nyathi, the social conscience becomes overwhelming. Although he displays indifference to it, it affects the only person who matters, his mother. His father is devastated to learn what has happened to his family (Mngadi, 167, 205) and, as a result he suffers from cardiac-related illness and a form of psychosis (Mngadi, 213–214).

Criminal networks

The novel postulates that it is not only Sokhele's secrecy that gives a longer reign to Nyathi's criminal syndicate, but also police institutions. Nyathi and his syndicate are only arrested when the Scorpions have been called in to investigate the failure of Sobantu police to crack the case. This necessitates an investigation of the connections between Captain Sibisi, Nyathi's cousin and Nyathi and Jabulani's activities (Mngadi, 134–137). The plot explores a three-pronged approach in dealing with Nyathi's criminal activities that includes the efforts of the local police, the community and the Scorpions. *Yizo Yizo* only portrayed attempts by the new principal, Grace Letsatsi, who galvanises the community into action; and the community involvement almost veered towards vigilantism, whereas the novel's exploration looks into the establishment of a Community Policing Forum, spearheaded by the ward councillor in collaboration with trusted, local police officials. It is through the combined efforts of the police and the Community Policing Forum that the Scorpions are called in to investigate (Mngadi, 159, 161, 164, 168). The novel's representation of the efforts made by the community to deal with crime is given credence because it draws on the vocabulary of political protests such as caucus meetings, community protection units, pickets and demonstrations against crime by both the community at large and women's groups (Mngadi, 173–175).

Mngadi does not romanticise the involvement of the community in addressing crime. He indicates that forms of adult vigilantism, such as the phenomenon called the 'fathers' that emerged in the late 1980s and acted as a counterweight to the intimidation politics of the comrades (Everett and Sisulu, 1992), can take the law into its own hands. In the novel, a youngster is suspected of stealing two taxis. The taxi drivers subject him to a kangaroo court, decide that he is guilty and seriously assault him (Mngadi, 175–176). Mngadi seems to suggest that the responsibility for dealing with crime cannot be placed solely on community policing forums as, at times, the community is overwhelmed by anger that easily translates into mob justice. This can promote violence and criminality in a society and result in unsolvable cases, such as in this case, where no one is arrested for brutally assaulting the youngster (Mngadi, 175).

Historically, the South African police have not earned the trust and respect of black South Africa because, among other things, they have been viewed as security agents of the apartheid government. After the elections these lingering sentiments remained whilst the police force attempted to change its image. This entailed more solved cases and arrests, effective detective methods and visible policing. In the text such police work is evident. Sergeant Gumede, whose partner has been killed by young drug addicts, is a dedicated, diligent and vigorous policeman. His behaviour represents that adopted by the police after elections, where effectiveness, competence and speed are central to resolving cases. However, his efforts are thwarted by the station commander who is on Nyathi's payroll. The narrative suggests that corrupt police officials not only perpetuate crime but also bring the whole image of the police force into disrepute. Furthermore, they also portray hardworking policeman or policewomen as incompetent.

In the narrative, this outcry against the police is among the major reasons for writing to the National Prosecuting Authority after their failed attempt to plead with the station commander. This suggests that, in South Africa, more hope and trust is placed in this elite force with its effective but, at times, underhand investigative methods. Mngadi seems to celebrate the Scorpions' approach to investigating crime as he asserts that it is through their rigorous undercover investigative tactics that the syndicate and its link to the corrupt station commander is discovered (Mngadi, 201–217).

According to Mngadi, crime in post-apartheid South Africa is a multi-layered structure with links between criminals in the community, law enforcement agencies and imprisoned criminals (Mngadi, 205). The fact that criminals or individuals who are sympathetic to criminal activities are at varying levels in institutions in the society makes crime fighting in the country a very difficult and dangerous task. The networks through which criminals operate involve widespread, interconnected groups in all corners of the country, including rural areas. For Mngadi, it seems the removal of criminals from society is not enough to deal with the scourge of crime. Inmates can control activities outside prison through a web of criminal contacts (Mngadi, 205). Repeat offenders recommit crimes, as is the case with Thekwane, one member of the syndicate, and these ex-convicts form important bridges between those still in prison and the criminal networks outside. It is through Thekwane that contacts and the planning of horrendous criminal activities are established inside the prisons and communicated to the outside (Mngadi, 98–103).

In an attempt to explain the rise of urban crime in the United States in the 1960's, Irvin Walker used an analogy of the crocodile pond: 'if you want to get rid of crocodiles, you can either try to club them all to death or you can drain the pond" (cited in Steinberg, 2000: 5–6). Irvin Walker was convinced that incarceration of criminals alone cannot solve the problem of crime. However, beginning to deal with structures that allow crime to fester, i.e. draining the pond, will go a long way toward combating crime. For Walker, the pond may be structural unemployment, the erosion of nuclear families (extended families in the South African context) and the perspectives of youth on the culture of crime and violence, which beckon them to crime. He concluded by pointing out that 'unless you tackle these [...] the pond will keep breeding crocodiles, no matter how many you club' (cited in Steinberg, 2000: 6).

Conclusion

The analysis of these texts reveals that there are competing perceptions of crime in South Africa because of the mutually exclusive manner in which white mainstream and African cultures have evolved since colonial times. The peculiarity brought about by this parallel existence complicates post-apartheid, crime-intervention strategies. Current crime debates increasingly lay the blame for the upsurge of crime on the current political leadership. These discourses ascribe this disconcerting increase in criminal acts to the (mal)administration of state resources, to the corruption of certain government figures as well as to the general feeling of betrayal of the national consciousness and the expression of this disaffection by re-marginalised black youth. Attempts at dissecting the pathology of crime are undermined by generic theories that fail to acknowledge the uniqueness of South Africa's political economy. However, new viewpoints are emerging that will bring about a paradigm shift in the manner in which crime is approached in South Africa.

These views emphasise the moral foundations of a collective ethos and invite an interrogation of the establishment of law in South Africa. Foremost amongst these is Steinberg (2001) whose studies have demonstrated that in post-apartheid South Africa, the views of some citizens regarding the law are not sufficiently understood and, as a result, some citizens have a conflicting and ambiguous interpretation of the law. Post-apartheid South Africans do not ascribe the same values to the law and this in turn affects their comprehension of what is legal or illegal. Gordon (2006), also focuses on South Africa's criminogenetic past as a logical springboard for discussing crime in post-apartheid South Africa. Through this focus, current patterns of crime, both by the state and citizens across the racial divide can be traced to their root causes. The current patterns of crime and the culture of retribution, according to Gordon, are traceable to colonial injustices which were, in essence, unlawful.

Endnotes

1 Reconstruction and Development Programme.

2 It was South Africa's elite crime fighting unit that was disbanded by President Zuma after he assumed office in 2009.

3 For comments on the problematic images of crime, misogyny, the glamorisation and celebration of crime in the series, see B. Peterson, 2001; R. Smith, 2000 and F. B. Andersson, 2004.

4 There are numerous media reports on nurses selling body parts and the murder of children and adults alike for their private organs for *muthi* purposes. The newspaper reports of 13 November 2007 carry an article about the decapitated torso of a boy that was discovered the previous week. It is believed that the head of the boy was needed for *muthi* purposes.

7

Conclusion

Declining interest in formal, written African-language fiction and the increase in the production and significance of other forms of artistic products in South Africa have encouraged the application of critical responses that, while seeking new ways to critique, also offer tools to appreciate emerging forms. This book takes the view that Barber's (1987, 1997, 2000) model is valuable when assessing African-language fiction as part of the African popular arts or popular culture. As a point of departure, the book argues that African narratives, old and new, share similar views and psychological outlooks. These views or discourses are generally found in the popular imagination of African society, the mainstay for creative compositions of any art form, and are generated and recycled in the society in numerous ways, taking into context the material conditions of the forms through which they are reproduced. The questions that arise relate to why new forms share allusive references with old ones and whether such repetitions will not yield to stagnation and reversion to old traditions, an aspect upon which the lack of development or under-development of Africa is blamed and for which the literary tradition is also lambasted. Another question might focus on issues of stylistic uniqueness which is observed in new art forms elsewhere.

A glance at the criticism produced in response to the African-language fiction crisis underlined, repeatedly, issues raised by these questions. None of this criticism has so far investigated the imperatives behind the continuation of discourses underpinning this literary tradition in the manner that Barber's model allows. Her insights into African art or African culture as a whole address the conundrum that has remained with the literary tradition for more than a hundred years. Her approach allows, for the first time in the context of the African-language literary tradition in South Africa, a conversation with other narrative and artistic forms in the continent and in the diaspora. It also allows for an exploration of how the products from these areas contribute in various ways in providing aesthetic tools for studying work produced by Africans or people of African descent. Irele (2001), who has conducted a groundbreaking study into the nature of African expressive forms, or what he calls the African imagination, offers explanations on how this relationship exists in black societies that were separated by time, space and other socio-economic and political disparities. He points out that the basic African traditional framework of thought in most black expressive forms is orality which in turn is a profound way of expressing everyday life experiences in contemporary black societies. Oral forms and genres become a Grand Narrative from which meta-narratives are derived and reproduced endlessly in the manner that Barber explains. Furthermore, the actual experiences of black people throughout the world have created a desire for a collective vision that reiterates conscious ways through which expressive forms must invoke a connection with Africa. By and large, Africa and its ethos have remained the main source of inspiration for the creative compositions of these diverse communities. The art forms from Caribbean (Cooper, 1994) and African-Americans communities (Watkins, 1998; Hall, 1997; Hooks, 1994) share interesting links with African ones. Equally criticism abounds where issues of aesthetics emphasise these links and in most instances these aesthetics taper down to orality as both the springboard for creative composition and as an analytical tool, in a manner very similar to Barber's suggestions. Significantly, the basis of Barber's model is an exploration of African orality and how it interconnects with popular culture.

Perhaps at this juncture we need to recapture what Barber's generative materialism is all about. Barber's (2000) version of popular culture is a theoretical paradigm that best suits the fundamental needs of composing and analysing African narratives and the vast taxonomy of other popular art forms, irrespective of whether these narratives are drawn from the elite or from subaltern cultures of African society. This model is a result of extensive research that explores the nature of orality and popular culture amongst modernising Africans. Contemporary African culture is a mixture of traditions from different societies which continue to influence one another in ways significant and meaningful to people who practise it. The coming together of cultures, also termed creolisation, is at the heart of Barber's analyses of African everyday culture, and to date this approach has opened and yielded many interesting research focus areas which have been overlooked. It has also fostered new perspectives in thinking about the relationship between local and transnational cultures during this globalisation stage.

The re-evaluation of orality implicit in Barber's approach is supported by Finnegan, who points out that

> oral texts are no longer automatically assumed to belong to the past with deep roots in traditional culture, fit objects to be scripturalised into written texts. Scholars now look for their examples to young people as well as old, to industrial workers and broadcast performers, and to disruptive and innovative forms, not just the old guards. Change and contemporaneity are now part of the picture (2007: 180).

Finnegan's views are a crystallisation of Barber (1987, 1997) and Appiah's (1991) views of the later 1980s and early 1990s when black urban popular cultures were subjected to systematic study and were found to have linkages with the oral tradition. This model reflects a genealogy of discursive traditions on paradigms that account for the historical, socio-economic and cultural issues affecting the black expressive tradition. In that way it engages with a vast repertoire of debates from across the African diaspora around issues of black expressive art.

In-depth discussion of further trajectories emanating from this model is not possible here. However, I cannot end this discussion without flagging some of the fascinating studies that enter into a dialogue with the stances and examples mentioned here. Currently there are numerous published studies that are offshoots of this paradigm (see Katrien Pype, 2004, 2006, 2007a, b, c, 2008, 2009, 2010, 2011a, b; Frederiksen and Wilson, 1997). Pype's work covers popular rituals, orthodox and charismatic churches, audience studies of television serials, visual culture and media. Most of her work is drawn from examples in Kinshasa. Frederiksen and Wilson's work studies Nigerian popular culture and its audiences. In South Africa, the most conspicuous researcher in the field is Liz Gunner, whose work on orality and its migrations stretches over three decades. Gunner, in her work, engages with Barber's theory in new and exciting ways. Her work on South African radio (Gunner 2000) and *isicathamiya* music (Gunner, 2003, 2009 and 2010) points to future trajectories for this theory and popular culture studies generally. At the University of Cape Town, there are currently studies underway on audiences and Nollywood films that draw from tenets of this theory. I have also conducted some research (to be published in a special issue of *African Identities* in 2012) on the use of mobile telephones and popular songs. This study investigates how popular forms composed by ordinary people as they negotiate everyday existence are appropriated by politics and corporate South Africa for political and commercial purposes. I argue that the 'unofficial' mass communication form embodied in mobile telephony, which is regarded as an alternative communication tool in media circles, has been used by political strategists to induce a false consciousness (Fabian, 1997) and by corporate South Africa to exploit, for profit, cultural notions of survival that have been formed by societies in the margin of South Africa's economy.

I have two projects underway: one on post-apartheid black opera and the other on black independent film production in South Africa. In the first project I investigate the African aesthetic in the composition of opera, which is a high-brow European art form. It should immediately be observed that South African black opera draws on the syncretic models identified by Barber. Both Mzilikazi Khumalo's *Princess Magogo*

(2002) and Vundla, Ndodana-Breen and Wilensky's *Winnie* (2011), integrate into their composition artistic and performance genealogies that have been sourced from the vast taxonomy of popular culture. These range in the case of the latter opera, from protest songs, choral music, urban popular music, theatre and media. In the case of the former opera, Khumalo has lavishly drawn from oral performances and choral traditions to compose his *Princess Magogo*. Yet the over-arching structure of the operas is that of traditional European opera.

In the second project on South African black independent films I investigate, firstly, Nollywood influence on the production of these films. Since the entry of Nollywood films into South African film space and culture four identifiable cineastes have emerged: Vendawood, Sollywood, Joziwood and Crazy Entertainers. These cineastes have drawn on Nollywood production styles and film circulation strategies to gain entry into the highly exclusionary and tightly controlled South African cinema industry and state, pay and satellite television. The films produced by these companies have been extremely successful with subaltern audiences to the extent that some film production companies drew the attention of corporate South Africa. The production company Crazy Entertainers, in particular, has been connected with the marketing strategies of Kentucky Fried Chicken. This company observed the commercial viability of Crazy Entertainers and positioned itself in such a way that it exploited the marginal markets that had been reached already by Crazy Entertainers through their films. Equally DSTV, which is South Africa's Multichoice's multi-channel digital satellite service, launched in 1995, took notice of the proliferation of films by these independent film companies and created a channel, Mzansi Magic, a sister channel to Africa Magic. Mzansi Magic gives space to South African productions in this category as well as other categories and Africa Magic, to Nollywood ones. The commercial viability of Nollywood and its influence on the South African popular arts scene have forced, for the first time in African Cinema politics, some recognition of a vast class of films that is giving space to voices from marginalised sections of Africa's population. As in many instances these films are made not by known production companies or professional directors, but are produced by ordinary people.

The second aspect I wish to investigate with these films is the kind of narratives that they foreground. Most of the narratives from these films have been conceptualised from a particular vantage point that gives credence to life as lived by ordinary people, some form of pedestrian knowledge, in a manner that Barber (2000) describes with her findings of Yoruba travelling theatre productions. Quite fascinatingly, the nature of stories churned out by these independent films has given rise to the epithet 'Ekasi' stories (Ghetto stories) which the South African pay television channel, etv, has jumped upon to market its brand of film programmes by some independent filmmakers whose outlook fits into etv's mainstream sensibilities. This epithet emphasises their locality and the fact that they are quotidian. Reading these films as texts of African authentic sensibilities rather than as the musings and escapism of the subalterns will help us to understand the depth and breadth of African popular imagination in South Africa.

I point to all these examples to demonstrate how far one can reach in the study of popular arts or popular culture using approaches like Barber's, that help excavate previously marginalised discourses. As pointed out by Liz Gunner (2011),[1] there is so much happening in our popular cultural scene where African languages are used as media to mediate modern experiences but, because we are not using the correct lenses to observe these happenings, everything is lost. With the correct lenses we are able to observe and reveal the richly-textured pedestrian knowledge and the constant making of meaning extrapolated from these art forms. This shift in paradigm, in terms of studying literature in African languages, is far reaching. Firstly, it encourages us to reconsider what falls into the African literary tradition. By opening up this category we are able to read interdisciplinarily across all art forms. Secondly, the aesthetic conundrum that has beset African-language literatures for the past hundred years is overcome through the application of this approach. Lastly, the application of this model will bring back enthusiasm for the study of literature and re-establish the reading culture of African-languages literature as was the case with the first mission-educated African intellectuals. It is my conviction that an appropriate theoretical model through which to assess expressive forms encourages lively debates that have far reaching results for growth.

Endnotes

1   Gunner mentioned this informally in our Performance Culture and Social Meaning reading group, at WISER, University of the Witwatersrand.

References

Abrahams, R. D. 1983. *The Man-of-words in the West Indies: Performance and the Emergence of Creole Cultures*. Baltimore: Johns Hopkins University Press.

Akinnaso, F. N. 1985. 'On the similarities between spoken and written language'. In *Language and Speech*, 28.4: 323–59.

Altbeker, A. 2001a. 'Policing the frontier: seven days with the hijacking investigating unit'. In J. Steinberg, (ed.), *Crime Wave: The South African Underworld and its Foes*. Johannesburg: University of the Witwatersrand Press: 24–40.

—2001b. 'Who are we burying? The death of a Soweto gangster'. In J. Steinberg, (ed.). *Crime Wave: The South African Underworld and its Foes*. Johannesburg: University of the Witwatersrand Press: 88–94.

Alvarez-Altman, G. 1981. 'A methodology to literary onomastics: an analytical guide for studying names in literature'. In *Literary Onomastics Studies*, 8: 220–230.

Andersson, F. B. 2004. *Intertextuality and Memory in Yizo Yizo*. PhD thesis. Johannesburg: University of the Witwatersrand.

Appiah, K. A. 1991. 'Is the Post – in Postmodernism the Post – in Postcolonial? In *Critical Inquiry*: 336–357.

Aschroft, B., Griffiths, G. and Tiffin, H. 1989. *The Empire Writes Back: Theory and Practice in Post-Colonial Literatures*. London: Routledge.

Azikiwe, M. 1969. *Renascent Africa*. New York: U Press.

Bakhtin, M. M. 1981. *The Dialogic Imagination. Four Essays*: Austin: University of Texas Press.

Barber, K. 1987. 'Popular arts in Africa'. In *African Studies Review* 30 (3): 1–78.

—1995. 'African-language literature and post-colonial criticism'. In *Research in African Literatures*, 26 (4): 3–30.

—1997. *Readings in African Popular Culture*. Bloomington and Indianapolis: Indiana University Press.

—1999. 'Quotation in the Constitution of Yoruba Oral Texts'. In *Research in African Literature*, 30 (2): 17–41.

—2000. *The Generation of Plays: Yoruba Popular Life in Theatre*. Bloomington and Indianapolis: Indiana University Press.

Barthes, R. 1985. *The Responsibility of Forms: Critical Essays on Music, Art and Representation*. (tr), by R. Howard. Berkeley: University of California Press.

Bartlet, O. 1996. *African Cinemas: Decolonising the Gaze*. London and New York: Zed Books.

Berglund, A. 1889. *Zulu Thought Patterns and Symbolism*. London: C Horst.

Bhavnani K., Foran, J., and Kurian, P. A. 2003. *Feminist Futures: Re-imaging Women, Culture and Development*. London, NY: Zed Books.

Bhengu, K. 1965. *UNyambose noZinitha*. Pietermaritzburg: Shuter and Shooter.

Bhengu, V. M. 1998. *Seziyosengwa Yinkehli*. Pietermaritzburg: Reach Out Publishers.

Biesele, M. 1993. *Women Like Meat*. Johannesburg: University of the Witwatersrand Press.

Boloka, G. 2003. 'Cultural studies and the transformation of the music industry: some reflections on kwaito'. In H. Wasserman and S. Jacobs (eds.). *Shifting Selves: Post-Apartheid Essays on Mass Media*. Cape Town: Kwela Books: 97–107.

Brecht, B. 2000 [1931] *The Threepenny Lawsuit. Brecht on Film and Radio.* Trans. M. Silberman, 147–199. London: Metheun.

Bryant, A. T. 1929. *Olden Times in Zululand and Natal*. London: Longmans, Green and Co.

Buthelezi, J. M. 1996. *Impi YaboMdabu Isethunjini*. Cape Town: Maskew Miller Longman.

Callaway, H. 1913. *The Religious System of AmaZulu*. Natal: Marianhill.

Caminero-Santangelo, B. 2005. *African Fiction and Joseph Conrad: Reading Postcolonial Intertextuality*. New York: University of New York Press.

Canonici, N. N. 1993. *The Zulu Folktale Tradition*. Durban: University of Natal, Zulu Language and Literature.

Cele, W. L. 1996. *Ngiyokhohlwa Ngifile*. Pietermaritzburg: Shuter and Shooter.

Chapman, M. 1996. *Southern African Literature*. London: Longman.

Chidi, A. 1989. *The Theory of African Literature: Implications for Practical Criticism*. London: ZED Books Ltd.

Chiji, A. 1998. 'Folklore and the African-Caribbean narrative imagination: The example of Roy Heath'. In *Research in African Literature* 29: 82–97.

Childers, J. and Hentzi, G. (eds.). 1995. *The Columbia Dictionary of Modern Literary and Cultural Criticism*. New York: Colombia University Press.

Chrispo, C. O. 2003. *Tradition, Identity, Performance: Black South African Popular Music on SABC Television*. Johannesburg: University of the Witwatersrand Press.

Cobley, A. G. 1990. *Class and consciousness: The Black Petty Bourgeoisie in South Africa, 1924 to 1950*. New York: Greenwood Press.

Cohen, Albert. 1955. *Delinquent Boys: The Subculture of the Gang*. London: Collier Macmillan.

Cohen, R. 2007. 'Creolization and cultural globalization: the soft sounds of fugitive power', *Globalization* 4(3): 369–373.

Comaroff, J. L and J. 1997. *Of Revelation and Revolution: The Dialectics of Modernity on a South African Frontier*. Chicago: Chicago University Press.

Cooper, C. 1993. *Noises in the Blood: Orality, Gender and the 'Vulgar' Body of Jamaican Popular Culture*. London: MacMillan Caribbean.

Coplan, D. 1985. *In Township Tonight! South Africa's Black City Music and Theatre*. Johannesburg: Ravan Press.

Cornwall, A. D. 1996. *For Money Children and Peace: Everyday Struggles in Southwestern Nigeria*. PhD Dissertation, S.O.A.S., University of London.

Couzens, Tim. 1985. *The New African: A Study of the Life and Work of HIE Dhlomo*. Johannesburg: Ravan Press.

Culleton, C. A. 1994. *Names and Naming in Joyce*. Madison: University of Wisconsin Press.

Davidson, B. 1964. *Which way Africa? The Search for a new society.* Harmondsworth: Penguin.

Davis, J. A. 1962. 'Pan Africanism: Nascent and mature'. In *Pan-Africanism Reconsidered* by the American Society of African Culture (ed.), Berkeley and Los Angeles: University of California Press.

Davis, P. 1994. *In Darkest Hollywood: Exploring the Jungles of Cinema's South Africa.* Randburg: Raven Press.

Dhlomo, H. I. E. 1977. 'Literary Theory and Criticism'. In N. Visser (ed.), *Special Issue of English in Africa* 4 (7).

Dhlomo, R. R. R. 1935. *Indlela Yababi.* Pietermaritzburg: Shuter and Shooter.

Dovey, L. 2009. *African film and film culture: Adapting violence to the screen.* New York: Columbia University Press.

Drummond, L. 1980. The transatlantic nanny: Notes on a comparative semiotics of the family in English-speaking societies. *American Ethnologist* 5: 30–43.

Dube, J. L. 1929. *Insila KaShaka.* Pietermaritzburg: Shuter and Shooter.

Duck, S. 1983. *Friends for Life: The Psychology of Close Relationships.* London: Harvester Press.

Ergang, R. 1967. *Europe: From the Rennaisance to Waterloo.* Longton, Massachussetts: D C Heath and Company.

Evans, M. 2010. Mandela and the televised birth of the rainbow nation. *National Identities* 12 (3): 309–326.

Evans, N. and M. Seeber (eds.) 2000. *The Politics of Publishing in South Africa.* London: Holger Ehling: 127–159.

Everett, D. and E. Sisulu, 1992. *Black Youth in Crisis: Facing the Future.* Johannesburg: Ravan Press.

Fabian, J. 1997. Popular culture in Africa, in *Readings in African popular culture*, K, Barber (ed.). Bloomington and Indianapolis: Indiana University Press: 18–28.

Fairclough, G. T. 1986. 'New Light on Old Zion'. In K. B. Harder, (ed.), *Names and their Varieties: A Collection of Essays on Onomastics.* Lanham: University Press of America. 89–99.

Finnegan, R. 1970. *Oral Literature in Africa.* Oxford: Oxford University Press.

—2007. *The Oral and Beyond: Doing Things with Words in Africa*. Chicago: University of Chicago Press.

Fletcher, A. 1964. *Allegory: The Theory of a Symbolic Mode*. Ithaca: Cornell University Press.

Flores, J. 2009. *The Diaspora Strikes Back: Carribeno Tales of Learning and Turning*. New York: Routledge.

Frederiksen, B. F. and Wilson, F. (eds.). 1997. *Livelihood, Identity and Instability*. Copenhagen: Centre for Development Research.

Fuery, P. 2000. *New Developments in Film Theory*. New York: St Martin's Press (Scholarly and Reference Division).

Gcumisa, M. S. S. 1978. *Inkatha Yabaphansi*. Pietermaritzburg: Shuter and Shooter.

Gérard, A. S. 1971. *Four African Literatures: Xhosa, Sotho, Zulu, Amharic*. Berkeley: University of California Press.

—1981. *African-languages literatures*. Washington DC: Three Continents.

—1983. *Comparative Literature and African Literatures*. Goodwood: Via Afrika.

Genette, G. 1999. *The Aesthetic Relation*. Ithaca, New York: Cornell University Press.

Gininda, J. M. 1997. *Ukukhanya Kokusa*. Pretoria: Van Schaik.

Gordon, D. 2006. *Transformation and Trouble: Crime, Justice and Participation in Democratic South Africa*. Ann Arbor: University of Michigan Press.

Granqvist, R. 1993. 'Storylines, Spellbinders and Heartbeats: Decentering the African Oral-Popular Discourse', in *Major Minorities: English Literature in Transit*, R. Granqvist (ed.) Netherlands: Rodopi B.V.

Green, G. and Kahn, C. 1985. *Making a Difference: Feminist Literary Criticism*. London: Metheun and Co. Ltd.

Grobbler, G. M. M. 1995. 'Creative African-language writing in South Africa: Writers unshackled after apartheid? In *South African Journal of African Languages* 15 (2): 56–59.

Groenewald, H. C. 2001. 'Tradition and reconstruction: The Culture Play in Zulu'. In *South African Journal of African Languages*, 21 (1): 33–44.

Guerrero, E. 1993. *Framing Blackness: The African American Image in Film*. Philadelphia: Temple University Press.

Gugler, J. 2003. *African Film: Re-imagining a Continent*. Bloomington: Indiana University Press.

Gunner, E. 1995. 'Clashes of interest: gender, status and power in Zulu praise poetry'. In G. Furniss and E. Gunner (eds.), *Power, Marginality and African Oral Literature*. Cambridge: Cambridge University Press: 185–196.

Gunner, L. 2000. Zulu Radio Drama in Sarah Nuttall and Cheryl-Ann Michael (eds.). *Senses of Culture: South African Culture Studies*. Cape Town: Oxford University Press, 216–230.

—2009. 'Post-apartheid Autobiographies and the Genre of Isicathamiya', in Ben Carton et al. eds., *Zulu Enigmas*. Pietermaritzburg: University of KwaZulu Natal Press.

—2010. 'The Road, The Song and The Citizen: Singing After Violence in KwaZulu Natal', in *Mediations of Violence in Africa: Fashioning New Futures from Contested Pasts*, Lidwien Kapteijns and Annemiek Richters (eds.), Leiden: Brill/Johannesburg: Wits University Press, 75–105.

Gwala, M. and Gunner, E. 1991. *Musho! Zulu Popular Praises*. East Lansing: Michigan State University.

Hall, S. 1997. 'What Is This "Black" in Black Popular Culture?', in *Representing Blackness: Issues in Film and Video*, Valerie Smith, (ed.). Rutgers: The State University: 123–135.

Hannerz, U. 1997. The world in creolization, in *Readings in African popular culture*, K. Barber (ed.). Bloomington and Indianapolis: Indiana University Press: 12–18.

Harder, K. B. 1986. *Names and their Varieties: A Collection of Essays on Onomastics*. Lanham: University Press of America.

Hawthorn, J. 1992. *A Concise Glossary of Contemporary Literary Theory*. Kent: Edward Arnold (a division of Hodder and Stoughton).

Haynes. J. 2000. *Nigerian video Film*. US: Ohio University Center for International Studies.

Herbert, R. K. 1995. 'The Sociolinguistics of Personal Names: Two South African case studies'. In *South African Journal of African Languages* 15 (1): 1–8.

Hofmeyr, I. 1993. *We Spend Our Years as a Tale that is Told.* Johannesburg: University of the Witwatersrand Press.

Holland, H. 2010. 'Drifting Down as Time Goes By'. *The Star* (2 March): 12.

Hondo Med 1996. 'What is Cinema for us?' In Imruh Bakari and Mbye Cham, (eds.). *African Experiences of Cinema.* London: British Film Institute: 39–41.

hooks, b. 1994. *Outlaw Culture: Resisting Representations.* New York: Routledge.

Imruh, B. & Mbye, C. 1996. *African Experiences of Cinema.* London: British Film Institute.

Irele, F. A. 2001. *The African Imagination: Literature in Africa and the Black Diaspora.* Oxford: Oxford University Press.

Ives, S. 2007. Mediating the neoliberal nation: Television in post-apartheid South Africa. In *ACME: An International E-Journal for Critical Geographies* 6 (1): 153–173.

Jabavu, D. T. 1921. *Bantu Literature.* Cape Town: Lovedale.

Jacobs, S. 2011. Post-apartheid South African social movements, in *Popular media, democracy and development,* Herman Wasserman (ed.). London and New York: Routledge Taylor Francis Group: 137–150.

Jeffries, J. 1992. 'Towards a redefinition of the urban: the collision of culture', in *Black Popular Culture.* Seattle: Centre for the Arts, New York and Bay Press: 156–163.

Jones, A. 2002. 'Historical writing about everyday life'. In *Journal of Cultural Studies* 15: (1) 5–16.

Kamwangamalu, N. M. 2004. 'The language planning situation in South Africa', in *Language Planning and Policy: Vol. 1: Botswana, Malawi, Mozambique and South Africa,* R. B. Baldauf et al. (ed.) Clevedon: Multilingual Language Matters: 197–281.

Kellog, R. and Scholes, R. E. 1966. *The Nature of Narrative.* London: Oxford University Press.

Khumalo, F. 1998. *Sunday Times,* 9th August: 17.

Knepper, W. 2006. 'Colonization, creolisation and globalization: the art and ruses of bricolage'. In *Small Axe* 10 (3): 70–86.

Koopman, A. 1987. 'The praises of Young Zulu men'. In *Theoria*
70: 41–54.

—1990. 'Some notes on the morphology of Zulu clan names'. In *South African Journal of African Languages* 10 (4): 333–337.

—1992. '-So and -No: Aged parents in new garb', in *South African Journal of African Languages* 12 (3): 97–100.

Kristeva, J. 1969. 'Word, Dialogue and Novel' in *Desire in Language: A Semiotic Approach to Literature and Art*. Roudiez, L.S. (tr.). New York: Columbia.

Kruger, L. 2010. Critique by stealth: aspiration, consumption and class in post-apartheid television drama. *Critical Arts* 24 (1): 75–98.

Kunene, D. P. 1992a. 'Language, literature and the struggle for liberation in South Africa', in *Perspectives on South African English Literature*, edited by M. Chapman, C. Gardener and E. Mphahlele. Johannesburg: A. D. Donker.

—1994. 'Characterization, realism and social inequality in the novels of C. L. S. Nyembezi'. In *South African Journal of African Languages* 14 (4): 155–162.

Kunene, M. 1989. 'Poetry and Society in South Africa', in Gibbons, R (ed.) *Writers from South Africa: fourteen writers on culture, politics and literary theory and activity in South Africa*. North-Western University: Evanston: TriQuarterly Books: 497–513.

Kutnick, P. 1988. *Relationships in the Primary School Classroom*. London: P. Chapman Publishers.

Laden, S. 1997. 'Middle class matters, or how to keep whites whiter, colours brighter, and blacks beautiful'. In *Critical Arts* 11 (1): 120–141.

Lardner, J. 1972 'Introduction to Tomorrow's Tomorrow: The Black Woman', in *Feminism and Methodology*, S. Harding, (ed.). Bloomington and Indianapolis: Indiana University Press.

Lefebvre, H. 1991. [1947]. *Critique of Everyday Life*, Vol. I. Trans. John Moore. London: Verso.

Lindfors, B. 1973. *Folklore in Nigerian Literature*. New York: Africana Publishing.

Maake, N. P. 1992. 'A brief survey of trends in the development of African Language Literature in South Africa: With Specific

Reference to Southern Sotho'. In *African Languages and Cultures* 5, (2): 157–188.

—2000. 'Publishing or perishing: Books, people and reading in African Languages in South Africa'. In *The Politics of Publishing in South Africa* by Nicholas Evans and Monica Seeber (eds.). London: Holger Ehling: 127–159.

Mabena, S. 1996. *Violence in Diepkloof: Youth Gang Subcultures in Diepkloof, Soweto*. Johannesburg: University of the Witwatersrand Press. Department of African Literature.

Makgamatha, P. M. 1992. 'The functionality of character in Northern Sotho narrative'. In *South African Journal of African Languages* 12 (2): 84–88.

Makhudu, K. D. P. 1995. 'Introduction to flaaitaal'. In J. Mesthrie, (ed.). *Social History: Studies in South African Sociolinguistics*. Cape Town: David Phillip: 298–304.

Masondo, M. M. 1990. *Isigcawu Senkantolo*. Johannesburg: Educum.

—1991. *Iphisi Nezinyoka*. Johannesburg: Educum.

—1994a. *Ingwe Nengonyama*. Midrand: Educum Publishers.

—1994b. *Ingalo Yomthetho*. Pietermaritzburg: Shuter and Shooter.

—1994c. *Kanti Nawe*. Pietermaritzburg: Shuter and Shooter.

—1994d. *Ngaze Ngazenza*. Pretoria: De Jager-HAUM.

—1994. *Kunjalo-ke Emhlabeni*. Midrand: Educum.

—1996. *Kungenxa Yakho Mama!*. Halfway House: Educum.

—1997. *Inkunzi Isematholeni*. Pretoria: Van Schaik Publishers.

—1998. *One Act Plays: A Collection of One Act Stage, radio and TV Plays*. Pretoria: Academica.

—2004. *Sixolele*. Braamfontein: Macmillan South Africa.

Mathenjwa, F. L. 1994. *Ithemba Lami*. Pretoria: Actua Press.

Mathonsi, N. 2002. 'Social commitment in *Ulaka LwabeNguni* (by I. S. Kubheka). In *South African Journal of African Languages* 3 (22): 206–214.

Mbatha, M. O. 1996. *Amanoni Empilo*. Pietermaritburg: Shuter and Shooter.

Mbhele, N. F. 1995. *Izivunguvungu Zempilo*. Pietermaritzburg: Reach Out Publishers.

McClusky, A. T. 2009. *The Devil you Dance With: Film Culture in the New South Africa*. Urbana and Chicago: University of Illinois Press.

Mkhize, D. 1965. *Ngavele Ngasho*. Shuter and Shooter.

Mncwango, L. J. 1951. *Manhla Iyokwendela Egodini*. Shuter and Shooter.

—1959 *Ngenzeni*. Pietermaritzburg: Shuter and Shooter.

Mngadi, J. M. 1995. *Umbele Wobubele*. Pretoria: Actua Press.

Mngadi, M. J. 1966. *Imiyalezo*. Edenvale: KwaZulu Booksellers.

—2005. *Usumenyezelwe-ke Umcebo*. Pietermaritzburg: Shuter and Shooter.

Mngadi, M. R. 2004. *Kuyoqhuma Nhlamvana*. Pietermaritzburg: Shuter and Shooter.

Mokitimi, M. 1997. *The Voice of the People: Proverbs of the Basotho*. Pretoria: UNISA Press.

Mokwena, S. 1992. 'Living on the wrong side of the law: marginalization, youth and violence', in *Black Youth in Crisis*, D. Everett and E. Sisulu, (eds.). Johannesburg: Raven Press: 30–51.

Molefe, L. 1991. *Ngiwafunge Amabomvu*. Pietermaritburg: Heinemann.

Monaco, J. 1980. *How to Read a Film: The Art, Technology, Language, and History and Theory of Film and Media*. Oxford: Oxford University Press.

Monye, A. A. 1996. *Proverbs in African Orature: The Aniocha-Igbo Experience*. New York: University Press of America, Inc.

Mpe, P. and Seeber, M. 2000. 'The politics of book publishing in South Africa: a critical Overview'. In N. Evans and M. Seeber, (eds.). *The Politics of Publishing in South Africa*. London: Holger Ehling: 15–42.

Msimang, C. T. 1976. *Izulu Eladuma eSandlwane*. Pretoria: Van Schaik.

—1986. *Folktale Influence on the Zulu Novel*. Pretoria. Acacia Books.

—1995. *Igula Lendlebe Aligcwali*. Pretoria: Kagiso Publishers.

—1996. *Walivuma Icala*. Pietermaritburg: Shuter and Shooter.

Mtuze, P. T. 1994. 'Tasks and challenges facing the indigenous literatures in South Africa'. In *South African Journal of African Languages* 14 (3): 128–132.

Mulaudzi, P. A. and Paulos, G. 'The "tsotsitaal" language variety of Venda'. In *South African Journal of African Languages* 2001 (22): 1–8.

Musila, Grace. 2009. 'Phallocracies and Gynocratic Transgressions: Gender, State Power and Kenyan Public Life.' *Africa Insight* 39 (1): 39–57.

Muthwa, S. K. R. 1996. *Isifungo*. Pretoria: Actua Press.

Ndebele, N. N. T. 1941. *UGubudele Namzimuzimu*. Johannesburg: University of the Witwatersrand.

Neethling, S. J. 1985. 'Naming in Xhosa folk-tales'. In *South African Journal of African Languages* 5 (3): 88–90.

—1988. 'Voorname in Xhosa'. In *Nomina Africa* 2 (2): 223–238.

—1994. 'Xhosa nicknames'. In *South African Journal of African Languages* 14 (2): 88–92.

—2000. 'An Onomastics Renaissance: African Names to the Fore'. In *South African Journal of African Languages* 20 (3): 207–216.

Ngonyani, D. 2001. 'Onomastic devices in Shaaban Robert's narratives'. In *Journal of African Cultural Studies* 14 (2): 125–136.

Ngubo, G. 1996. *Yekanini Ukuzenza*. Roggebaai: Kwela.

Ngugi wa Thiong'o 1986. *Decolonising the Mind: The Politics of Language in African Literature*. London: J. Currey.

Nhlapho, Phindile J. 1998. *Maskanda: The Zulu Strolling Musicians*. Johannesburg: University of the Witwatersrand Press.

Noakes, B. O. and Aub-Buscher, G. 2003. *The Franchophone Caribbean Today: Literature, Language Culture*. Barbados: University of the West Indies Press.

Ntombela, T. E. 1995. 'Characterization in C. T. Msimang's novel *Akuyiwe Emhlahlweni*'. In *South African Journal of African Languages* 15 (3): 125–136.

Ntshangase, D. K. 1993. *The Social History of Iscamtho*. MA Thesis. Johannesburg: University of the Witwatersrand).

—1995. 'Indaba yami i-straight: language practices of Soweto'. In R. Mesthrie (ed.), *Social History: Studies in South African Sociolinguistics*. Cape Town: David Phillip: 291–297.

Ntuli, D. B. Z. 1968. 'A Brief Survey of Modern Literature in the South African Bantu Languages: Zulu'. In *LIMI* 6: 28–36.

—1985. *Ngamafuphi: Izindaba Ezimfushane*. Pretoria: De Jager HAUM.

—1992. *Phumelela Ekuhlolweni isiZulu Std 10: A Study Guide*. Pietermaritzburg: Reach Out Publishers.

—1993. *Zulu Literature: Comparative Literature and African Literatures.* Pretoria: Via Afrika.

Ntuli, D. B. and Swanepoel, C. F. 1993. *South African Literature in African Languages: A Concise Historical Perspective.* Pretoria: Arcadia.

Nxumalo, O. E. H. 1969. *Ngisinga Empumalanga.* Shuter and Shooter.

Nyembezi, C. L. S. 1949. *The Proverb in Zulu.* MA Thesis. Johannesburg: University of the Witwatersrand Press.

—1958. *Izibongo Zamakhosi.* Pietermaritzburg: Shuter and Shooter.

—1961. 'A Review of Zulu Literature, in *African Studies.* 21.

—1975. *Mntanami Mntanami.* Shuter and Shooter.

Obiechina, E. 1972. *Onitsha Market literature.* London: Heinemann.

—1973. *An African popular Literature. A Study of Onitsha Market Pamphlets.* Cambridge: Cambridge University Press.

Ogude, J. 1996. *Ngugi's Novels and African History: Narrating the Nation.* London: Pluto Press.

Oguibe, O. and Enwezor, O. 1999. Introduction. In Olu Oguibe and Okwui Enwezor, (eds.). *Reading the contemporary: African art from theory to the marketplace.* London: Institute for International Visual Art: 8–14.

Okpewho, I. 1992. *African Oral Literature: Backgrounds, Character, and Continuity.* Bloomington: Indiana University Press.

Orbach, S. and Eichenbaum, L. 1987. *Bittersweet.* London: Arrow.

Pan South African Language Board (PanSALB). South African Languages/Multilingualism in South Africa. http://salanguages.com/multilingualism.htm. Accessed April 2009.

Pelling, J. N. 1977. *Ndebele Proverbs and Other Sayings.* Rhodesai: Mambo Press.

Peterson, B. 1997. *Monarchs, Missionaries, and African Intellectuals: Redemption and Revolution in South African Theatre.* Johannesburg: University of the Witwatersrand.

—2000. *Monarchs, Missionaries, and African Intellectuals: African Theatre and the Unmaking of Colonial Marginality.* Johannesburg: University of the Witwatersrand Press.

—2001. 'Yizo Yizo: reading the swagger in Soweto youth culture. Paper presented at annual international conference, *Africa's*

Young Majority: Meanings, Victims, Actors, Center of African Studies, University of Edinburgh.

—2003. 'Kwaito, "dawgs" and the antimonies of hustling'. In *African Identities* 1 (2): 197–213.

—2006. The Bantu world and the world of books: Reading, writing and 'enlightenment'. In Karin Barber (ed.). *Africa's hidden histories: Everyday literacy and making the self*. Bloomington, IN: Indiana University Press: 236–257.

Posel, D. 2010. Races to consume: Revisiting South Africa's history of race, consumption and the struggle for freedom. In *Ethnic and Racial Studies* 33 (2): 157–175.

Pyles, T. 1986. 'Bible Belt Onomastics or Some Curiosities of Anti-Pedobaptist Nomenclature'. In K. B. Harder, (ed.). *Names and their Varieties: a collection of essays on onomastics*. Lanham: University Press of America: 72–88.

Pype, Katryien 2004. Transgressiviteit in rituelen van Vlaamse wicca's. *Volkskunde [Transgressivity in the rituals of Flemish Wiccans]* 105: 243–273.

—2006. Dancing for God or the Devil: pentecostal discourse on popular dance in Kinshasa. *Journal of Religion in Africa* 36 (3–4): 296–318.

—2007a. We need to open up the country: development and the Christian key scenario in the social space of Kinshasa's teleserials. *Journal of African Media Studies* 1 (1): 101–116.

—2007b. Audience Participation and Performance in the Production of Kinshasa's Television Serials. *Recherches en Communication* (28): 27–36.

—2007c. Fighting boys, strong men and gorillas: notes on the imagination of masculinities in Kinshasa. *Journal of the international African institute* 77 (2): 250–271 (citations : 1) (IF publication year : 0.4) (IF most recent : 0.64).

—2008. Comment on B. Straight's article 'Killing God: Exceptional Moments in the Colonial Missionary'. *Current Anthropology: a World Journal of the Sciences of Man* 49 (5): 837–860 (IF publication year: 2.03) (IF most recent : 2.03).

—2009. The Noise of Still Images. Encounters in/with Sub-Saharan Africa. *Visual Anthropology* 22 (4): 247–251.

—2010. Of Fools and False Pastors: Tricksters in Kinshasa's Television Fiction. *Visual Anthropology* 23 (2): 115–135.

—2011. Confession-cum-Deliverance. In/Dividuality of the Subject among Kinshasa's Born-Again Christians. *Journal of Religion in Africa* 41 (3): 280–310.

—2011. Dreaming the Apocalypse. Mimesis and the Pentecostal Imagination in Kinshasa. *Paideuma* 57: 81–96.

Radebe, M. E. (1996) *Aphelile Agambaqa*. Cape Town: Maskew Miller Longman (Pty) Ltd.

Ragussis, M. 1986. *Acts of Naming*. New York: Oxford University Press.

Ramphele, M. 1992. 'Social disintegration in black community: implications for social transformation'. In E. D. Everett and E. Sisulu, (eds.), *Black Youth in Crisis: Facing the Future*. Johannesburg: Kwela Books: 10–29.

Ramsaran, J. A. 1965. *New Approaches to African Literature: A New Guide to Negro-African Writing and Related Studies*. Ibadan: Ibadan University Press.

Rudwick, S. 2005. 'Township language dynamics: isiZulu and isiTsotsi in Umlazi'. In *Southern African Linguistics and Applied Language Studies* 23 (3): 305–317.

Scheub, H. 1985. 'Zulu Oral Tradition and Written Literature'. In B. W. Andrzejewiski et. al. *Literature in African Languages: A Sample Survey*. Cambridge: Cambridge University Press.

Segal, L.; Pelo, J. and Rampa, P. 2001. 'Into the heart of darkness: journeys of the amagents in crime, violence and death', in, *Crime Wave: The South African Underworld and its Foes*, J. Steinberg, (ed.) Johannesburg: University of the Witwatersrand Press: 95–114.

Serudu, M. S. 1996. 'Literary History: The Case of Northern Sotho'. In A. J. Smit, Johan van Wyka and Wade Sean-Philipe, (eds.). *Rethinking South African Literary History*, Durban: Y Press: 93–109.

Shabangu, M. T. 1997. *Kade Sasibona*. Johannesburg: Heinemann.

Shabangu, S. S. 1966. *Imiyalezo*. Pietermaritzburg: Shuter and Shooter.

—1977. *Imvu Yolahleko*. Pietermaritzburg: Shuter and Shooter.

—1982. *Bamngcwaba Ephila*. Pietermaritzburg: Shuter and Shooter.

—1982. *Isithunzi sikamufi*. Johannesburg: Educum.

—1987. *Bamngcwaba Ephila*: Pietermaritzburg. Shuter and Shooter.

Shabangu, S, S. and De Kock, J. 1995. *Ifa lakwaMthethwa*. Isando: Cantaur Publications.

Shohat, E. and Stam, R. 2003. *Multiculturalism. Postcoloniality, and Transnational Media*. New Brunswick: Rugters University Press.

Sibiya, D. 2002 *Kungasa Ngifile*. Cape Town: Tafelberg.

—2006. *Ngidedele Ngife*. Cape Town: Tafelberg.

Sibiya, N. 2002. *Kuxolelwa Abanjani*. Pietermaritzburg: Shuter and Shooter.

Sidbury, J. 2007. 'Globalization, creolisation and the not-so-peculiar institution', *Journal of Southern History* 73 (3): 617–630.

Simamane, K. S. C. 1995. *Kuhaza Impophoma*. Pietermaritzburg: Shuter and Shooter.

Slabbert, S. 1994. 'A re-evaluation of the sociology of Tsotsitaal'. In *South African Journal of Linguistics* 12 (1): 31–41.

Smith, R. 2000. *Yizo Yizo This is it?: Representation and Receptions of Violence and Gender Relations*. Durban: University of Kwazulu Natal Press.

Smith, V. 1997. 'Introduction', in *Representing Blackness: Issues in Film and Video*, Valerie Smith, (ed.). Rutgers: The State University Press.

Smith, V. 1998. *Not just race, not just gender: Black Feminist Readings*. New York: Routledge.

Stam, R. 2005. *Literature Through Film: Realism, Magic and the Art of Adaptation*. Malden, MA: Blackwell Publishers.

Steinberg, J. (ed.). 2001. *Crime Wave: The South African Underworld and its Foes*. Johannesburg: University of the Witwatersrand Press.

Stephens, S. 2000. 'Kwaito', in *Senses of Culture: South African Culture Studies*, S. Nuttall and C. Michael (eds.). Cape Town: Oxford University Press.

Stewart, C. 2007. 'Creolization: history, ethnography, theory'. In Charles Stewart (ed.). *Creolization, History, Ethography, Theory*. California: Left Coast Press: 1–25.

Stewart, G. R. 1986. 'A classification of place names'. In Harder, K. B. (ed.). *Names and their Varieties: A Collection of Essays on Onomastics.* Lanham: University Press of America: 23–35.

Sucksmith, H. P. 1970. *The Narrative Art of Charles Dickens.* Oxford: Clarendon Press.

Swanepoel, C. F. 1996. 'Merging African-Language Literature into South African Literary History', A. J. Smit, J. van Wyke and W. Sean-Philipe, (eds.) *Rethinking South African Literary History.* Durban: Y Press.

Teer-Tomaselli, R. 1997. Shifting spaces: Popular culture and national identity. In *Critical Arts* 11 (1): i–xvi.

Teshome, Gabriel 1982. *Third Cinema in the Third World: The Aesthetics of Liberation.* Ann Arbor: UMI Research Press.

Thackway Melissa 2003. *Africa Shoots Back: Alternative Perspectives in Sub-Sahara Francophone African Film.* Indianapolis: Indiana University Press.

Thipa, H. M. 1984. 'What shall we call him'. In *South African Journal of African Languages* 1: 84–99.

Thosago, C. M. 2004. 'The postmodern era: tombstone or cornerstone of folklore'. In *Southern African Journal of Folklore Studies* 14 (1): 12–18.

Tomaselli, K. 1986. *Myth, Race and Power: South Africans Imaged on Film and Television.* Bellville Publishers: Anthropos.

—1989a. *The Cinema of Apartheid: Race and Class in South African Film.* London: Routledge.

—1989b. *Broadcasting in South Africa.* London: J. Currey.

Turner, N. S. 1999. 'Representations of masculinity in the contemporary oral praise poetry of Zulu men'. In *South African Journal of African Languages* 19 (3): 196–203.

—2001. 'Humorous names, verbal weapons'. In *South African Journal of African Languages* 21 (4): 449–458.

Vilakazi, B. W. 1935. *Noma Nini.* Pietermaritzburg: Marianhill.

—1944. *Nje Nempela.* Pietermaritzburg: Marianhill.

—1945. *The Oral and The Written Literature in Nguni.* PhD Thesis. Johannesburg: University of the Witwatersrand Press.

Vilakazi, P. B. 1998. *Aphume Nobomvu*. Pietermaritzburg: Reach Out
    Publishers.

Walshe, P. 1970. *The Rise of African Nationalism: The African National
    Congress 1912–1952*. London: C. Hurst.

Walton, K. 1990. *Mimesis as Make-Believe: On the Foundations of
    the Representational Arts*. Cambridge Massachusetts: Harvard
    University Press.

Wanda, M. E. 1997. *Izibiba Ziyeqana*. Pietermaritzburg: Shuter and
    Shooter.

Watkins, S. C. 1998. *Representing: Hip Hop Culture and the Production of
    Black Cinema*. Chicago: University of Chicago Press.

Welsh, D. 1971. *The Roots of Segregation: Native Policy in Colonial Natal,
    1845–1910*. Cape Town: Oxford University Press.

Whitman, J. 1987. *Allegory: The Dynamics of an Ancient and Medieval
    Technique*. Oxford: Clarendon Press.

Widdicombe, S. and Wooffitt, R. 1995. *The Language of Youth
    Subcultures: Social Identity in Action*. New York: Wheatsheaf.

Worton, M and Still, J. 1990. *Intertextualities: Theories and Practices*.
    Manchester: Manchester University Press.

Xulu, M. 1994. *Udwendwe LukaKoto*. Pietermaritburg: Reach Out
    Publishers.

Yanga, T. 1999. 'Ubuntu as a social lever', Occasional paper,
    Department of African Languages. Johannesburg: University of
    the Witwatersrand.

Yearwood, G. L. 2000. *Black Film as a Signifying Practice: Cinema,
    Narration and the African-American Aesthetic Tradition*. Trenton:
    Africa World Press, Inc.

Zondi, E. 2001. Personal interview, Durban.

Zounmenou, M. V. 2004. *The Function of Oral Genres and the Question
    of the African Renaissance: A Comparative Study of Goun and
    Zulu proverbs and Folktales*. Johannesburg: University of the
    Witwatersrand.

Zulu, N. S. 2000. 'African Literature in the Next Millennium'. In *South
    African Journal of African Languages* 19 (4): 290–301.

Films

Landis, J. 1988. *Coming to America*. Paramount.

Mahlatse, T. 2001. *Yizo Yizo I*. Johannesburg: SABC Education.

—2002. *Yizo Yizo II*. Johannesburg: SABC Education.

—2004. *Yizo Yizo III*. Johannesburg: SABC Education.

Shabangu, S. and De Kock J. 1995. *Ifa LakwaMthethwa*. Philo Pieterse Productions.

Shabangu, Pixley and Sidney 2000. *Umuzi Wezinsizwa*. Shambe Productions.

Swanson, D. 1949. *Africa Jim*: USA: Villion Pictures.

Whener, M. 1994. *Hlala Kwabafileyo*. Scholtz Film Productions.

Yazbek, A. 2003. *Gaz' Lam I*. Johannesburg: SABC Education.

Music

Mfeka, Nkosinathi a.k.a. Mgarimbe. 2006. *Sister Bethina*. Ghetto Ruff.

Newspapers

Mail and Guardian 13th November 2007.

Mail and Guardian 12 February 2008.

Star 29th October 2006.

Sunday Times 9th August 1998.

Opera

Khumalo, Mzilikazi 2002. *Princess Magogo kaDinizulu*. SAMRO. Braamfontein.

Vundla, M; Ndodana-Breen, B. and Willensky, W. 2001. *Winnie*. Johannesburg: Vundowill Pty. Ltd.

Index

Printed and bound by CPI Group (UK) Ltd, Croydon, CR0 4YY

09/06/2025

14685819-0004